Adventure
NEW ENGLAND

Adventure
NEW ENGLAND

An Outdoor Vacation Guide

Diane Bair
and Pamela Wright

Ragged Mountain Press
Camden, Maine

International Marine/
Ragged Mountain Press

A Division of The McGraw-Hill Companies

2 4 6 8 10 9 7 5 3 1

Library of Congress Cataloging-in-Publication Data
Bair, Diane.
Adventure New England : an outdoor vacation guide / Diane Bair and Pamela Wright.
p. cm.
Includes bibliographical references and index.
ISBN 0-07-003309-9
1. New England—Guidebooks. 2. Outdoor recreation—New England—Guidebooks. I. Wright, Pamela, 1953- . II. Title.
F2.3.B3 1996
917.404'43—dc20   96-1413
                                                    CIP

Questions regarding the content of this book should be addressed to:

Ragged Mountain Press
P.O. Box 220
Camden, ME 04843

Questions regarding the ordering of this book should be addressed to:

The McGraw-Hill Companies
Customer Service Department
P.O. Box 547
Blacklick, OH 43004
Retail customers:
1-800-822-8158
Bookstores: 1-800-722-4726

A portion of the profits from the sale of each Ragged Mountain Press book is donated to an environmental cause.

Adventure New England is printed on 45-pound Editors Eggshell, a recycled, acid-free paper containing a minimum 50% recycled deinked fiber. ♻

Printed by R.R. Donnelley

Illustrations by Chris Van Dusen. Maps on pages xiii-xvii by Paul Mirto

Design by Eugenie S. Delaney

No promotional fees were requested or colllected from commercial establishments mentioned in this book.

Contents

CANOEING

KAYAKING

SAILING

WINDJAMMING

WHITEWATER RAFTING

FISHING

SAILBOARDING

SCUBA DIVING

HIKING

HORSE PACKING AND TRAIL RIDING

BICYCLE TOURING

MOUNTAIN BIKING

ROCK CLIMBING AND CAVING

WILDERNESS EXPLORATION

HOT AIR BALLOONING

SOARING, GLIDING, AND SKYDIVING

CROSS-COUNTRY SKIING

DOWNHILL SKIING AND SNOWBOARDING

WINTER ADVENTURE

Maine

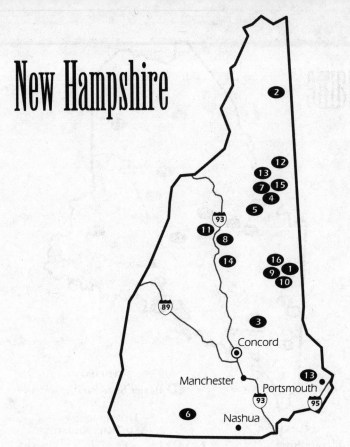

New Hampshire

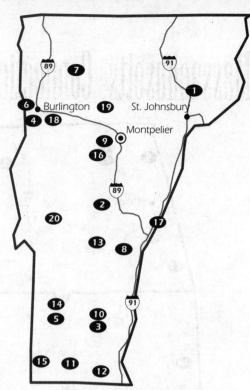

Vermont

Massachusetts, Connecticut, and

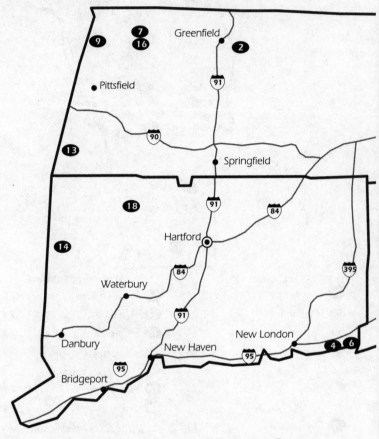

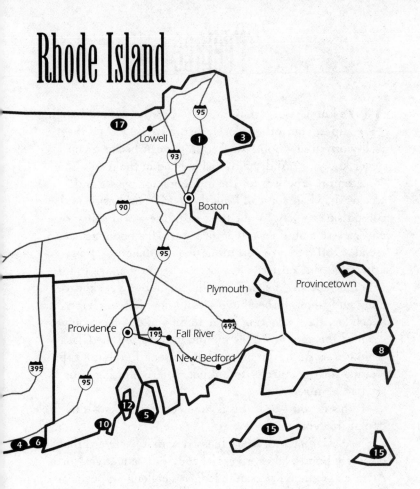

Rhode Island

95

17

Lowell

1

3

93

90

Boston

95

Plymouth

Provincetown

Providence

195

Fall River

495

New Bedford

395

95

12

5

10

8

4   6

15

15

Preface

We know you. You're the one with the wetsuit hanging up in your office closet, just in case . . . And the well-worn hiking boots stashed in the car, because you never know . . . And the fly-fishing rod in the trunk. . . .

Admit it. You live for the outdoors, for weeks and weekends when you can fling the work-world aside and run outside to play. While the rest of the world is just discovering this outdoor adventure stuff (It's booming! It's a trend! Outfitters are sprouting like dandelions!), you know that the outdoors has always been the place to be. Whether you paddle, sail, ski, hike, climb, dive, skydive, hang glide—or all the above—you know it beats lying on a beach any day. Relaxing is the thing you do after you've reached the summit of the mountain or rafted the Class-V whitewater. And even as you loll, or soak in the hot tub, waiting for the muscles to unkink, you're plotting your next adventure.

If this is you—or if this is how you daydream—this book is for you.

In New England, we're blessed with a backyard that has it all: ponds, lakes, rivers, the icy-but-seductive North Atlantic; gentle hills, granite ledges, challenging peaks; and don't even get us started on the lush forests, salt marshes, and watchable wildlife. All this, in an area that would fit into Montana with room to spare. (We've got our wide-open spaces, though, you just don't have to drive very far to get to them.) Virtually anything you can do out West, you can do in New England, except stuff like bungee-jumping (which is a decidedly un-Yankee thing to do).

You won't find every single, possible New England adventure in this book. There are, we've discovered, approximately a zillion of them, and you'd spend so much time reading you'd never get outside. So, we've focused on 75 or so really good and unique experiences, aiming for lots of variety in the mix. And, a few surprises: Ever tracked a bear? Or belly-crawled for fifty yards in total darkness into the bowels of an all-marble cave? We have, and we'll share the highlights, lowlights, and how-tos with you. As veterans of more action and adventure than Sylvester Stallone, we'll reveal all the inside stuff, so maybe you can avoid some of the bruises and bugbites that we didn't.

Happy trails!

Diane Bair and Pamela Wright

Acknowledgments

We would like to thank the following people for their help, enthusiasm, and insights: Arvrum Belzer; Ailsa Bennel; Wally and Jeanna Brown; Minna Casser; John and Judi Churchill; John Clippinger; Robin Cross; Jerry and Michael Dee; Judy Eitler; Cheryl Goodson; Eve and Sam Hamlin; Cindy Hirsch; Wendy Harris; Peter Harriss; Marcia Glassman-Jaffe, Marisa and Mark Jaffe; Steve and Debbie Johnson; Carroll Jones; Steve Jones; Skip King; Polly Mahoney; Steve and Rhys Martin; Greg Nikas; Steve and Denise Palmer; Betsy and Bob Renshaw; Myra and Roy Ruff; Cindy Schram; Scott Schulz; Rick Semonian; Steve Smith; Jonathon Wagman; Joel Weisman; Tom Willett and Maxie Russell-Willett.

And, special thanks to our families: Chuck, Jared, Sadie, Steve, Charlotte, and Connor, who hiked, biked, paddled, climbed, crawled, jumped, soared, surfed, and sailed right along with us. You were great sports.

Canoeing

1

Allagash River, Maine: Six Days on the Wild and Scenic Allagash

Seduced by Silent Woods and Rippling Water

Sometimes you need to splash the soul with wonder, awaken your senses with a touch of wildness. A wilderness canoe trip down northern Maine's Allagash River will do that for you. It gives a change of scenery and a change of attitude.

The Allagash Wilderness Waterway is a ninety-eight-mile corridor stretching from the northwest corner of Baxter State Park to the frontier village of Allagash, just ten miles from the Canadian border. It encompasses nearly 170,000 acres of lakes, rivers, forests, and woods—most of it owned by large paper companies. Despite the encroachment of tandem logging trucks and the maze of dirt roads they travel on, the Allagash's wild side has not yet been tamed.

It's best to travel the Allagash with someone who knows it well and respects its primitiveness. Also, plan to stay long enough for the special silence of the river and woods to work its calming magic on you. We joined Mahoosuc Guide Service's six-day trip, led by Polly Mahoney and Kevin Slater. Mahoosuc is not well publicized, but still has a well-earned, top-notch reputation among outdoor enthusiasts. Mahoney and Slater own and operate the company, offering a variety of trips year-round, including Native American cultural journeys, dogsledding, mountaineering, and white-water and wilderness canoe trips. Their forte: traditional canoeing and camping techniques. You might enjoy a

CONTACT: Mahoosuc Guide Service, Bear River Road, Newry, ME 04261; (207) 824-2073.

HOW TO GET THERE: Mahoosuc will designate a meeting spot depending on the trip. Pickup for the Allagash trip is at the Hampstead Farm Bed and Breakfast, RD 3, Box 703, Bangor, ME 04401; (207) 848-3749. The farm is located just west of I-95 in Hermon.

RATES: Six-day trips, including all equipment (tents, sleeping bags, dry bags, canoes, life jackets), meals, and transportation to and from river, are $650 per person. Room rates at the Hampstead are $35 to $50 per room, per night.

WHAT TO BRING: Mahoosuc will send a suggested clothing list. In general, bring warm clothing, river shoes, flashlight, binoculars, and bug repellent.

KIDS: Twelve and up, if they can handle six days in a canoe.

SKILL LEVEL: All levels; no paddling experience necessary.

ON YOUR OWN: Several outfitters rent canoes and offer drop-off and pickup services on the Allagash. For a list of registered guides, write or call the Allagash Wilderness Waterway, Maine Department of Conservation, State House 22, Augusta, ME 04333; (207) 723-8518. Camping is allowed at designated sites only; first-come, first-served. The North Maine Woods, P.O. Box 421, Ashland, ME; (207) 435-6213, provides maps and regulations. We like DeLorme's *Map and Guide of the Allagash and St. John;* it's available at selected sports stores, or order it from DeLorme Mapping Co., P.O. Box 298, Freeport, ME 04032.

dinner hung from a hand-carved *spunhungan* (a wooden stick notched to hold a pot) and cooked over an open fire. Or a peach cobbler baked in an ember-layered Dutch oven, flavored with just a hint of the spruce branch that was used to clean the oven the night before. You'll learn to use the Native American setting pole for shallow-river travel, and you'll practice standing paddling techniques. Mahoney and Slater eschew modern equipment; in fact, they make much of the gear used on their trips, such as ash dogsleds, cedar canvas canoes, maple paddles, and snubbing poles.

We met them early one morning at the Farmstead Bed and Breakfast, just outside Bangor, Maine. Seven of us "sports" (guide slang for customers) piled into a van and endured a bumpy six-hour ride on dirt and gravel roads to our put-in spot on Umsaskis Lake. It felt like the middle of nowhere—a long, long way from home. Finally, we reached the shores of the Allagash, the hunting and fishing grounds of the Abenaki Indians and the pristine wilderness of which Henry David Thoreau wrote so eloquently. It was at once quiet and humbling.

We had paddled only a short distance when someone sang out, "Is that a moose?" We stopped paddling and scoured the landscape. It was a rock, but the confusion was understandable. At dusk, the huge black rock, set against the dense wall of spruce and fir, looked remarkably mooselike. That night we camped on a hill overlooking Long Lake and feasted on fresh salmon steaks grilled over an open wood fire. Perfect, except for the mosquitoes and blackflies that swarmed around us. (Remember to bring plenty of bug repellent.)

The next few days progressed at a slow, almost rhythmic pace. We awoke early to the smell of coffee and the sound of Slater chopping wood. We paddled across the lakes and down the river of the Allagash Wilderness, framed by mountains and the tall, wooded slopes of northern Maine. We learned to slide our canoes quietly through the water, to slip our paddles in and out with barely a whisper of a splash. We began to notice things: an immature eagle riding updrafts, hugging the shoreline; an osprey, diving feet first for its dinner; a deer grazing on the shoreline brush. Some days we paddled until dusk before reaching camp; other days we stopped early and spent the afternoon swimming, identifying wildflowers, reading, or napping.

A ranger told us there were several groups on the Allagash, but we met few people while paddling. A couple of times, however, we shared our campsite. Slater laments even these small intrusions of civilization. He talked about a trip they'll make in the winter, dogsledding with the Inuit of

Maine River Classics

Canoe voyaging on the remote, wild, scenic waterways of northern Maine is an experience you won't soon forget. The classically beautiful Machias River, the St. Croix, and the St. John offer spectacular scenery, quiet beauty, and some of the best canoeing anywhere.

The Machias River snakes through the remote interior of eastern Maine, mixing technically challenging whitewater with long stretches of wilderness travel. You'll paddle by dramatic glacier formations, tall stands of pine, and dense woods, and you'll cross pristine, isolated Machias Lake.

The tranquil St. Croix rises in a chain of wilderness lakes and flows along the Canadian border through never-ending woodlands and vast meadows. Moderate rips and gentle reaches make it the perfect wilderness journey for novices.

The St. John has been called the "most magnificent wilderness run east of the Mississippi River." It offers the granddaddy of all Maine canoe trips. You'll paddle waters running through the great northern Maine woods, across remote ponds, through narrow stretches and wide-open runs. Plan to paddle this classic beauty in the spring—it becomes too shallow later in the year.

There are a number of outfitters offering multiday wilderness canoeing and camping trips of these classics. (See the resource guide list at the end of this chapter.) We like Sunrise County Canoe Expeditions, Cathance Lake, Grove Post Office, ME 04638; (207) 454-7708.

Baffin Island. And of another, when he'll be out for three or four weeks but take food to last only seven days. He'll hunt and fish for the rest.

Most canoeists will be sufficiently challenged by what the Allagash dishes out: rips and riffles, shallow rapids, jutting boulders, and rocks lurking just below the surface. We spent several hours at a stretch bumping off and just missing rocks, getting thrown around, backward, sideways, and, yes, over.

"It's like canoeing in a minefield," someone said. "It's like driving in a blizzard."

But after a while, we learned to read the river and to know something about the rocks. We found the channel, looking for the vee pointing upstream (not down); we stopped holding our breath.

One day, we woke to a dark dawn and light rain. Fog rising from the river mixed with the drizzle, erasing the border between air and ground. In our canoes, we seemed to be floating in space, part of a scene created by an impressionist painter. As we rounded the bend, we spotted a large bull moose halfway submerged in the river, feeding on weeds. He eyed us and then went on eating as we floated by. Farther down the river, we were awarded a quick glimpse of a black bear as it lumbered into the woods. We paddled on in silence.

Our final night was spent at the base of beautiful Allagash Falls. From there, it is a half-day's paddle to the end of the Allagash Wilderness Waterway and to Allagash village.

"What's that noise?" someone asked. We heard a soft rumble in the distance that was, at first, foreign. Cars. We didn't realize until that moment how thoroughly we'd been seduced by the sound of the river and the silence of the woods.

Jackman, Maine: Earth-Friendly Canoe-Camping in the North Woods

Native American–Style River Travel with the Chewonki Foundation

CONTACT: The Chewonki Foundation, RR 2 Box 1200, Wiscasset, ME 04578; (207) 882-7323. Chewonki runs a couple of family canoe-camping trips each summer, depending on interest.

RATES: Trips cost $300 for adults, $225 for children twelve and under.

HOW TO GET THERE: The trip meets at the canoe landing of Jackman Landing Campground. Jackman is a 3.5-hour drive north from Portland. Take the Maine Turnpike north to Waterville, then catch Route 201 north to Jackman. The campground is on your left.

WHAT TO BRING: No room to list all the required gear here; they'll send you a list when you register. Borrow whatever you can. Certain items are available for a nominal rental fee.

KIDS: This trip is appropriate for children eight years old and up; paddling experience is not essential.

SKILL LEVEL: Beginner. Count on getting tired and a little sore.

Call it wood shop, home economics, earth science, and phys. ed. class rolled into one. You'd expect a canoe-camping trip to put more power into your paddling, but it's the unexpected that sets this trip apart. On this adventure you'll learn how to bake a cake in a Dutch oven; how to split wood like a lumberjack; even how to clean greasy pots with leaves and dirt. And you'll discover just how much work it can be to load all your belongings into a canoe, then paddle the whole shebang to a far-flung campsite.

"This is no catered trip; everybody pitches in," the Chewonki people tell you when you call them to sign up. Think outhouses, not hot showers. The emphasis here is on personal growth, not personal grooming. Stewardship of the planet and respect for nature form the basis of Chewonki's philosophy. Their main business (since 1917) is running a boy's camp in Wiscasset, Maine, and leading wilderness expeditions for teens in Maine and Labrador. Famed ornithologist/painter Roger Tory Peterson wrote the first edition of *A Field Guide to the Birds* while at Chewonki. Expeditions for adults and families feature hiking, sea kayaking, sailing, cross-country ski-camping, and canoe-camping.

We opted for a family trip, "Introduction to Canoe-Camping," suitable for kids aged eight and up. The lure: the remote

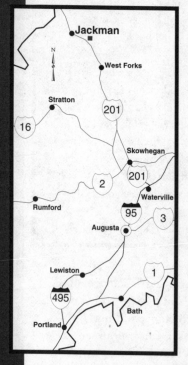

location, in northwest Maine near the Canadian border. This is north woods territory, near the headwaters of the Moose River, and we'd heard the ponds were secluded, beautiful, and studded with pine-covered islands.

Our first clue that this was no ordinary outing came with the equipment list, which was more than a page long and included items like an insect head-net. We managed to borrow, rent, and buy everything on the list except for the extra-large waterproof river bag (too pricey); these can be rented from Chewonki. (Tip: forget the canvas high-top sneakers Chewonki recommends. They're squeegy when wet and take forever to dry. Wear river sandals instead.)

In spite of all the gear, this trip is decidedly low-tech, with equipment fashioned after traditional Cree and Abenaki Indian materials. "The Cree (from Canada) were great canoeists," guide Dave McWethy told us, as he described "wanagans" (wooden boxes) and Duluth packs. We'd be hauling these babies a lot, first to Chewonki's field station on Big Wood Pond, where we'd stay for two nights, then to a remote campsite on the beach at Attean Pond, where we'd stay for our third and final night. We all admired a traditional Cree paddle made of spruce. "The Cree can carve one of these out of a tree in just twenty minutes," guide Chad Toomey told us. "Awesome, huh?"

After a quick paddling lesson, we headed to the base camp. The sight of three canoes is such a rarity in these parts, a resident moose wandered to the shore to watch us. The lone child in the group, from Massachusetts, was thrilled. "It's the first moose I've ever seen, except for Bullwinkle!" she said.

After setting up camp, we made a tasty dinner of shish kebabs, baked potatoes, and banana cake—our first lesson in campfire culinary arts, presented by Toomey. He described the process of Dutch oven cooking with the zeal of Julia Child whipping up a pot au feu (if she were a twenty-something male with golden dreadlocks, anyway). "There's a lot of trial and error involved in not burning a cake," he told us. "Once you get the hang of it, you can bake pizza, bread— anything you can bake in a traditional oven, you can bake on a campfire." Before we ate, one of the participants gave a reading from the book *Earth Prayers*, by Roberts and Amidon. This became an evening ritual. After some campfire chat, we spread out our sleeping bags in Chewonki's two yurts and fell asleep to the eerie call of the loons.

With no modern distractions (happily, there wasn't so much as a cellular phone among us) we fell into a satisfying back-to-basics routine: up, cook, eat, clean, pack, paddle, unpack, eat, clean, sleep; up, cook, eat, clean, pack, paddle. On our first full day, we paddled across the pond to a sandy beach for lunch and a swim, then back to base camp for a woodcraft lesson. McWethy gave a wood-chopping demonstration, then we all had a go at the billet. The child in the group was a quick study, proving that skill, not raw strength, rules here. "Woodcraft is an art," McWethy told us solemnly. "The Native Americans and loggers who were up here had incredible wood skills, and now those skills are disappearing."

As for low-impact camping, if you think that means no Budweiser cans left behind, consider this: Chewonki guides demonstrate how to spit toothpaste through your teeth, in a spraying fashion, so the toxins are spread around, not saturated in one place. Finicky? Maybe. But it's that kind of Earth-first attitude that makes a Chewonki trip so interesting. That, and the communal job-sharing that's part of the experience, especially when you bring kids along. Children who balk at making their beds at home seem to attack tent setup with relish. What this proves, we don't know. But we like it.

The next day we rose at 5 A.M., loaded all the gear, and paddled to Attean Pond through a section of the Moose River. We landed on a perfectly inviting (read, deserted) stretch of beach to set up camp. After a day of breaking camp and paddling for hours, all we really wanted to do was sleep on the beach. What we ended up doing was climbing a mountain.

Sally Mountain had looked tempting from a distance, lush and green, with but a 1.6-mile hike to the summit. Even the little kid was game. In reality, though, the trail was buggy, boggy, muddy, wet, and rocky. Just when we were ready to call it quits, a couple of seventy-somethings and two old canines literally sprinted past us down the trail. "Super hike, huh?" they called. Uh, yeah. If they could, we could, so we did. At the top, we were amply rewarded with panoramic views of bluer-than-blue water speckled with gemlike islands.

Wild blueberries covered the mountaintop. We collected enough to bake a pie in the Dutch oven for dinner, and headed back, spirits buoyed. We followed our noses to camp, led by the aroma of a Chewonki classic, Sheila's Adirondack Chili. Beef stew from a can will never taste the same. Bone-weary, smelling of woodsmoke and bug repellent, we crawled into our sleeping bags, soon to wake up and do it over again.

North Conway, New Hampshire: Running Wild Water on the (Very) Swift River

Better Start Swimmin' or You'll Sink Like a Stone

CONTACT: You're on your own; it's impossible to schedule Swift River runs, so commercial guide service is not available. There is a water gauge on a rock in Cabin Gorge. Minimum running level is 1.5; maximum (know your abilities!) is 2.5 to 3. If you're an experienced boater with your own equipment, stop in at Saco Bound in North Conway, New Hampshire, and ask for Craig Niiler. He'll chat with you about the trouble spots and point out the best put-in and take-out locations on the river.

HOW TO GET THERE: From Route 16 north, take a left onto Route 112 (Kancamagus Highway). From I-93 north, take Exit 32 to Route 112. You can put in at Upper Falls, just below the Rocky Gorge Scenic Area, off the highway; or at Lower Falls, just below the covered bridge (this is the very tough section of the Swift), off the highway.

WHAT TO BRING: All your own equipment and a buddy, in case you need help. Canoes should be fully equipped with flotation. Safety ropes are a must.

KIDS: Not likely.

SKILL LEVEL: Strong and very experienced whitewater paddlers only. You have to know what you're doing to tackle this river.

Y ou've got to be a little crazy—and a whole lotta good—
to run the Swift River in springtime. The pretty little
stream that trickles along the Kancamagus Highway and
attracts sunbathers and waders in summer and fall turns
into a snarling beast when the snow melts. In a "good Swift
year" (one with lots of snow and spring rain), paddlers line
the shores, staring down at one of the toughest, meanest
stretches of water in New England.

"Pretty scary," said one paddler as he scouted from the
shore. "I can probably do it but I'm not so sure it'll be worth
it." His paddling buddies nodded in agreement, but began
to talk about the trouble spots on the river, and how they
might negotiate them. "You're going to have to forget using
the cross stroke on this off-side drop," someone suggested.
"Just try to balance through the hole." "No, I think you're
going to have to brace," another said. Their voices were
barely audible over the rush of wild water.

Another animated onshore group broke into a rendition
of a Bob Dylan classic:

> Gather 'round people wherever you roam,
> And admit that the waters around you have grown,
> And accept that you'll soon be drenched to the bone,
> Oh, the waters, they are a changin'

Changin' is the key word, here. The Swift is steep, fast,
and narrow, but its unpredictability is what throws most
paddlers for a loop.

"You can't memorize the Swift," says Craig Niiler,
general manager of Saco Bound in
North Conway, New Hampshire. "It
changes day by day, hour by hour.
You have to be able to actively read
the water as it comes at you." Niiler
has run the Swift more times than he
can remember. "It's never been the
same run twice," he says.

The Swift's flow is in the hands
of Mother Nature; it is one of only a
handful of New England rivers with
a natural release rather than a dam-
controlled one. Originating out of

the Sandwich Range of the White Mountains, its waters are clear and cold, with more faces than Eve. Generally, if the water is running high, the Swift is a rough, pushy Class IV, with some drops rating a Class V. At medium levels, it's a fast, technical Class IV, with some Class III pauses. In both cases, you'd better know what you're doing up against the narrow, challenging chutes, sudden, deep holes, and rocky ledges. And be ready: The Swift always pops surprises.

"A few years back, I caught the sweetest surfing wave I've ever seen," reminisces Niiler. "I haven't seen it since. You just never know what you're going to get on the Swift."

Paddlers can put in at Lower Falls, above the bridge on the Conway side of the Kancamagus Highway, and potentially run all the way to the Davis Covered Bridge at the Saco River. But it's a long, tough ride with lots of turbulence and obstacles. It has two dramatic drops that require scouting from the shoreline. Cabin Gorge is a twelve- to fifteen-foot drop running more than 100 yards, and Staircase is an intense set of rocky rapids, requiring precise moves. Paddlers often take the drops one at a time, with someone standing on shore with a safety line.

"I'm going for it," said one confident paddler, after several minutes of scouting and mustering up courage. Word had gotten out: It was a good Swift day; the river was running at medium to high level. A group of onlookers gathered to witness the skills of some of the best boaters in the region.

The paddler slid his canoe into the swollen river, dropped four feet, then another eight feet, through a rock-lined gorge. After a tense near-encounter with a boulder, he completed the run successfully. A small cheer sprang up from the crowd. An onlooker walked over to shake his hand. "Quite a run," he shouted above the sound of the water. "Got more luck than brains, boy."

East Burke, Vermont: Women-Only Hike and Paddle in the Northeast Kingdom

Where the Rivers Run North

CONTACT: North Country Journeys for Women Over 40, RR 2, Box 2114, Charlotte, VT 05445; (802) 425-4121. North Country offers a variety of women-only trips, including llama treks, full-moon canoe trips, wildlife viewing, and tracking and hiking workshops.

HOW TO GET THERE: Meet at the Mountain View Creamery for this adventure. From Exit 23 off I-91, take Route 5 through Lyndonville, then take a right onto Route 114. Follow for 4.4 miles, then turn left at the Burke Hollow sign. Bear left up the hill; at the top of the hill, take a left onto Darling Hill Road. The creamery is on the right.

RATES: For $315 you are provided with all meals, two nights' lodging, gratuities, guide service, canoes, and gear.

WHAT TO BRING: Personal gear; plan for any kind of weather.

KIDS: Not appropriate.

SKILL LEVEL: All levels; no experience necessary.

We were teetering on the ridge of Mt. Pisgah. At least, it felt that way. The sheer cliffs drop almost vertically, some 2,700 feet below, into the gleaming, glacier-carved waters of Lake Willoughby. Beside us was a seventy-year-old grandmother of thirteen. Petite and sprightly, she had hair like a wolf's tail, and joie de vivre oozed from her like some exotic perfume. We couldn't decide what was more inspiring: the spectacular view or this lively septuagenarian.

We had joined a group of women for a weekend of canoeing and hiking in Vermont's fabled Northeast Kingdom. Adrenaline junkies, seek your thrills elsewhere; this is not a trip for peak baggers. Rather, it's a simple weekend designed for the sometimes difficult task of slowing down.

"I think everyone needs to be coddled sometimes," says Judy Rowe, our group leader. "We provide a safe haven, surrounded by physical beauty, and then let nature do its work."

Rowe heads up North Country Journeys for Women Over 40. Why forty? "It's arbitrary," says Rowe. "In fact, we get lots of interest from thirty-year-old mothers who want to get away." The average age of women on North Country trips is fifty-four, she says.

This weekend, we were the youngest in a largely post-menopausal group. Our base for the weekend was the lovely Mountain View Creamery Bed and Breakfast in East Burke, Vermont. This is one gorgeous piece of real estate. The elegant farmhouse sits on 440 acres, with 360-degree views of rolling hills and valleys. It would be easy to spend the entire weekend at the creamery, curled in the Adirondack chairs overlooking the free-flowing gardens, or walking the miles of trails that wind through classic Vermont countryside.

It was clear from the start that this would be a warm and fuzzy, deeply relaxing experience. Rowe believes that no adventure is complete without some journey inward, and incorporates a holistic approach to travel. Each morning, before heading out, we reached into a

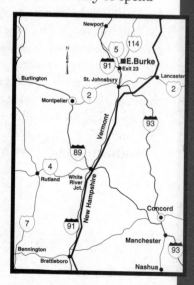

small basket and selected our "angel card." The card contained one word and, Rowe told us, represented "a gift from an angel for the day." Flexibility. Peace. Delight. Transformation. Balance. Release. It provided a reflective, inward focus for the day's adventures.

The first day, after an early morning walk and an elegant breakfast, we piled into a van for our canoe trip on the Connecticut River. We put in on the New Hampshire side, just below Moore Dam. This is a slow-moving section of the river, which allowed plenty of time to practice paddling strokes and techniques and to appreciate the scenery at the river's edge. The leisurely canoe trip took us eight miles downstream, much of it along forested shoreline, to Comeford Dam. We paddled softly, canoe slipping through the water like a hot knife through butter. Above, we noticed a red-tailed hawk riding the thermals with equal effortlessness.

The day unfolded peacefully. We stopped for lunch in a sheltered inlet. Later, a dangling rope swing proved too inviting to resist. With childlike glee, we swung and dropped into a deep river pool. The day ended with a scrumptious dinner at the Creamery and a sunset walk on its countryside trails.

On our final day, we drove to the Mt. Pisgah trail-head for the 2.2-mile hike up to its summit, then to Lake Willoughby for more canoeing. We paddled past the crowded public beach in search of quieter shores and ended up at a lovely spot reserved for sunning and swimming au naturel. We exchanged a few quick "Should we?" glances, then peeled off our sweaty hiking shorts and shirts to skinny-dip in the refreshingly cool waters of Lake Willoughby.

Girls just wanna have fun.

Randolph, Vermont: Inn-Based Adventure on the White and Winooski Rivers

*Inexperienced Canoeists Are in Over
Their Heads on This Trip*

CONTACT: BattenKill Canoe, Ltd., P.O. Box 65, Arlington, VT 05250; (802) 362-2800. The company offers day trips on the Batten Kill and canoe rentals from mid-April to November. Other trips range from two days to ten days in duration. Most trips are inn-based; some are camping trips; and others are a combination of the two. Trip dates may change, depending on interest, but there are usually one or two guaranteed dates per trip.

HOW TO GET THERE: Our trip, "Safari on the White," met at the Three Stallion Inn at Green Mountain Stock Farm, Lower Stock Farm Road, Randolph, VT; (800) 424-5575. From I-89 north or south, take Exit 4; the inn is 4 miles west of the highway.

RATES: The trip costs $327 per person; canoe rental is $45. If there is a low sign-up (six or seven people, as opposed to eight to twelve) on a trip date that's not guaranteed, a ten percent surcharge may be added. Advance reservations and deposit are required.

WHAT TO BRING: They'll send you a list upon confirmation. In general, bring light clothing to be layered, swimsuit, rain gear, hat, sunblock, and insect repellent. BattenKill Canoe will provide a dry bag for gear.

KIDS: This trip is not for them, but the company runs a number of family trips, appropriate for kids age five and up, throughout the season.

SKILL LEVEL: Moderate. We'd recommend some whitewater paddling experience to make the trip more fun.

W e should have known what we were getting into when the guides started joking about making the "BattenKill swim team."

"If you capsize, you make the team," BattenKill Canoe guide Carolyn Parker explained, a twinkle in her eye.

So we all took bets, not believing that anyone in this bunch of fit, active types would run into trouble. Among us were skiers, hikers, divers, tennis players, and Outward Bound canoe-trip grads. Okay, so maybe some of us hadn't paddled a lot, but this trip was rated "beginner to moderate" by BattenKill Canoe. Surely we could handle it. And by our standards, this trip was posh indeed. We'd be staying at the Three Stallion Inn, a bastion of fine food and comfort.

About the inn, we were right. It's an ultrawelcoming place with a main house, a Victorian building with additional guest rooms, an indoor hot tub, stables, and a very good dining room. Outdoors is another hot tub, a pool, gardens, a trout pond, and, as if this wasn't enough atmosphere, horses grazing the lawns.

About the paddling, we were to find that the only easy thing would be making the BattenKill swim team.

Day one, we were to attack the Winooski River, about forty minutes away by van, near Burlington. We looked

down into some very rapid water. "It's smoother downriver," the guides reassured us. So we loaded the canoes with equipment (including a lunch trunk) and got a paddling lesson. We practiced the *draw stroke*—propelling the canoe toward the paddle and away from an object—and the opposite motion, the *pry*. These strokes would prove important to our survival.

Within minutes, we faced Class III rapids, over a ledge, with a three- to four-foot drop. Gulp. Our guide would wait over the drop and gesture to the point of entry. We were to watch the water for an upside-down vee, the best entry point, then go down the waterfall, forward or backward. Any way but sideways.

Couple number three went over—sideways. Diane and Neil were soaked and shaken. It took forty-five minutes to retrieve them, their paddles, the canoe, and the lunch trunk. The other six of us made it.

The next stretch of river was pretty and placid, complete with paddling ducks. Now this is more like it, we thought. Then, more falls.

"You guys can walk downstream, and we'll bring your canoes down," our guides told us, "or you can challenge yourselves."

Hmmm. Which to choose: adrenaline rush or wimp-out? Couple number one braved it and aced it. Couple number two had a bad spill; so bad, the husband was having a difficult time keeping his head above water, even with a life jacket on. Quick rethink, and we decided to split up and tackle the falls with a secret weapon—a guide—in each of our canoes. We soared. And we learned a trick: keep paddling after going over the falls, right through the quickwater, to maintain stability.

The river widened, and it was time for lunch, served buffet-style on an island, complete with table and stools. The last couple of miles downriver were pleasant and uneventful. All told, we paddled about eight miles, enough to feel guilt-free about a stop at Ben & Jerry's Ice Cream Factory in Waterbury. Later, a soak in the hot tub, followed by a tasty dinner at the inn.

Day two, we tackled the White River, an obstacle course of shallow waters and rocky outcroppings for the first few miles after our put-in. We had the responsibility for the lunch trunk (a hex on our canoe?), so we paddled carefully toward Sharon Dam. This time, everyone negotiated the falls successfully. We sailed through effortlessly, feeling downright smug. Lesson: Never tempt the river gods.

After another elegantly presented lunch, our luck ran out. We paddled left and got stuck on a rock. We paddled right and got stuck on a rock. We pried like the devil to free ourselves. Then, quickly, we had to negotiate a dangerous passage—around an island marked with an American flag, then through a waterfall. Instantly we were out of control. The current grabbed us and we headed—sideways, naturally—over the falls. Out we flew, the newest members of the BattenKill swim team. Chastened but giggling, we reboarded our craft.

Eventually, we reached a stretch of river popular with tubing families. We passed them, waved merrily, and got stuck on a rock. Then we ran aground in a shallow spot. I jumped out to drag the boat into deeper water, swamped it, and dumped my no-longer-laughing paddling partner out of the canoe. Parker had warned us that paddling was a test of any relationship.

We redeemed ourselves by going over the last drop of the day, Cadillac Falls, as if we had sprouted fins.

Is this a good trip for beginning paddlers? Only those blessed with plenty of derring-do, who aren't afraid to get wet. We recommend it heartily for more experienced types. Personally, though, we'd rather swim laps in the pool at the inn than make like a salmon in the White.

Topsfield, Massachusetts: Twilight Paddle on the Ipswich River

Creatures — and Canoeists — Come Out at Night

CONTACT: The Massachusetts Audubon Society, Ipswich River Wildlife Sanctuary, 87 Perkins Row, Topsfield, MA 01983; (508) 887-9264. Canoe trips run throughout summer and fall. In addition to twilight trips, the sanctuary runs gourmet breakfast canoe trips, family paddles, and a full program of events and activities.

HOW TO GET THERE: From the junction of Route 1 and Route 97 in Topsfield, turn south (toward Beverly and Danvers) on Route 97, then take the second left onto Perkins Row. Follow Perkins Row for one mile; the sanctuary is on the right.

RATES: Our trip cost $20 per person for Massachusetts Audubon members and $25 for nonmembers.

WHAT TO BRING: Rubber-soled shoes, a water bottle, and a plastic bag or river duffel with a change of clothes in case you get wet.

KIDS: This trip is not recommended for children. Sign up for a family trip—some of these are run in the evenings—if you wish to bring kids.

SKILL LEVEL: This trip is fine for beginners.

ON YOUR OWN: From May 1 to October 31, the Ipswich River Wildlife Sanctuary rents canoes to Massachusetts Audubon members on a first-come, first-served basis for $5 per hour. Canoes go out between 9 A.M. and 3 P.M. and must be in by 4:30 P.M. Call ahead to be sure they won't be in use for a program on the day you plan to visit. Canoe rentals are also available from Foote Brothers, 230 Topsfield Road, Ipswich; (508) 356-9771.

Y ou're paddling under a new moon on an inky stretch of river. Silently, you listen to the night chorus of grasshoppers, crickets, and bullfrogs, dipping your paddle into the water oh so gently to remain unobtrusive. A great brown bat circles overhead, then another; a screech owl's eerie call breaks your reverie. The woods are alive as you maneuver your way around the sinuous twists and turns of the river. Night has fallen. You can see very little, but, senses atingle, you're aware of everything.

Such is the delicious pleasure of a twilight-to-dark canoe trip. The merely beautiful by day becomes magical by night. Even a familiar-as-an-old-friend stretch of river takes on a mysterious presence when shrouded in darkness.

Of course, it never hurts to have some company on an after-dark river adventure, especially if you're exploring an area for the first time or after a long absence. We joined a group from the Massachusetts Audubon Society/Ipswich River Wildlife Sanctuary for a twilight-to-dark paddle on the Ipswich River, in Topsfield, Massachusetts. The trip is run on a weeknight—Thursday, in this case—so harried commuters can unwind on the river after work.

The Ipswich River is more familiar to residents of Boston's North Shore than they might realize; the ground-water supplies drinking water to much of the region.

"This is a great night for a paddle; it's cloudy so it'll be really dark," sanctuary director Carol Decker said as she handed out life vests and paddles to the seven of us.

Decker and naturalist Bob Speare, our guides, couldn't resist pointing out signs of wildlife as we walked to the canoe launch site.

"Does anybody smell that? Kind of skunky? It's fox; hey, here's proof, fox scat," Decker said. We sniffed. She told us later that if we wet a nostril, we'd have a keener sense of smell, as animals do. That set the tone for the trip—a "be one with nature" theme that we eagerly embraced.

Speare gave us a quick paddle-stroke refresher course, then he and Decker demonstrated how to enter and exit a canoe without getting wet, acknowledging that the water level was so low, it really didn't matter. "If you fall in, we'll holler, 'Stand up,'" Decker said, laughing.

Her major advice for night-paddlers: communicate with your partner. "There might be a giant log in front of you that your partner can't see," she noted. "Makes sense to say, 'Big log ahead' to avoid upending yourself."

We paddled upriver, taking in the deep, earthy smell of decaying leaves that marked the approaching autumn equinox. We entered the realm of wooded swamp, a river-scape dominated by trees and shrubs. Some of the larger trees bear high-water marks from past floods. Downstream, the tree-lined banks give way to an open marshland, a popular feeding and nesting ground for wetland birds. Canoeists flock here, too, and the appeal is obvious; the river's serpentine twists provide an interesting ride and the chance to employ the whole repertoire of strokes, especially the sweepstroke.

On this late-September weeknight, the river was void of human life except for us, but rife with wild things. Decker shushed us and pointed up. "A barn owl, in that tree!" she whispered. We spotted it, a dark form on the outline of a tree limb, just before it took flight.

Eyes attuned to the darkness, ears at the ready, we sensed the presence of creatures all around us. We spotted bats overhead, then picked up the sound of a flying squirrel, then what sounded like the shriek of a mugging victim but turned out to be the cry of a screech owl. Decker screeched back with a call so authentic that Speare, three boats behind, answered her call with his own. We paddled as quietly as possible (forget the communicating stuff, we were communing with nature); then Decker pierced the silence with another owl call.

"I'm trying to say, 'We're here in your territory, come see us,' but I could be saying anything in owl talk," she told us. The owls talked back. Eventually, we came to a place where the river forked to the right and an island was on our left. We disembarked at the island for a campfire and a snack.

Perkins Island, about forty acres of pine, is owned by the sanctuary. Massachusetts Audubon Society members can camp overnight here from May through October, the same time period that canoes are available at the sanctuary.

Decker started building a fire in a fire ring while Speare put out snacks and cider on a folding table. All that's missing are the marshmallows, we thought. Then Speare pulled out a bag. Now, these people know how to put on a canoe trip; they've brought along the makings of s'mores. As every Girl Scout and Boy Scout knows, a s'more is the ultimate sandwich: roasted marshmallow and a square of chocolate, sandwiched between two graham crackers. Outrageously good.

Judging by the happy, marshmallow-streaked grownup faces around the campfire, nobody was having any trouble relaxing. "I've paddled this river a dozen times," said one participant. "But this was truly enchanting. It's like another world." The respectful hush as we paddled back to the landing said it all; we felt privileged to witness nightlife on the river.

Resources

Additional Outfitters

Allagash Canoe Trips, P.O. Box 713, Greenville, ME 04441; (207) 695-3668.

Allagash Wilderness Outfitters, Box 620, Star Route 76, Greenville, ME 04441; (207) 695-2821 (May through November); 36 Minuteman Drive, Millinocket, ME 04462; (207) 723-6622 (December through April).

Appalachian Mountain Club, P.O. Box 298, Gorham, NH 03581; (603) 466-2727.

Clarke Outdoors, 163 Route 7, West Cornwall, CT 06796; (203) 672-6365.

Connecticut River Safari, 451 Putney Road, Brattleboro, VT 05301; (802) 257-5008.

Huck Finn Adventures, P.O. Box 137, Collinsville, CT 06022; (203) 693-0385.

Maine Canoe Adventures, RFD #1 Box 105, Allagash, ME 04774; (207) 398-3191.

Maine Sport Outdoor School, P.O. Box 956, Rockport, ME 04856; (207) 236-8797.

Northern Pack and Paddle, P.O. Box 624, Woodstock, VT 05091; (802) 457-1409.

Outdoor Center of New England, 10 Pleasant Street, Millers Falls, MA 01349; (413) 659-3926.

Sunrise County Canoe Expeditions, Inc., Cathance Lake, Grove Post Office, ME 04638; (207) 454-7708.

Umiak Outfitters, 1880 Mountain Road, Gale Farm Center #6, Stowe, VT 05672; (800) 479-3380.

Vermont Waterways, RR 1 Box 322, East Hardwick, VT 05836; (800) 492-8271

Zoar Outdoor, Mohawk Trail, Charlemont, MA 01339; (800) 532-7483.

BOOKS

AMC River Guide: Maine. Appalachian Mountain Club Books.

AMC River Guide: Massachusetts, Connecticut, Rhode Island. Appalachian Mountain Club Books.

Canoe Camping: Vermont, New Hampshire. Roioli Schweiker, Backcountry Publications.

Canoeing Massachusetts, Rhode Island and Connecticut. Ken Weber, Backcountry Publications.

Quiet Water Canoe Guide: Maine. Alex Wilson and John Hayes, Appalachian Mountain Club Books.

Quiet Water Canoe Guide: Massachusetts, Connecticut, Rhode Island. Alex Wilson, Appalachian Mountain Club Books.

Quiet Water Canoe Guide: New Hampshire, Vermont. Alex Wilson, Appalachian Mountain Club Books.

Whitewater Handbook. Bruce Lessels, Appalachian Mountain Club Books.

Kayaking

Deer Isle, Maine: Island-to-Island Tour

Flexibility Is the Key on This Trip

CONTACT: L.L. Bean Outdoor Discovery Program, Freeport, ME 04033; (800) 341-4341, ext. 6666. L.L. Bean offers a number of courses and trips, including fly-fishing clinics, cycling, canoeing, archery, hunting, and outdoor skills workshops.

HOW TO GET THERE: Take I-95 north to just past Portland, then take Exit 9 (you're leaving the Maine Turnpike, but you're still on I-95). Continue to the Freeport exit and into town; you can't miss L.L. Bean on your left.

RATES: The five-day kayak-camping trip, including all paddling and camping equipment, instruction, meals, and transportation from Freeport to put-in and take-out spots, costs $595.

WHAT TO BRING: L.L. Bean will supply a list. All supplies and equipment must fit in the boats, so they are very specific about what to pack. Instructors often call registrants before the trip to go over questions and to check on clothing and equipment needs. Just follow the list, and you'll be fine.

KIDS: Minimum age is fourteen.

SKILL LEVEL: No experience necessary; you should be comfortable in and around water.

We were standing on the dock, watching the sky get darker, the waves get higher, and the drizzle turn to a steady downpour. We were ready to embark on a five-day Maine island-to-island kayak tour. The prognosis did not look good.

"Do you think the rain is going to stop?" we asked the

lobsterman. Surely, he knows something about forecasting weather, we thought.

"Always has," he replied.

Down East humor. We laughed in spite of the gloomy outlook. We had signed up for L.L. Bean's Penobscot Bay kayak and camping trip. The brochure promised a tour along protected and open waters, with stops at several secluded, uninhabited islands, hikes along scenic trails, and a visit to Isle au Haut, part of Acadia National Park.

On day one, we met at L.L. Bean in Freeport, packed the van, and headed to Sunshine Campground on Deer Isle. On the way, we stopped at popular Moody's Diner. So far, so good. According to plan, we devoured giant portions of pancakes, sausages, handcut fries, and slices of homemade pie—and hoped that the boat would stay afloat with the added weight.

On to our campsite. Under gray, threatening skies, we began our lessons. First, our instructors, John Bradley, Jim Kaiser, and Bob Myron, went over paddle and boat nomenclature and design. Ho-hum; full bellies, fresh air, nomenclature. Time for a nap? No way; they had us on the water before we could catch a wink. We practiced forward strokes and backstrokes, forward and reverse sweeps, draw strokes and bracing strokes. We were getting pretty darned good, and then the instructors mentioned the ever-popular wet exit. Moans, groans. "Do we have to?" "In this water?" "I don't think so." But, good sports that we are, we gave it a whirl. It was not as difficult as it first seemed, but it was work. We went to sleep very quickly that evening to the pitter-patter of rain on the roof of the tent.

Day two: Overcast skies and a steady wind from the north, just enough to make paddling slow and tough. Plans called for lunch on Hell's Half Acre, about six miles away, and overnight on Harbor Island, another four

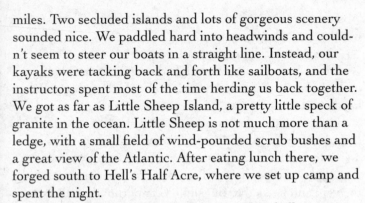

miles. Two secluded islands and lots of gorgeous scenery sounded nice. We paddled hard into headwinds and couldn't seem to steer our boats in a straight line. Instead, our kayaks were tacking back and forth like sailboats, and the instructors spent most of the time herding us back together. We got as far as Little Sheep Island, a pretty little speck of granite in the ocean. Little Sheep is not much more than a ledge, with a small field of wind-pounded scrub bushes and a great view of the Atlantic. After eating lunch there, we forged south to Hell's Half Acre, where we set up camp and spent the night.

This island is much closer to heaven than hell. From a distance it looks like a giant beach; it wears a carpet of green bushes like a toupee. It's actually a solid piece of granite, worn smooth by the wind and pounding salt water. Protected by large islands on all sides, with sweeping ocean views, it's paradise found for coastal kayakers.

Day three: The wind was a blowin'! "We'll do whatever the group wants," said Kaiser. "Should we try to make Harbor Island today?" No one wanted to be the one to wimp out, so we loaded the boats and slid them into the water. Yikes! We had to cross a slot with lots of fetch (we learned this word the first day of class). We paddled about 100 yards, maybe less, before we hurried back to the protected shores of Hell's Half Acre. Paradise revisited.

Left with time on our hands, we explored Hell (who else can say that?) and had a short, impromptu class on foraging and plant and tree identification. Two of the more aggressive paddlers cruised out into the surf, where they were pummeled, tossed, and turned, and all the happier for it.

A note about our guides: they were always willing to accommodate each guest. If you wanted to relax, that was fine. If you felt like paddling, someone would take you out. They also knew a great deal about outdoor survival techniques and skills. What was billed as a kayaking learning vacation turned out to be much more. We learned about maps and compassing, navigational skills, camping and island etiquette, and more. On top of all this, Myron is a gourmet cook.

Day four: The winds had died down a bit, but now we

were running out of time. If we went on to Harbor Island to camp overnight, would we make it back on time? What the heck? We'd stay on Hell's. But we needed water. According to our proposed plan, we would have reached the shores of Isle au Haut by now, and been able to refill our bottles. The group decided to paddle to Stonington. (Actually, two people wanted to remain on the island. The instructors played Paper, Scissors, Rock to see who would stay with them. We know what you're thinking. You're wrong; the loser stayed behind.)

As we left the island, the sun peeked out, the skies cleared, and the wind died. We paddled gently through water as smooth as glass. On the way back, water jugs full, we stopped at Russ Island, climbed to its highest point, and gazed out at the open sea in one direction and a protected bay littered with islands in the other. Penobscot Bay is where Maine must have dumped all its extra islands; it's a haven for coastal travelers. We explored Russ, coming across an old farm, a quarry, and a flock of sheep. Kaiser explained that sheep are common on Maine's uninhabited islands. Farmers dump the sheep on the islands, where there are no predators.

We left Russ Island at sunset. It was a full-moon, low-tide evening, and we floated through inches of water, gazing down at a remarkable carpet of starfish. We made one more stop—this time to pick up mussels for our evening appetizer.

Day five: Time to pack up and go. So, we didn't make it to Harbor Island. We didn't make it to Isle au Haut, either. But no one was complaining. We started the trip as a class with instructors sheep-dogging us around the water. By the end, we were a group of friends gone paddling.

And sometimes the best part of an adventure is not knowing where you'll end up.

Rockport, Maine:
Campout in Muscongus Bay

Exploring an Island Wilderness

CONTACT: Maine Sport Outdoor School, P.O. Box 956, Rockport, ME 04856; (800) 722-0826. Maine Sport offers an assortment of tours, from a two-hour circuit of Camden harbor to four days of island hopping. On two-, three-, or four-day tours, participants camp on an island each night. Kayak instructional courses and family adventures are also offered.

HOW TO GET THERE: Take Exit 22 (Brunswick) off I-95 north to coastal Route 1; take Route 90 until you pick up Route 1 again in Rockport, then go left on Route 1 north to Maine Sport, about a half-mile on the left.

RATES: A two-night, three-day Muscongus Bay tour, including paddling equipment, wetsuit (if needed), guides, shuttle to and from the put-in, group camping, cooking gear, and meals, costs $275.

WHAT TO BRING: Maine Sport will supply a specific equipment list. All gear must fit in kayaks, so participants are asked to bring no more, no less than what is suggested. Tents, sleeping bags, and dry bags are available for rent from Maine Sport.

KIDS: This tour is not appropriate for children. Look into Maine Sport's youth adventures and special family kayak trips, from half-day trips to custom one- to four-day island tours.

SKILL LEVEL: No experience necessary, but you should be comfortable around water and with wilderness camping.

S teady, gentle strokes glide the kayak through broad
sweeps of deep-blue water studded with boreal scenery.
Islands of wind-stunted trees and rocky ledges spill into the
sea. As far as the eyes can see is an astounding length of
coastline weaving in and out for 3,478 squiggly miles. An
open, restless sea is broken by calm inlets and quiet coves,
and peppered with clusters of rocky islets. The setting pre-
sents a world that few tourists see: an untouched watery
wilderness with nearly 3,000 saltwater islands to explore. It
is the promise and lure of Down East coastal kayaking.

"Sea kayaking is something that everyone can do," says
Kristen Oehler, assistant director of Maine Sport Outdoor
School in Rockport, Maine. "And it really gets you away
from it all. Imagine, being on your own — or with a chosen
few — on an isolated island. That's pretty appealing." Oehler
says interest in the sport of coastal kayaking is taking off,
and Maine Sport classes and trips fill up fast. Maine Sport
is one of the premier sea kayaking schools in the Northeast,
offering a variety of instructional programs and learning
vacations. You can pick from an extensive menu; we liked
the sound of the popular three-day Muscongus Bay trip.
"The ultimate Maine coast experience," the brochure
promises. "Spend your days paddling and exploring the
protected waters of Muscongus Bay, your evenings relaxing
beneath the stars at a private island campsite." We were
reassured that previous kayaking experience was not necessary; the guides would teach us what we needed to know.

Class began bright and
early in the morning on Round
Pond, about a forty-five-
minute drive from the Maine
Sport headquarters. We stood
on the banks, dressed in poly,
fleece-lined layers and
wrapped in life jackets big
enough to save a drowning
moose. This was clearly not the
island paradise promised. What
about the romantic images of
Inuit coastal travel in the Arc-

tic? Apparently, we've come a long way in 5,000 years; we were staring up at a mountain of miracle-fiber equipment and gear. The better to keep us warm, dry, and safe, our instructors told us. We kept an open mind.

It was instantly apparent how different kayaking would be from other boat travel. Each of us was fitted with a waterproof elastic skirt that sealed the cockpit. We were basically wearing our boats. Mermaidlike, we floated on water that was inches deep.

We took off with decisive, pushy draw strokes. "Slow down. You're working far too hard," said Martha Garfield, our instructor. "Kayaking requires graceful, gentle movements. If you do it right, you'll be able to paddle long distances without getting tired." Working less sounded good to us, so we gave it a try. So much different than aggressive canoe strokes; the kayak stroke is a light touch on the paddle. It works, and before long we were gliding gracefully across Round Pond.

There was no talk of Eskimo rolls, wet exits, or any of the more publicized aspects of whitewater river kayaking. "The trick to staying upright in a sea kayak is a gentle rock of the torso counterpoint to the rhythm of the waves," Garfield said. Huh? Comprehending the instructions proved more difficult than mastering the technique. After only a few hours, we had mastered the docile, enclosed waters of Round Pond and were ready for the Atlantic. We put our kayaks in at a local harbor and paddled out slowly into Muscongus Bay.

Muscongus is the Abenaki Indian name for "fishing place," and it's still an accurate description. Lobsters are bountiful in the warm, shallow waters and mussel-rich shoals of the bay. Lobster buoys are everywhere, dotting the expanse of sea like colorful bobbers, and testing our newly acquired paddling skills. We shared the tranquil waters with seabirds, marine mammals, and lobstermen.

We followed the rocky coastline, poked around coves, and circled uninhabited islands with names like Louds, Thief, and Cow Wreck. We reached our destination, Crow Island, with plenty of daylight left to set up camp. Maine Sport groups camp only on public islands or at their own

Maine Island Trails

No wonder the lure of sea kayaking has hooked you: Down East waters boast some of the most spectacular and wild scenery in the world. The Maine coastline stretches in and out for 3,478 miles, and its cold, savage Atlantic waters are peppered with more than 3,000 islands. Less than 200 of them are inhabited; most are privately owned or belong to the Bureau of Public Lands or the Bureau of Parks and Recreation.

So where do you go? Your first step should be to join the Maine Island Trail Association. The association has put together a string of seventy-eight islands from Casco Bay to Machias Bay, whose owners graciously allow public use. As a member, you'll take over responsibility for certain islands, patrolling regularly for litter and other signs of abuse. You'll also get the best island guide on the market: *The Maine Island Trail Guidebook*, available only to members.

permanent site on Gay Island. Low-impact camping rules and island etiquette are strongly followed. This means, among other things, that there are no bathroom facilities. Solid waste is packed out in an airtight (thankfully) container. Luckily, we were on large enough islands to afford ample privacy.

Crow Island is beautiful, rugged, and deserted. Towering pine trees and rocky beaches sweep down to the sea. Standing on a granite outcrop overlooking the mighty Atlantic, we felt the day's last shafts of sun shine through the trees, giving us the wonderful, wild feeling that we were, perhaps, the first to land here. The romantic images of coastal travel had returned. We set our tents where the ocean breeze blew all night, clear and cool from the open seas.

The next morning, we broke camp and paddled at a leisurely pace all day, with stops to explore an uninhabited island or to take a swim break. It was easy to be calmed, almost mesmerized by the surrounding scenery: dark, jutting islands contrasted against the deep blue of the water. Flocks of seabirds and families of eider ducks exploded as we paddled near, and we got so close to the gulls, terns, loons, and herons that we felt the swish of air as they scattered away. Once, the tranquil waters around us began to quiver. We felt the tiny vibrations of rippling water, and up popped a seal, inches from us.

Our second night we spent on Gay Island, home of Maine Sport's lodge and private island base from May through October. They even had an outhouse, which seemed downright luxurious by this point. We shed our kayaks and walked the island fields, a tangle of sea-tolerant bushes and shrubs, edged with meandering stone walls. We sunbathed on a pebble beach and, later, watched the sun sink below the horizon.

The last day we had a short paddle back to our pick-up point at Pleasant Point in Cushing, Maine. We dawdled. We poked around. We paddled slowly. We were in no hurry. We were tempted to drop a note in a bottle and send it out to sea: "Not homesick yet."

Errol, New Hampshire: Whitewater School on the Androscoggin

Go with the Flow

CONTACT: Saco Bound Northern Waters Canoe and Kayak, P.O. Box 119, Route 302, Center Conway, NH 03813; (603) 447-3002.

HOW TO GET THERE: Follow Route 16 north into Errol. Northern Waters School is on Main Street.

RATES: The two-day beginning course, including all paddling equipment, instruction, transportation, and a campsite, costs $160.

WHAT TO BRING: Count on getting wet. Bring an extra change of clothing, a swimsuit, two pairs of sneakers, polypropylene or wool underwear, a polypropylene shirt, a sweater, and a hat. If you have a wet suit, bring it; otherwise Northern Waters will supply one if necessary.

KIDS: Minimum age thirteen; must also be five feet tall and weigh at least 100 pounds.

SKILL LEVEL: Whitewater kayaking is a strenuous activity. You should be in good shape and have no fear of water. Northern Waters suggest participants spend some time becoming both physically and mentally prepared for instruction.

ETCETERA: Participants can camp at Northern Waters for free (hot showers and toilets, but very rustic). The town of Errol has one restaurant, a general store, and the modest Errol Motel, (603) 482-3256. Within a 30-minute drive you'll find Berlin, and the luxurious Balsams Resort in Dixville Notch. The vacation town of Rangeley, Maine, is about 45 minutes farther on Route 16.

K ayakers are at the top of the food chain. There are none higher."

That's the gospel according to Northern Waters' kayaking guru, Jeff Laveirede. And it won't take long before you're a believer. If anyone can get you dreaming of white holes and praying to the river gods, the instructors at Saco Bound's Northern Waters can.

Five of us stood at river's edge, surrounded by enough equipment to outfit a high school athletic department. We had gathered on the banks of the Androscoggin River in Errol, New Hampshire, for Saco Bound's Northern Waters' Whitewater Kayak Clinic. We had spent the morning in class, learning the basics of paddling and boat handling. Now, we were playing patty-cake with our paddles, rotating our torsos, limbering up our muscles. "Stretching is the ignition that turns on the body and mind," Laveirede told us. We ended with a prayer (albeit tongue in cheek) to Otar the River God.

Prayers. Helmets. Lifejackets. Spray skirts. Perhaps there was a message here. Yet optimism reigned; we were ready to glide through the currents, surf the waves, conquer the rapids.

Our instructions were to paddle a stone's throw distance to a quiet, deep spot across the river. We each slid into the cockpit of our kayak (which proved much easier than putting on the spray skirt) and launched the craft. Whoa. We took off, slip-sliding away with the current; we had no control. It was like driving a Ferrari with a brick tied to the accelerator. No, like steering a banana peel. We all managed to make it to the other side without getting wet. Thank you, Otar; we were humbled.

Our next onwater exercise was practicing a wet exit and aggressive self-rescue techniques. The three steps to remember: one, tuck, to keep your head up and avoid hitting something; two, pull the spray skirt off; and three, push the boat off of you so you can swim to the surface. How bad could it be?

The water was surprisingly warm. The Androscoggin runs from Umbagog Lake, which is very shallow and quickly heated by the summer sun. Tipping over wasn't nearly as bad as it first seemed.

Still, shouldn't we have been practicing ways to *avoid* wet exits? "Always keep your self-rescue skills concurrent with your boating skills," Laveirede explained to the more impatient ones in the group. Before long, we were practicing rightside-up moves, too—paddle strokes, ferries, body movements, balance. As we moved down the river, our guide told us to "sense the water through the paddle. Close your eyes and feel the water and the boat."

That's the seduction of kayaking. You are the elusive trout swimming the currents, a feather dipping and reemerging across the meringue surface. You are in the water, not on it; the boat becomes an extension of yourself. But the Zen of kayaking does not come without paying your dues. We went trout-scouting (dumped, overboard, flipped, submerged, swimming—call it what you want) several times that afternoon.

"Don't try to muscle the boat," Laveirede cautioned us. "Kayaking is a grace and finesse sport, not a muscle sport."

The first day ended with a Class II rapids run—a kayak disposal, Laveirede joked. After a quick mental review of our lessons, we eased into the current and took off. Waves hit the boat and splashed our faces. Paddle. Lean. Remember balance. Water sprays. Stroke. Stretch. Lean again. The boat picked up speed. Final stroke and . . . the silence and calm of the eddy. What a rush!

It's amazing how fast you can learn to kayak, with the right instruction. The next day we paddled the river like it was a playground, seeking out eddies and holes, paddling close to the edge of our newly acquired abilities. Too soon, the clinic was over. "You're walking away with a tool box," Laveirede told us. "You have the tools to work with to get better. Reach into the box as you progress."

We said good-bye, with well-meant promises to stay in touch, to our top-of-the-chain mates. The following week we bumped into two of them at the Kittery Trading Post, pricing kayaks.

Jamaica, Vermont: End Over End on the Wild West River

Getting Air Time

CONTACT: Vermont Department of Forests, Parks, and Recreation, RR 1, Box 33, North Springfield, VT 05150, (802) 886-2215, will provide you with dam release dates. Everett River and Mountain in Wakefield, RI, (401) 783-4547, runs a fall group trip for experienced paddlers.

HOW TO GET THERE: From Brattleboro, take Route 30 north about 25 miles to the village of Jamaica. Turn right at the white church in the center of the village (there's only one; you can't miss it). The Jamaica State Park entrance is a half-mile on the left.

WHAT TO BRING: You'll need all your own equipment, a change of clothes, and lunch.

KIDS: This trip is not appropriate for children, unless you have a teen who's an experienced paddler.

SKILL LEVEL: Very experienced on the upper West; moderate skill level needed on the lower West.

You've played the river, a beautiful stretch of kayaking heaven, surfing the waves, hitting the eddies. Now, ahead, is an enormous sheet of rocks. The river rushes and deflects against the granite, forming an eddy wall: the perfect place for an end-over-end maneuver. You drive the bow of the boat into the wall of water; it plunges, standing you on end, then squirting you out, sending you airborne. Blast off!

Ender Rock. If you're a seasoned kayaker, you undoubtedly have a story about this place. It's the West River in Vermont, and there's no better fall water release in the Northeast. Just when the rivers are dry and New England kayakers are getting the whitewater jones, the Bald Mountain Dam release sends forth the perfect amount of white, frothy boil. For one weekend in the fall (usually late September or early October), kayakers from all over the region — and beyond — clamor to the shores of the wild, wild West.

"When I first started coming here, from about 1969 to 1975, there were only around 200 of us," says Russ Everett, kayaking instructor and owner of Everett River and Mountain in Wakefield, Rhode Island. "We knew everybody; it was like a small community affair. Now, there are 2,000 to 2,500 paddlers doing the weekend."

It is, indeed, a special happening, and probably the most excitement the little town of Jamaica, Vermont, sees in a year. There's often gridlock in Jamaica State Park, where this whitewater adventure begins. To control traffic, the park operates a shuttle service. Paddlers pile in the back of a pickup truck with twenty or so other people and hang on for the short ride up an old railroad grade. Another truck brings their boats.

The Upper West is a two-mile stretch of water that ignites enthusiasm and sparks descriptions. "It's craziness." "It's a wonderful, delightful piece of water." "Perfect." "There is none better." "Ya-hoo! Let's do it again."

Paddlers must negotiate a continuous run of Class III rapids. (Some say III-plus, others argue IV-minus. This provides fodder for many heated discussions.) Two-thirds of the way down, you'll meet "The Dumplings." Sounds cute; it's not. It's a series of enormous rocks jutting out of the water (there's one that must be at least ten feet high), and it requires experienced moves.

GREG NIKAS

*His kayak nearly lost in the boil, a paddler works his way
through a Class IV rapid on the West River.*

Of course, kayakers all have their own style, and the
West brings out the best in them. There are the Players; they
surf every wave, ferry across the currents, hit all the eddies.
They paddle the river as if they were playing a game of chess.
How many moves can they make? How many ways can they
play it? They put in early in the morning, skip lunch, and by
late afternoon, they've made one run of this two-mile stretch.
Then there are the River Runners. Straight down, in and out
in twenty minutes; they'll make five runs a day.

However you do it, you'll end up at Ender Rock. By the
time you get there, there'll be a line in the eddy and a crowd
on the banks watching and cheering. Good luck.

So, what if you're not up to this whitewater craziness?
Here's a secret: show up for the dam release anyway. Then
take your kayak downstream, below Townshend Dam.
There are plenty of put-in spots above and below Newfane
(where Route 30 crosses the bridge is a great spot; or just
below the Townshend Dam). The paddling on the lower
West offers eight to ten miles of Class I to Class III water,
with enough shoots, currents, and eddies to keep even the
wildest kayaker wet, sassy, and happy.

Millers Falls, Massachusetts: Rips and Rapids on the Deerfield

To Be One with the River Is the Thing at OCNE

There's nothing in life that truly prepares you for your first wet exit. Hanging upside down, under water, snapped into a boat, doesn't sound like something you'd ever do on purpose. Yet this unseemly act is what separates serious kayakers from rookies.

For your first time, you want to be in good hands. We went to one of the best, Outdoor Centre of New England. *Outside* magazine named OCNE the top paddling school in the Northeast; many consider it one of the best in the country. Founder Tom Foster has been called "the godfather of contemporary paddling instruction" (yes, he's heard a million bad Marlon Brando imitations). He will likely answer the phone himself when you call, saying "Come on up, we'll teach you how to put a blade in the water."

Up, in this case, is Millers Falls, Massachusetts, a couple of hours west of Boston. We signed up for a weekend pond-to-river whitewater paddling class, with two nights at OCNE's bunk and breakfast lodge. The two-story lodge is rustic, but beautifully landscaped; bunk rooms and bathrooms are communal, so you get to know your classmates well. (Tip: arrive early to stake out your bunk.) There are also two private rooms reserved for couples. A popular hangout is the video room, with a collection of whitewater action flicks.

There's a 10 P.M. noise curfew, for good reason: coffee at 6:15 A.M., breakfast until 7:15. Between bites of tater-tot, instructors told whitewater war stories (which made absolutely no sense to us beginners). Then, the day began in earnest for paddler wanna-bes; until 5 P.M., beginners and

CONTACT: The Outdoor Centre of New England, 10 Pleasant Street, Millers Falls, MA 01349; (413) 659-3926. OCNE runs two-day and five-day paddling workshops, specializing in whitewater canoeing and kayaking.

HOW TO GET THERE: From north or south, take I-91 to Exit 27, Route 2 east. Go 7.3 miles, then turn right on Union Street and right again to Pleasant Street.

WHERE TO STAY: Your best bet is OCNE's lodge for bunk and breakfast. The $30 rate includes group-style bunks (bring a sleeping bag) and breakfast. Private rooms ($60 per couple) are also available.

RATES: Beginner/Intermediate (B/I) kayak workshops are $179; four-day workshops are $319. Kayak and gear, wetsuit and booties, and lunch each day are included. A deposit is required.

WHAT TO BRING: Polypropylene or polyester underwear and socks (available for purchase at OCNE's retail store), post-paddling clothes, sunblock, and sunglasses.

KIDS: Check out "Kayak Kids," a three-day program for beginners and intermediates age twelve and up.

SKILL LEVEL: Participants in B/I workshops range from pure beginners (never paddled) to those who have had instruction and are working on precise river maneuvering and rolls. Staffed at a three-to-one ratio, groups are split up according to ability, so beginners paddle with beginners, intermediates with intermediates. OCNE also offers Intermediate/Advanced workshops.

ETCETERA: Once you've taken a workshop or private lesson with OCNE, you can join the OCNE Paddling Club for free. Weekends, paddlers meet at OCNE, load boats, and travel to the Deerfield (shuttle provided by OCNE). The group puts in below Fife Dam, paddles to Zoar Gap, then plays in the gap until the release stops (about five hours). Back to OCNE for free munchies, swapping of paddling tales, and going out to dinner. It's a good way to get paddling experience with paddlers of varying abilities.

intermediates would be stroking, spinning, drawing, sculling, sweeping, and circling; generally, learning to be one with the river, "playing in harmony with it," in one guide's words. The student-instructor ratio is three to one, and students are divided into groups on the basis of ability and personality. (Personality? This they've determined over toast and tater-tots?)

Groups designated and gear assigned, we piled into vans and headed for the Deerfield River. Turns out the "pond" is a placid section of the Deerfield just above a dam. We're ready to put in and paddle, but, whoa! Not yet. Stretching exercises are an important part of the OCNE regime. Since your legs and feet are stuffed into a skinny little boat for five or six hours a day, it probably makes sense to get the blood flowing first.

After a demonstration of launching and landing techniques, it's wet exit time. Feeling like Batman in the bat cave, we hung upside down in the cold water, overturned by instructor Brian Totten. We hung there as long as we could stand it (seconds? minutes?), then banged on the bottom of the boat, signaling Totten to turn us rightside up, unprepared for the rush of icy water that runs down one's chest and back at this juncture.

Teeth chattering, shivering, we do it again. And just when we're starting to think this exercise is as much fun as childbirth and gum surgery, (or childbirth during gum surgery), an amazing thing happens: We start to enjoy it.

After what was deceptively billed as a "gourmet lunch" in the OCNE brochure—turkey sandwiches or peanut butter and jelly—we piled into the blessedly heated van again and headed for the Fife Brook Dam section of the river. We put in at an eddy and attempted some C-turns, which looked easy until three of us flipped.

Once our fear of flipping had passed, we found it easier to concentrate on paddling. We envied instructors Totten and Peter "P. J." Giampetro for their fluidity on the water; each move they made showed skill and grace, and they moved with such ease, it was frustrating

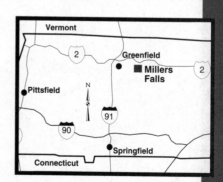

when our own attempts to follow suit were awkward and jerky. But they were good teachers, encouraging us and instantly picking out the one tiny movement or flaw that was screwing us up, so we could make it right. In spite of their far superior skill level, they seemed like part of the group. The dam release was coming to an end that day, so we headed back to the base, making jokes about who'd win the "most flips for the weekend" award at workshop's end.

The locations were the same on day two, with new material to cover, including river strategies (ferrying, eddy turns, peel outs) and more advanced strokes and maneuvers. But we had time for a game called Sharks and Minnows—basically, tag in a kayak. This was a fun way to practice boat control, and we paddled like crazy to avoid becoming a shark.

Our added confidence would come in handy later, when we took on a Class II rapids called S Turn. It was easy to distinguish the guides and intermediates on this one: they glided smoothly from one side of the river to the other, while the beginners paddled in a frenzy just to stay upright. As if this weren't humbling enough, halfway down, an eddy called "The Elevator" sucks you back up to the top of the rapid again. We flailed, we flipped, we floated in the fast-moving water—we were becoming one with the river, all right—and then it was over. Back in the van, we made plans to come back and do it again. Even the guy with the most flips to his credit that weekend (nineteen) vowed to return.

Gloucester, Massachusetts: Whale-Watching in a Sea Kayak

Eye to Eye with a Gentle Giant

CONTACT: Adventure Learning, 67 Bear Hill Road, Merrimac, MA 01860; (800) 649-9728 or (508) 346-9728. Ask for a schedule; trips are generally run Fridays and Sundays in July and August, from 8 A.M. to 4 P.M. You're usually in the water between 10:30 and 1:30.

HOW TO GET THERE: Trips meet at the boat dock on Gloucester harbor. Take Route 128 north to the very end, Exit 9. Bear right onto Route 127 south. Bear left onto Rogers Street. Go past the Gorton's sign and take a left onto Harbor Loop. Look for the pier between a red brick building and the Coast Guard station; you should see a sign for Rainbow Chaser Charters. Park on Harbor Loop or across the street in the parking lot near the doughnut shop.

RATES: Trips cost $130 per person, which includes kayak equipment and motor cruiser transportation. Important: Reserve two months in advance; these trips fill up fast.

WHAT TO BRING: A wetsuit with water sandals or booties (not required but recommended), long underwear, wind or rain jacket, pre- and postpaddling clothes, deck shoes or sneakers, hat, sunglasses, sunblock, waterproof camera, lunch, snack, water bottle, seasick medication if necessary (take before boarding). Note: Whales seem attracted to bright colors, so you might want to wear a vivid hat to get their attention.

KIDS: By individual evaluation.

SKILL LEVEL: Adventure Learning insists you take their one-day sea kayak clinic or equivalent; you need good bracing strokes and must be comfortable in open water.

"This trip will ruin you for any other wildlife encounter," trip leader John Halloran warned us. Imagine being right in the water with the largest mammal on earth, having seventy tons of finback whale coming toward you, coming so close you get wet from the spray of its blowhole . . . that's whale-watching in a sea kayak. Forget those tourist-laden whale-watch boats. This is an adventure.

Like rubber duckies in a gigantic bathtub. That's how we felt, twenty miles out to sea, bobbing along in sixteen-foot sea kayaks. We felt plenty vulnerable, knowing that the seasonal cetaceans are curious about the brightly colored boats. Although Coast Guard regulations state that a human cannot intentionally come within 100 feet of a whale, who's to say it's vice-versa? Even the slowest whale can move faster than a kayak can.

"Not to worry. We've had three years of whale-watch trips without incident," Halloran told us.

Halloran and his wife, Nancy, run Adventure Learning, based in Merrimac, Massachusetts. Whale-watching by sea kayak is not unusual on the West Coast, but on the East Coast it's almost as rare as the northern right whale (the most endangered species in the world). Adventure Learning runs about ten such trips a season; all are sell-outs. Capacity is limited to six kayakers and two guides, "so we won't impact the whales' activities," Halloran explained.

Recently spotted in the area: two species of dolphin, harbor porpoises, and five species of whale, along with myriad seabirds. Twice, Adventure Learning groups have sighted northern white whales (only a few hundred of these are left); more typically, they encounter minkes, finbacks, and humpbacks. "At times, we've seen twenty or more, other times we've seen just one," Halloran told us, noting that many of the great whales travel solo when they head to feeding grounds. (Would you want to tell a football team if you were heading to the buffet table?)

Of course, there's no guarantee that the whales will make an appearance. They're more elusive than ever, having migrated from their usual feeding grounds at Stellwagen Bank to Jeffrey's Ledge, a shoal farther north. Potentially rough water in this unprotected area makes the trip a no-go for inexperienced paddlers. Despite the added challenge, Adventure Learning kayakers have encountered whales on every trip this season. If the sought-after cetaceans turn out to be no-shows, we'll be hugely disappointed.

We and our kayaks were transported from Gloucester harbor to Jeffrey's Ledge via *Rainbow Chaser*, a thirty-foot motor cruiser with the latest tracking equipment. After a ninety-minute boat ride, we off-loaded at Pigeon Hill, a shallow (150 feet or so) underwater hill. The water here in the hills, we were told, is full of nutrients, which attract fish, which attract whales. We paddled around in the open water, out of sight of land, looking and listening for a sign that we were not alone. We tried to spot a "spout," the water fountain–like breath that appears when a whale surfaces. Whales species can be identified by their spouts. (Whoever spots one first gets to say, "Thar she blows!" surely one of the highlights of any whale-watch trip.) Spouting can be heard as well as seen—it makes a blasting noise audible from as far as a mile away. But all was quiet on this hazy July day. . . .

Whooossshhhh! Where did that come from? We didn't see anything; then a black humplike shape appeared as if from nowhere. It was up, and it was gone. We paddled in the general direction it moved, but never saw it again. No time for frustration, because at that moment Halloran shouted, "Finback whale!" The finback had popped up just twenty to thirty feet away, between us and *Rainbow Chaser*. We did as we were told: we just sat there watching, jaws agape. This majestic mammal—the second-largest animal that ever lived (the blue whale is largest)—came so close we could have touched it. A perfect swimming machine, it glided under our boats with nary a ripple. For one magical hour, this frolicking finback teased and played with us, as we snapped pictures and Halloran kept the whale facts coming. (Is there anything this biology teacher doesn't know about whales?)

Then we heard a fainter whooshing sound and saw, a half-mile or so away, more spouts. More finbacks. We started paddling toward them, but they got to us first. (Finbacks can reach a size of more than seventy feet and seventy tons, but their streamlined bodies allow them to move as fast as twenty-eight miles per hour.) The pair were headed toward the Pigeon Hill sushi bars. They'd go under, disappear, then reappear, never popping up where we'd expect. But the original finback wasn't through with us yet. The playful whale kept coming between us and the other two, as if to say, "Hey, what about me?" We now had three finbacks in our midst, often within four kayak-lengths of us, so close we could look down and see an eye blink. Often, we could see their throat pleats, swollen with water and food, as they broke the surface of the water. In fact, they were so close, they ruined our pictures, filling the frame with their massive gray bodies. We could barely contain our excitement, but managed to keep from capsizing. (Adventure Learning guides say they can rescue people in thirty seconds. We didn't want to put them to the test.) Since the whales had come right up to us in delightfully sociable fashion, we'd only paddled two or three miles. So we weren't tired, just exhilarated, tingly, and humbled—dwarfed by the immensity of these astonishing creatures, and honored to have been part of their world. Halloran was right; this close encounter will be tough to top.

Resources

Additional Outfitters

Atlantic Kayak Tours, 320 W. Saugerties Road, Saugerties, NY 12477; (914) 246-2187.

Atlantic Outfitters, 152 Bellevue Avenue, Newport, RI 02840; (401) 848-2920.

Clarke Outdoors, 163 Route 7, West Cornwall, CT 06796; (203) 672-6365.

Essex River Basin Adventures, P.O. Box 270, Essex, MA 01929; (800) KAYAK-04.

Everett River and Mountain, P.O. Box 723, Wakefield, RI 02880; (401) 783-4547.

Maine Island Kayak Company, 70 Luther Street, Peaks Island, ME 04108; (800) 796-2373.

Mountain Workshop, P.O. Box 625, Ridgefield, CT 06877; (203) 438-3640.

Riverrunning Expeditions, 85 Main Street, Falls Village, CT 06031; (203) 824-5579.

Sakonnet Boathouse, 169 Riverside Drive, Tiverton, RI 02878; (401) 624-1440.

True North Outfitters, 4 University Drive, Burlington, VT 05401; (802) 860-1910.

Umbagog Outfitters, P.O. Box 268, Errol, NH 03579; (603) 356-3292.

Umiak Outfitters, 1880 Mountain Road, Gale Farm Center #6, Stowe, VT 05672; (800) 479-3380.

Zoar Outdoor, Mohawk Trail, Charlemont, MA 01339; (800) 532-7483.

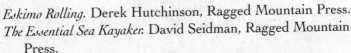

BOOKS

Eskimo Rolling. Derek Hutchinson, Ragged Mountain Press.

The Essential Sea Kayaker. David Seidman, Ragged Mountain Press.

Kayaking Whitewater and Touring Basics, A Trailside Series Guide. Steven Krauzer, W. W. Norton & Company.

The Maine Island Trail Guidebook. Maine Island Trail Association. (This is available only to members of the Association; worth joining to get it.)

Sea Kayaking Along the New England Coast. Tamsin Venn, Appalachian Mountain Club Books.

Whitewater Handbook. Bruce Lessels, Appalachian Mountain Club Books.

Sailing

Burlington, Vermont:
Become a Sailor in a Weekend
on Lake Champlain

Just Don't Call It a Crash Course

Question: How much can a novice sailor learn about the sport in just two days? Answer: Alas, not enough to skipper a fifty-footer through the coral reefs of Bora Bora, but enough to handle, say, a twenty-seven-foot Soling under normal wind conditions with a smidgen of confidence.

Ideally, of course, one should spend a week or more learning to sail, preferably in crystalline, bathtub-warm waters dotted with inviting isles. But, when time and money are at a premium, a weekend course can provide a solid introduction to sailing, and enough of a trial run to reveal whether the Topsiders-and-topsails lifestyle is the one for you.

"Our programs are compact and intense," explained Robin Doyle, owner/director of the International Sailing School in Colchester, Vermont. The fifteen-year-old school is based on Malletts Bay in Lake Champlain, a 120-mile-long expanse of fresh water studded with more than fifty islands. I.S.S. offers plenty of longer courses, but we decided the real test would be a two-day learn-to-sail program. Could Doyle & Co. possibly turn a forty-plus-year-old landlubber into a salty dawg in just two days?

With a student-instructor ratio of just three to one, and all-day sessions, the school crams a lot of knowledge into a short course. Beforehand, students are asked to read Gary Jobson's *Fundamentals of Sailing*, and it helps to be highly motivated. Despite the temptations of nearby Burlington (home of fifty-seven bars, at last count), this ain't no party.

CONTACT: International Sailing School, 253 Lake Shore Drive, Malletts Bay, Colchester, VT 05446; (802) 864-9065. A sister school is operated in Punta Gorda, Florida. Summer courses on Lake Champlain run from mid-May through mid-September.

HOW TO GET THERE: From I-89, take Exit 16 to Route 7north. Follow Route 7 for 2.5 miles, then go through a series of lights and enter a valley to a four-way intersection. Take Blakely Road for 2 miles, heading into Malletts Bay. Go straight (you'll see water). Go about 400 yards up the road; on your left you'll see a yellow building marked International Sailing Center.

WHERE TO STAY: The I.S.S. office has information about local campgrounds, waterfront cottages, and motels near the school. Reasonably priced ($40 to $50 per night) and within walking distance of the school is the Beach 'N Boat Motel, on Lake Shore Drive; (802) 863-6577. Less than 3 miles away is the Marble Island Resort, on Marble Island Road; (802) 864-6800. The resort offers golf and tennis, which is good if you're bringing a nonsailing companion. Rooms are $80 to $100 per night.

RATES: The two-day "Learn to Sail" course is $275 for a single participant, $245 per person for groups of two. Included are free sailing privileges through the Friday following your class, a school T-shirt, a sailing textbook, an ASA logbook, ASA certification, an I.S.S. wallet card, and a certificate of achievement.

WHAT TO BRING: Nonskid boating shoes (no black soles), comfortable clothing, rain gear, sunglasses, sunblock, and visor. Carry your gear in a collapsible bag or duffel.

KIDS: This course is not appropriate for them. Ask about two- or five-day children's courses.

SKILL LEVEL: Beginner, but you should be able to handle extended time on the water.

Students drive home at night or stay at nearby lodgings, and are on their own in the evening; no socializing required. That was fine with our test student, Greg. "We went at such a fast pace during the day, it was nice to knock off and be on my own, without the pressure to party," he said.

Class began at 8:30 A.M. with an onshore "chalk-talk" by instructor John Townsend, who used a model boat to demonstrate the principles of sailing. Then, a go at the real thing, a twenty-seven-foot Soling, an Olympic-class keelboat. After rigging the boat and getting a lesson in safety gear, the two students (a third would arrive on day two) and their instructor were underway, plying the deep-blue waters of Lake Champlain.

Time to put the chalk-talk stuff into practice. After getting a feel for the boat by trying to steer a constant course, each sailor wanna-be practiced taking the helm and tacking and sailing on different points of sail, while the crew of one trimmed the sails and the instructor provided a play-by-play account of what was going on. If instructor Townsend was made nervous or amused by his neophyte skippers, he didn't let on. When someone screwed up, Townsend kept repeating himself, voice rising. "Head up, Charles. Head up, Charles! HEAD UP, CHARLES!" he said at one point, grabbing a lifeline in a mock attempt to save himself.

"John never criticized us or lost his sense of humor," Greg said.

At noon, the group sailed back to the mooring for lunch. Then, another hour of "ashore knowledge," as I.S.S. calls it, followed by an afternoon of sailing.

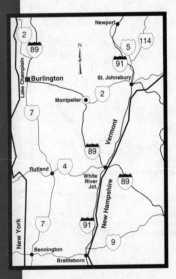

This time, the focus was on the *controlled jibe*, meaning moving the stern of the boat through the wind on purpose, as opposed to swinging wildly in an uncontrolled manner (the mark of a rookie at sea). The twosome jibed away until class ended at 4:30.

On day two, students Greg and Charles were joined by not-quite-novice Rebecca for the morning chalk-talk. Topics included jibing, and reefing the mainsail (reducing the size of the sail's surface) in case of heavy wind. The class put this into practice immediately, jibing to the other side of the bay. Then, as if on cue, the wind picked up and it started to rain. "Perfect!" Townsend said. The class rigged the boat for heavy weather (to flatten it out) and practiced maneuvers in the steady, light rain.

Back ashore for lunch, and more discussion. This time, Townsend used the model boat to illustrate person-overboard techniques. ("All that was missing was the drowning Barbie doll," Greg said.) Aboard the Soling, students practiced "saving" a boat cushion, each skipper doing the drill — turning the boat, stopping the boat, trying not to run over the victim — until each had successfully rescued the cushion. By now, the wind had died, providing a chance to practice light-air sail trim and maneuvers. Everyone worked hard, processing as much information as possible for what was to come: the American Sailing Association (ASA) Basic Keelboat standard test, a written test to be administered ashore. This was when the truth would be revealed: would anybody remember anything, given all the material crammed into their heads in just fourteen hours?

Everybody passed the test, receiving certificates stating that said sailor is "able to sail a twenty-foot boat in light to moderate winds and sea conditions in familiar waters without supervision." Daysailing in one's backyard, in other words, but hey, that's how Dennis Conner got started. Not bad for a weekend. (If even a weekend is too much of a commitment, I.S.S. offers a free "learn to sail" day every spring, to promote the sport.) The next logical step: I.S.S.'s intermediate course, or a similar offering, which goes beyond the basics to navigational skills, sail trim for maximum boat speed, dealing with common emergencies, and so on.

Of course, learning to sail is one thing. But to be a sailor? As any old salt will tell you, that takes a lifetime.

Newport, Rhode Island: Couples-Only Weekend

Taken by Storm

The winds were raging twenty-five to thirty knots, churning the seas like a Maytag on heavy-duty wash cycle. We were sloshing around in the middle of it, on a twenty-seven-foot Soling sailboat, heeling over, hanging on, and recalling the words of our instructor: "It's impossible to capsize this boat." Won't capsize … won't capsize … won't capsize … the words ran through our minds like a mantra as we struggled with the tiller and fought the insistent waves. In one quick blast, a squall hit the bow of the boat, jerking the tiller from the white-knuckled grip of the helmsman and knocking us all to the deck of the boat.

"Guess this is trial by fire," our instructor said as we regained control of our vessel. "Just think how much easier it'll be after you master sailing in this weather!"

Master? We were barely managing. Our onwater instruction was to last until six o'clock. By four we were soaking wet, layered with sea salt, frazzled, and, yes, ready to call it quits. At least for the day. "If you feel like going out again, I'll be here 'til six," he said as we docked. Fat chance. We scurried for dry clothes and a sunny table at a cafe overlooking Newport Harbor.

Of course, Offshore has no control over the weather; you might have gentle, warm breezes every day of this three-day weekend course. No matter, this school will make sailors out of you, ready or not! Offshore is one of the oldest and largest sailing schools in the country, with bases in Captiva, Florida; Tortola, British Virgin Islands; and Newport. The school has turned more than 75,000 landlubbers into sailors, offering myriad courses, including learn-to-sail,

CONTACT: Offshore Sailing School, 16731 McGregor Boulevard, Ft. Myers, FL 33908; (800) 221-4326. Offshore also runs classes in Florida, New York, New Jersey, Connecticut, Washington's San Juan Islands, the British Virgin Islands, St. Lucia in the West Indies, and Mexico. All arrangements are made through the Florida office.

HOW TO GET THERE/WHERE TO STAY: Offshore students get a discount on lodging at the Admiral Farragut Inn, 31 Clarke Street, Newport, RI 02840; (800) 343-2863 or (401) 846-4526. (Check in the night before class.) It's about 1.5 hours from Boston and Hartford, and 3.5 hours from New York City. From the Newport Bridge, take the first exit, then turn right on Farewell Street. Take Farewell Street to Thames Street, turn right, and continue to Touro Street. Take Touro to Clarke Street. The inn is just far enough from the center-of-town hustle and bustle, yet still within walking distance of the harbor, restaurants, shops, and other sites. Offshore's classroom is at 2 Dean Avenue, 2nd floor, above Zelda's restaurant, on the corner of Dean Avenue and Thames Street.

RATES: The weekend package includes the sailing course, a textbook, a logbook, breakfast each morning, and four days/three nights accommodations at the Admiral Farragut, a historic colonial inn (circa 1702) tucked away on a quiet street. Rooms and tuition are $795 for a single, $695 for a double, per person. Tuition only is $595 per person.

WHAT TO BRING: Shorts, T-shirts, swimsuits, nonskid shoes, rain gear, warm-up clothes, sunscreen, visor or hat, and sunglasses. Life jackets are provided.

KIDS: Not on the couples-only weekend, but ask about other learn-to-sail programs. Offshore also offers parent-child classes.

SKILL LEVEL: No previous experience is necessary, but you must feel comfortable being out on the water for long periods of time.

advanced sailing, bareboat cruising, liveaboard cruising, and special accelerated courses.

We liked their couples-only course—it was a great way to combine a weekend getaway in lovely Newport with learning to sail.

Each day began with in-class instruction, held at Offshore's headquarters in the center of town. Nautical terminology, types of boats, rigging, knot-tying, the mechanics of wind and sail, and more were covered with slides, diagrams, and discussion. (Listen up: the next morning's class begins with a test!) After lunch, we boarded the Soling and headed out of Newport Harbor. This, in itself, was a navigational nightmare. There were big boats and small boats; fishing boats and Coast Guard boats; motorboats and sailboats; charter boats and cruise ships; boats coming and boats going; boats docked and boats moored; boats, boats, boats everywhere. What appears as a picturesque harbor from ashore became a battleground for us beginning navigators. Our amazingly calm instructor provided just the right mix of positive encouragement, instruction, and humor, however.

The second day, the wind was blowing fifteen to twenty knots. The mountainous waves were more like rolling hills, and the sun was sparkling. We each got plenty of practice at all the boat tasks. (There are never more than four students per boat.) To our surprise, what had seemed, only a day ago, like an intimidating, complicated sport—with a language of its own—had become familiar and doable.

The final day, Offshore lived up to its promise of teaching us how to sail by inviting us to chart a course and sail on our own, without the instructor. No quitting early today. We barely had time to change from our sailing clothes and make 7:30 dinner reservations. We watched the last rays of sun burnish the seas, soaking in the nautical atmosphere, feeling like sailors.

Massachusetts

Providence

Fall River

6

395

Connecticut

1

138

Newport

Adventure New England

Stonington, Connecticut: Guys Need Not Apply for This Long Island Sound Adventure

Power to the Deck Monkeys!

CONTACT: Sea Sense, Inc., 25 Thames Street, New London, CT 06320; (800) 332-1404. Sea Sense offers women-only liveaboard sailing courses of three, five, and seven days. Special Adventures in Maine, the British Virgin Islands, and Greece, as well as offshore passagemaking from Camden, Maine, to New London, Connecticut, are among the current offerings.

HOW TO GET THERE: The three-day coastal cruise sails from Dodson Boat Yard, 194 Water Street, Stonington, Connecticut. To reach the boatyard, take I-95 to exit 91 (Stonington). From I-95 North, turn right onto Route 234; from I-95 South, turn left onto Route 234.

RATES: The $485 fee includes everything except optional dinners ashore.

WHAT TO BRING: They'll provide a list: Generally, shorts and T-shirts, a swimsuit, towels, light cotton long-sleeved pants and shirts for layering, rain gear, and toiletries.

KIDS: This trip is not appropriate for them.

SKILL LEVEL: Beginning to intermediate sailing skills. On our cruise, everyone had had some previous sailing experience, and three of the four students were boatowners.

"Where are the guys?" the yachtsmen in Stonington Harbor asked as we headed out of the harbor. "They're below decks, cooking," one of us answered. "Barefoot and pregnant, too," another said, tittering.

Put six women on a thirty-six-foot sailboat in Long Island Sound and what do you get (besides a lot of irreverent humor)? A little kvetching about Captain Ahab–type husbands at the helm, and enough hands-on sailing experience to be able to tell 'em to blow it out their portholes.

Started in New London six years ago by captains Patti Moore and Carol Cuddyer, Sea Sense has expanded to include courses in Lake Michigan (out of Wisconsin), Florida, and the British Virgin Islands in winter. The idea: to teach women to operate and understand the mechanics of sailboats and powerboats as well as any man.

Why isn't the school coed? "Women as a group learn better when there's not a man on the boat," Moore explained. "They get intimidated, so they just sit back and let him do it." On a Sea Sense cruise, you can't sit and watch.

To a woman, we had the same story: We'd been sailing with guys and acting like well-trained "deck monkeys," in instructor Pat Markl's words. We had our boat jobs ("honey, pull in the jib"), and we did them, never questioning why. Well, enough of that! No more galley wench/winch wench stuff. We wanted power—to be in control, take command, and, yeah, issue a few orders ourselves.

So we took off on a thirty-six-foot Sabre sloop called

Bolero to harness the power of skipperhood and the power of the wind. Sea Sense chartered the boat from a local owner, but plans to buy boats to use for teaching. Before we set off, we provisioned the vessel (loaded her up with food and drink) for our three-day sail, as we'd be living aboard. Then we spent a couple of hours getting acquainted with what would be our home and classroom at sea. The sky was clear, and we had a strong westerly wind—about twenty knots, enough to get us to Fisher Island, our anchorage for the night, real quick.

Nothing doing. This was sailing school, so we zigged, we zagged (tacking and jibing, in sailorspeak)—we could have swum it faster than we sailed it. Which was exactly the point. We rookies had control of the boat, faced with doing the same maneuvers over and over again until we got the point—the why, not just the what.

"You have the power. Tell your crew what to do!" instructor Markl said as the first student-skipper got behind the wheel. "Power! I love it! But I'm terrified," Skipper Number One confessed, clutching the wheel in a death-grip. That pretty much summed it up for all of us. To be in control of a six-ton hunk of fiberglass, possessing an alarming tendency to heel way over to starboard, is a fairly daunting concept for a novice. So we dealt with it the way gals do, by cracking jokes and giving each other lots of encouragement. And we got lots of warm fuzzies and positive reinforcement from our instructor, right?

Wrong. Markl is, shall we say, the no-nonsense type. Gravel-voiced, chain-smoking, with a vocabulary that can only be described as colorful, Markl is Tallulah Bankhead on a yacht. "Whaddya gonna do now? Hit 'em? No, no, watch it! Watch it!" is typical Pat-patter; this, balanced by the gentle manner of her volunteer/assistant, Sylvia Lachter. The student-teacher ratio on our cruise, and most Sea Sense cruises, is four to two. Markl's been sailing forever, and has lived aboard a boat on the Chesapeake Bay. She's been an instructor with Sea Sense for three years, proving the company chooses its instructors based on sea smarts, not perkiness. Fine with us. We were at sailing school, not charm school; given that, Markl was a perfect choice. She knows her stuff.

We learned how to determine the direction of the wind. We learned the points of sail. We learned the Rules of the Road (and how it makes no difference at all that a sailboat has right-of-way when a powerboat filled with yahoos is coming right at you). We learned the difference between heading up and hardening up. All this in the first couple of hours. And nervous as we were, we got a taste of the pure, unfettered joy of sailing, spiked with those sweet "Aha!" moments, when an elusive concept suddenly becomes crystal-clear. Even Markl waxed a bit sentimental about this.

"I do this job to see people's eyes light up, when they understand something for the first time," she confessed. "Men can't explain things to women on a boat, because they know what to do but they don't understand it enough to explain how to do it," she theorized. "They just do it. Women always ask why."

We got to the moment some of us feared—the dreaded anchor-drop maneuver—but we managed to do it right the first time, and determined we were, indeed, "holding ground." At that point, it seemed like a good idea to open the bar, so we did, six women crammed into the tiny galley and saloon to cook, drink, tend bar, and relive those glorious moments at sea.

What do you do at sailing school when there's not a breath of wind? We found out the next day. We had a chart talk and a navigation lesson; Markl used a lime to represent the planet when she demonstrated compassing. We learned how to plot courses. Then we took a look at *Bolero*'s Volvo engine, and the bilge. Still no wind. So, like the old salts we were fast becoming, we set out to find some, dammit. No dice. We were "in the doldrums," stuck. Poker, anybody?

Nope. Markl engaged the engine and we did some power turns, a maneuver useful for getting a boat in and out of a dock space—essentially, backing the boat up. This was fine until the engine fumes, combined with ninety-degree weather, nearly knocked us out. So we motored through the passage from Stonington Point to Napatree Beach, via the Pawcatuck River, which separates Connecticut from Rhode Island. Napatree Beach is on the Rhode Island side, a skinny arm off the tip of Watch Hill. Several boats were anchored off Napatree, so we joined them, jumping off the boat for a swim.

Reboarding *Bolero*, we discovered something we'd barely noticed before: the handsome vessel had developed an alarming stink. Lesson learned: always make sure your holding tank is pumped out before it's too late. (This was supposed to have been done before we boarded. Pat was peeved.) Quickly, leaving an unpleasant aroma behind us, we headed back to Stonington Harbor for an emergency pumpout. What to do but make the best of it? We raced to the showers, and then to the pay phones, to call home to brag to the guys about all the stuff we'd learned.

Resources

For lists of commercial schools and community sailing programs in your area, contact: American Sailing Association, 13922 Marquesas Way, Marina del Rey, CA 90292; (213) 822-7171; or U.S. Sailing, Box 1260, 15 Maritime Drive, Portsmouth, RI 02871; (401) 683-0800.

Here are some highly regarded sailing schools:

Bay Island Sailing School, 21 Elm Street, Camden, ME 04843; (800) 421-2492 or (207) 236-2776.

Coastline Sailing School, Eldridge Yard, Marsh Road, Noank, CT 06340; (800) 749-7245.

J World Newport, P.O. Box 1509, Newport, RI 02840; (800) 343-2255 or (401) 849-5492.

Womanship, The Boat House, 410 Severn Avenue, Annapolis, MD 21403; (800) 342-9295.

Women's Sailing Adventures, 39 Woodside Avenue, Westport, CT 06880; (800) 328-8053.

WoodenBoat Sailing School, P.O. Box 78, Naskeag Road, Brooklin, ME 01616; (207) 359-4651.

BOOKS

Colgate's Basic Sailing. Steve Colgate, published by Steve Colgate.

Cruising Fundamentals. Harry Munns, International Marine.

Cruising Guide to the New England Coast. Duncan, Fenn, Fenn & Ware, W.W. Norton & Company.

Sail, Race & Win. Eric Twiname, Sheridan House.

Sailing Fundamentals. Gary Jobson, Simon & Schuster.

The Boating Bible. Jim Murrant, Sheridan House.

The Coast of Summer: Sailing New England Waters from Shelter Island to Cape Cod. Anthony Bailey, HarperCollins Publishers.

The Complete Sailor: Learning the Art of Sailing. David Seidman, International Marine.

Around the Buoys: A Manual of Sailboat Racing Tactics and Strategy. Michael Huck, Jr., International Marine.

A Cruising Guide to Narragansett Bay, Buzzards Bay, and Cape Cod's South Shore. Childress, Childress, and Martin, International Marine.

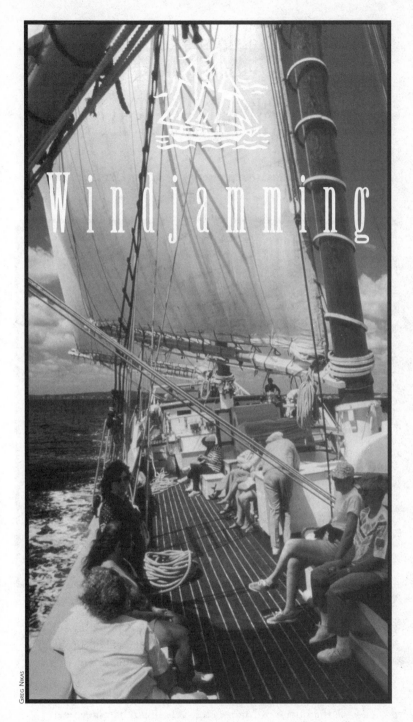

Windjamming

GREG NIKAS

Rockland, Maine: Cruising the Coast

Sail Back in Time on Victory Chimes

CONTACT: *Victory Chimes*, P.O. Box 1401, Rockland, ME 04841; (800) 745-5651. *Victory Chimes* sails out of Rockland from June through September.

HOW TO GET THERE: Take Route 1 north to downtown Rockland (about 2 hours north of Portland), then turn right on Tillson Avenue. Turn right into the boat terminal area; parking is inside the terminal.

RATES: Half-week cruises cost $400 to $450 per person; six-day cruises are $650 to $700 per person. A deposit is required. Prices include lodging (aboard) the night before the cruise.

WHAT TO BRING: They'll provide a list. In general, bring warmer clothes than you think you'll need, nonskid shoes, light cotton pieces for layering, a hat or visor, sunblock, and bug repellent. Pack in a collapsible bag or duffel; there's very little room to stow gear in bunks. Casual clothes are fine for trips ashore.

KIDS: Aged ten and up okay; however, we'd recommend bringing kids who are extremely good at entertainmenting themselves. There's no TV or Nintendo here.

SKILL LEVEL: All levels.

Catching a glimpse of one of Maine's spectacular schooners under sail is a perfect photo op. Better still is sailing aboard one yourself, recapturing the feel of those distant days when boats were powered by the wind, not engines; when hearty crews, not sophisticated electronics, did all the work. Welcome aboard the three-masted schooner *Victory Chimes*, the queen of Maine's ten-vessel windjammer fleet.

Now, this is one gorgeous ninety-five-year-old; she's all polished brass, gleaming wood, and tightly coiled lines. Although this 170-foot schooner looks the same as she did almost a century ago, some creature comforts have been added to woo twentieth-century seafarers—namely, hot showers and flush heads (toilets). But if your big-boat experience has been limited to cruise ships, take heed: the *QEII*, she ain't. Berths are smallish, with bunks, sinks, and portholes. Downright cozy, in fact. If you talk in your sleep, make snorting sounds, or plan on a night of passion with your partner, it'll be no secret to your shipmates.

But we were interested in capturing the romance of the sea, not the other kind. That was easy. The breakfast bell rang at 8 A.M., and we consumed vast stacks of blueberry-studded pancakes. Then, Captain Kip Files began radioing commands to the crew from the helm: "Sarah, cast your spring line off"; "Stand by to centerboard." The twenty-nine crewmembers sprang to action; even the chef was fending off as we departed Rockland for parts unknown.

We couldn't have asked for a more splendid cruising day on Penobscot Bay. Sea and sky were Technicolor blue, the breeze a fifteen-knot northwesterly. And the views! Suffice it to say, Maine's fabled dramatic coastline deserves all the superlatives. We glided past rocky, pine-covered islands, including (in case you have a chart handy) Mark Island, Saddle Island, and Islesboro. The latter is the home of the Islesboro Inn, owned by actress Kirstie Alley. "There she is!" said a guy with binoculars. "Sunbathing naked on that rock!" Lots of jockeying for position, until someone realized it was a seal, not a human female. (So that's how those mermaid stories got started.) Looking over Captain Files's shoulder at the chart, we dis-

covered that even the rocks have names out here — so hapless skippers can identify what they've hit, no doubt.

We had expected to earn some calluses and break some fingernails on this adventure at sea. Nothing doing. Aboard the *Victory Chimes,* shipboard tasks are strictly voluntary. Passengers can help hoist the sails — a bit like tug-of-war for twenty people — and lend a hand with that old navy standby, peeling spuds for dinner. Occasionally, one of us greenhorns would have a go at the wheel, with Captain Files discreetly muttering "two spokes to the right," "four spokes to the left," in our ear.

The most promising guest skipper turned out to be thirteen-year-old Emily Garvin, who handled the helm with such deftness she probably could have parallel parked the vessel. She might have rounded Cape Horn, for all we cared. The order of the day is, kick back and enjoy the view, feel the sun on your face, curl up in a corner with that book you've been meaning to tackle. Or track your route on the ship's chart; or take in the sights along Maine's picturesque coast with a pair of binoculars or a sketch pad.

Ports of call included sleepy fishing villages, such as Stonington, and quiet anchorages with views you'd never see from Route 1. But the destination isn't really the point; the journey's the thing. As Captain Files told guests on the first night at sea, "When you come aboard, you've arrived. Where we go from here is up to Mother Nature."

Mother Nature may or may not smile on you. As the saying goes, "Summer in Maine: blink and you'll miss it." A typical summer day in these parts can mean warmth and brilliant skies or cold, fog, and drizzle. No matter what, the boat sails. Mainers (all New Englanders, for that matter) take a perverse pride in their endurance of the nastiest of weather.

Tip: the weather is warmest in August, but, by no coincidence, that's the busiest month for boating here, so you'll probably share the choicest anchorages with other boats. Insider's secret (tip from a former first mate): Consider September. "Gorgeous days, sweater weather, no traffic," is how he put it.

On our three-day adventure, clear skies prevailed. It was so sunny (and there's no awning rigged to provide shade)

GREG NIKAS

Victory Chimes *lies at anchor on a flat calm*
Penobscot Bay off Owls Head.

that the hopelessly fair-skinned among us used copious
quantities of sunblock, and still we burned. We definitely
recommend bringing long-sleeved cotton T-shirts, cotton
pants, and a baseball cap or wide-brimmed hat, along with a
sweater and jacket. And earplugs, in case there's a serious
snorer aboard. (Since the maximum capacity of *Victory
Chimes* is forty people, you can pretty much count on it.)

We curious types took the opportunity to poke around
our home at sea, squinting up at the tall spruce masts and
heavy canvas sails, all held in place by thick oiled-rope hal-
yards. Amazing to think this stately vessel could have ended
up as a floating restaurant in Japan. Domino's Pizza for-
merly owned the schooner (renamed *Domino Effect*), but
when the pizza company hit hard times, they put it up for
sale. Files and his partner, Paul DeGaeta, bid on the boat
and, to their surprise, got it. "We tried to talk each other out
of it," Files confessed, "but it didn't work!"

Eventually, we glided into Bucks Harbor, our first port
of call. The dinner bell rang, and we were all more than
ready for a boiled lobster dinner, topped off by the chef's
signature strawberry rhubarb pie. Files was right when he
said the most important person aboard a boat is the cook.

Meals aboard *Victory Chimes* are hearty, not fancy, but fit in with the retro theme of the excursion.

After dinner, we boarded the dinghy in shifts to play tourist at Bucks Harbor. We strolled to Bucks Harbor General Store, where we fortified our beer supply (it's BYOB on the *Victory Chimes*) and used the pay phone to say "wish you were here" to kinfolk. Back aboard, we chatted like old chums, prompting one passenger to remark, "I like the fact that the boat puts you in close contact with strangers; within hours, you're having lengthy discussions about anything and everything." If that sounds good to you, then this is probably the kind of low-key adventure you'll adore. We found the most striking thing about this trip is how quickly we adjusted to the slower rhythms of the sailing life.

Perhaps the best moment came at 7 A.M. on our third and final day, while we were still at anchor. Suddenly, crewmember Peter Allen shouted, "Moose! Moose!" Half awake, we stumbled onto the deck to see a moose in the distance, grazing at the tip of Monroe Island. Yeah, it was early, and we were on vacation. But nobody seemed to mind the wake-up call.

Mystic, Connecticut: You're Part of the Crew on This Vintage Vessel

Never Hauled a Gollywobbler or Polished a Winch? You Will on This Trip

CONTACT: Mystic Seaport Museum, Sail Education Program, 75 Greenmanville Avenue, P.O. Box 6000, Mystic, CT 06355; (203) 572-5323. Adult programs run Friday through Monday from mid-May through mid-June, and September through mid-October.

HOW TO GET THERE: Take Exit 90 off I-95; Mystic Seaport Museum is almost immediately on your right. Park in the south parking lot and proceed to the south gate, where the attendant will direct you to *Brilliant*.

RATES: The adult program (age twenty and older), including all meals, costs $495.

WHAT TO BRING: A sleeping bag and pillowcase, two towels, a swimsuit, comfortable clothing, rubber-soled shoes (no black soles), a wool sweater, a jacket or windbreaker, rain gear, a flashlight, and antiseasickness tablets. All gear, except your sleeping bag, should fit into one moderately sized duffel bag.

KIDS: Not on this trip. There is a teen program for those aged fifteen to nineteen.

SKILL LEVEL: No sailing experience is necessary, but all participants must be fit and agile. This is a hands-on experience requiring energetic participation.

W hen you look at the dazzling *Brilliant*, one of the finest schooners ever built, you don't have to wonder what a thrill it would be to sail her. You can sail her yourself.

This classic wooden boat, built in 1932 and measuring seventy-four feet from bowsprit to stern, is owned by Mystic Seaport Museum. The museum is one of the most visited sites in New England, but the *Brilliant* program is a well-kept secret. Few people realize that they can slip back in time and be a working crewmember aboard this vintage vessel.

And we don't mean, help hoist a sail and then go back to your John Grisham novel. With just two experienced crewmembers, Captain George Moffett and Mate Amy Hagberg, it's "All hands on deck" to undertake the tasks necessary to get the boat from port to port. Even if it's a full house (capacity is two crew, ten passengers), you'll get a most thorough taste of the seafaring life.

When you arrive at *Brilliant* with your duffel bag of essentials and sleeping bag in hand, you may well feel like a swabbie of yore, joining your ship to sail for foreign ports. Or maybe not. But by the time you disembark, you'll have earned your stripes, matey. Even by schooner standards, *Brilliant* is a busy rig. "She's a lively boat, and requires a lively crew," Captain Moffett told us. During the course of your four-day voyage, you'll be called upon to steer the thirty-ton vessel; hoist the sails (at least four are flying most of the time); trim, drop, and furl same; navigate; work the galley (cook); clean; polish; and perhaps even stand a night watch. Those postcards will have to wait.

The point of all this is not to give captain and mate a holiday, but to provide an enriching experience to participants. "Our philosophy is 'Learn by doing,'" Moffett explained. Initially, Mate Hagberg's job assignments — "You take the peak halyard, you take the throat" — will sound like so much mumbo jumbo, until you've memorized the parts of the boat and learned how everything works together.

Landlubber personas are quickly shed as individuals become a crew. Knowing that a serious mistake could lead to injury or boat damage, everyone gives it his or her all. Whatever your job on land, it won't matter at sea; CEO or waitress, everybody is equal when it comes to hauling a golly-wobbler or polishing a winch. Of course, a crew is only as good as its bosses, and Moffett (*Brilliant*'s captain since 1983) and Hagberg are an able, enthusiastic team.

Our first day aboard, we plotted a course for Newport, Rhode Island. With a fair wind blowing and four sails flying, we outran every boat in the harbor. On a yacht like this, you're sure to draw attention; count on admiring glances, bald-faced envy, and comments from other skippers, like, "She sure looks pretty," and "You've really got her moving." That's one constant aboard *Brilliant*; the other constant is, the itinerary isn't. Our plans to head to Newport were scuttled when the wind shifted. The shift favored Block Island, so Block Island it would be. A couple of passengers nearly kissed the ground when we reached our destination, as the rolling seas had left them feeling a little green. (Antiseasickness tablets are a sensible addition to anyone's ditty bag.)

We explored the island a bit, then hiked back to *Brilliant* for dinner. No one minded forgoing Block Island's eateries; the communally made meals aboard ship are tasty, featuring lots of fresh fish and produce.

One advantage to sailing on a ship without a shower: getting ready for the day is a cinch. Those who don't relish this much authenticity can shower at most of *Brilliant*'s ports of call. At 7 A.M., Hagberg lit a fire in the boat's original coal stove to heat the main cabin. Outside, it was pouring. Gamely, we donned foul-weather gear, hoisted sails, and again plotted a course to Newport. Again, this was not to be. The wind had changed, blowing directly from our destination, so we changed our plans and sailed with the wind to Sag Harbor, New York.

The sky cleared, and we gratefully peeled off layers of clothing. Everyone took a turn at the helm, carefully maneuvering *Brilliant* between shoals. By now, we'd all found our sea legs. Working together, we made the boat fairly dance as we entered port. First order of business at upscale Sag Harbor—showers. Nobody wanted to look scruffy here, where celebrity types (Billy Joel, Mick Jagger) and assorted beautiful people hang out. Turns out it wouldn't have mattered; *Brilliant*'s reputation preceded us. The harbormaster welcomed us, and a nice berth was waiting. Arriving in *Brilliant* is like pulling up in a Rolls Royce limo. Heads turn, people stare. We never grew accustomed to her beauty; perhaps nobody does. In his book *Brilliant Passage*, Philip Gerard wrote, "She had the look that a vintage Martin guitar has, or a Steinway baby grand: a look that invited touching."

The following day, we set sail for Hamburg Cove, a lovely, secluded spot on the Connecticut River. Again, other boats sailed by as close as possible to get a good look at *Brilliant*. We all beamed proudly, as though she were ours. In truth, we were hers, for far too short a time.

Resources

The Maine Windjammer Association's roster includes ten
ships, most of them genuine working schooners—the
world's largest fleet of historic windjammers. Member
vessels are: *Angelique, Grace Bailey, J. & E. Riggin, Lewis
R. French, Mary Day, Mercantile, Nathaniel Bowditch, Rose-
way, Timberwind,* and *Victory Chimes.* Contact the association at P.O. Box 1144, Blue Hill, ME 04614; (800)
807-WIND. To see these majestic schooners gathered
together, check out: Maine's annual Windjammer Days,
held in June in Boothbay Harbor; the Great Schooner
Race from North Haven to Rockland, on the Friday of
July Fourth week; Windjammer Weekend in Camden
over Labor Day weekend; and the *WoodenBoat* Sail-In,
held in mid-September in Brooklin to mark the end of
the season.

In Connecticut, try the *Mystic Whaler,* a recreated New England schooner sailing out of Mystic on three- and five-
day cruises. The eighty-three-foot boat departs from
Whaler's Wharf. Contact Mystic Whaler Cruises, Inc.,
P.O. Box 189, Mystic, CT 06355; (800) 697-8420, or try
the *Sylvina W. Beale,* an 84-foot schooner built in Maine
in 1911; 120 School Street, Mystic, CT 06355;
(800) 333-MYSTIC.

OTHER POSSIBILITIES INCLUDE:

American Eagle, Heritage, or *Isaac Evans,* P.O. Box 482, Rockland, ME 04841; (800) 648-4544 or (207) 594-8007.

Pauline or *Stephen Taber,* P.O. Box 1050, Rockland, ME
04841; (800) 999-7352 or (207) 236-3520.

Schooner *Ernestina,* State Pier, New Bedford, MA 02741-
2010; (508) 992-4900.

Schooner *Shenandoah*, Coastwise Packet Company, Box 429,
Vineyard Haven, MA 02568; (508) 693-1699.
Senta, P.O. Box 18, Castine, ME 04421; (207) 326-4135.
Wendameen, P.O. Box 506, Camden, ME 04843; (207) 236-3472.

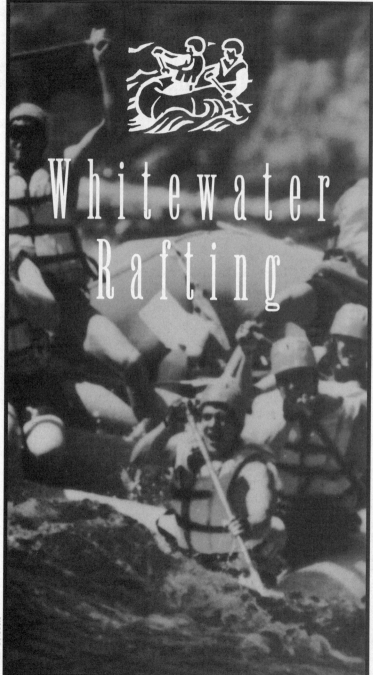

Whitewater Rafting

The Forks, Maine:
Family Hike and Raft Weekend
on the Kennebec

*Between the Rapids, the Waterfalls, and the
Hot Tubs, You're Sure to Be Wet, but Never Bored*

T*he scenario:* A weekend off. No overtime. No Little
League games. The laundry can wait.

The players: A frazzled Mom and Dad. One very bored
teenager. An antsy little brother.

Cut to: A whitewater river in northern Maine.

Sound like the makings of a *National Lampoon* vacation
disaster flick? It's not. A rafting weekend on the Kennebec
River may well be the perfect family getaway.

The rafting business has changed since the days when
only daredevils rode the waves. Participation in whitewater rafting is surging faster than New England rivers
in springtime—drawing folks of all ages and abilities.
Since 1976, when less than 600 people ventured down
the Kennebec River, the sport has grown nearly 1,000
percent. Now, more than 65,000 river rookies take the
plunge in Maine waters annually. Today, the New England
rafting industry is luring families with special minivacation
packages that combine a trip down the river with mountain biking, canoeing, kayaking, horseback riding, hiking,
and more.

After viewing *The River Wild* a couple of times to stir
our collective imagination, our family of four headed up to
Downeast Whitewater's base on the Kennebec in West
Forks, Maine. The plan was to stay at one of their log cabins, opt for the meal package (what's a vacation if you have

CONTACT: Downeast Whitewater, P.O. Box 119, Center Conway, NH 03813; (603) 447-3002.

HOW TO GET THERE: Take Exit 36 off I-95. Take Route 201 north through Skowhegan and Bingham. Look for the Dew Drop Inn, about 15 miles north of Bingham on 201.

RATES: All Kennebec River packages include lodging (cabin, inn, or campground), meals, bus shuttle to and from the river, and a rafting trip with a barbecue lunch. Two nights at the inn cost $175; cabins are $185; tents, $155; and campsites, $135. Rates are per person, based on double occupancy (quad occupancy for cabins), weekends. Children sixteen and under can raft the Kennebec for half price on Sundays and weekdays. Other weekday packages are available.

WHAT TO BRING: A swimsuit, sneakers, a sweater, a windbreaker or rain suit, a change of clothes, and a towel. Also, if you're staying in the cabins, bring a flashlight for walking the paths, and additional lighting (lantern, candles) for inside the cabin. (Cabins are lit by gas lights and can be dim.)

KIDS: Yes, they want them. Children must be eight years old and weigh at least fifty pounds. Minimum age on the upper Kennebec is twelve.

SKILL LEVEL: No experience necessary. Rafters don't have to be exceptionally fit or athletic. Pregnant women are not allowed on the river.

WHEN TO GO: Kennebec trips are run May 1 through Columbus Day.

to cook?), raft the Kennebec River one day, and spend another enjoying Maine's great outdoors. The cabin was nestled in the woods, with footpaths to the river. Each cabin has a porch, bedroom, loft, living room, and full bath. Hearty, all-you-can-eat meals are served at the Dew Drop Inn, located a short stroll from the cabin. The inn sits atop a hill overlooking Pleasant Pond. Downeast Whitewater guests are invited to use the hot tub and sauna, beach, restaurant, bar, and game room. Also available for use are canoes, a windsurfer, and a paddleboat. Not bad for an outdoor escape. After dinner and a soak in the hot tub, Mom and Dad began to unfrazzle.

The next morning, the Downeast Whitewater bus arrived at the inn around 8:30, with helmets, life jackets, and instructions for the day's rafters. Within a half-hour, the rafts were put in at the Harris Station Dam on the upper Kennebec.

Make no mistake: the upper Kennebec is not for babies. The rock-and-roll rumble of its dam-released rundown will knock the dreaded "B" (as in boring) word right out of your teenager's vocabulary. The upper Kennebec's Class IV to Class V rapids are some of the finest around, and we hit them head on.

The minimum age on this run is twelve. While older family members challenged the gorge, Downeast Whitewater bused younger siblings to the halfway point to meet their families for lunch and join them for the second half of the trip. (The daily release of water from the dam creates Class IV to V surges at the start, but slows to a Class I float downstream.)

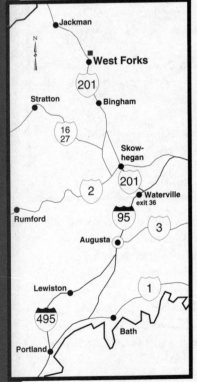

Ready or not, they waved good-bye. Got in. Sat down. And hung on. For the next couple of hours they bounced and lurched up and over mountains of screaming whitewater, attacking rapids with names like Magic Falls (because it makes rafts disappear), Tierney's Turmoil, Alleyway, and Three Sisters.

After being pummeled with sheets of water, splashed, showered, and soaked, seven Downeast Whitewater rafts stopped at Carry Brook to pick up the little ones. The river turned from chaos to calm, with only a few rips, and lots of opportunity for body surfing, water fights, and sightseeing. A few rafters, boasting a little experience and a lot of chutzpah, practiced paddling maneuvers, turning the rafts to hit the whitewater backwards, sending them spinning.

The trip was over twelve miles from the start, where the Kennebec meets the Dead River. Then, dinner, sauna, and lullabies.

It's tough to compete with the excitement of a day rafting the wild river. But this area offers an abundance of outdoor activity and great scenery. Anglers can test the local waters, well known for their plenitude. Or bring your bikes; there are miles of back roads to explore, and fat-tire enthusiasts will find numerous off-road trails to climb. Our family opted for an afternoon hike to nearby Moxie Falls. A short walk through the woods put them at the base of a gorgeous cascade—Maine's tallest waterfall.

"Yeah, it's real pretty," the kids agreed. "But we'd rather go over it in a raft!"

The Forks, Maine: Doing the Dead's Big-Water Release

New England's Wild Ride

CONTACT: Northern Outdoors, P.O. Box 100, Route 201, The Forks, ME 04985; (800) 765-7238.

HOW TO GET THERE: Take Exit 36 off I-95. Take Route 201 north, through Skowhegan and Bingham. Northern Outdoors' Forks Resort Center is 18 miles north of Bingham on Route 201.

RATES: A fee of $79 per person includes a registered Maine guide in each raft, a cookout, bus transportation to and from the river, and full use of the resort's facilities. You can rent a full wetsuit for $12. Lodging costs $8 per person, per night, for a campsite and $17 for a cabin tent (see below). A lodge room is $30 for one person, $45 for two; logdominium space is $25 apiece for seven or eight people, $30 for five or six people, and $40 for three or four people. A deposit is required.

Be sure to reserve spaces several weeks in advance; high-water Dead River runs fill up fast. If Northern Outdoors cannot accommodate you, they will try to arrange a trip with another local company.

WHAT TO BRING: A swimsuit, sneakers, a wool or fleece sweater, a windbreaker or rain suit, a change of clothes, and a towel.

KIDS: No one under fifteen.

SKILL LEVEL: No experience necessary. Come with a positive, let's-go-for-it attitude and you'll be fine.

WHEN TO GO: Dead River trips are run on high-water releases in the spring and fall. Call ahead for a schedule.

B ig. Intense. The longest stretch of continuous white-water in the East. The Dead River. Even its name is ominous. Zigzagging through the gorgeous northern Maine woods, the Dead has earned a unique reputation among whitewater rafters and adrenaline junkies. Six times a year, upriver dams let go high-water releases, turning the always challenging Dead into a snarling white serpent.

That's when the circus comes to town. Thousands of thrill-seekers come to run the river wild, crowding the banks for a ride on Maine's natural roller-coaster. Forget Kumba. Who needs Mr. Toad's Wild Ride? We've got The Dead.

If you're looking for a relaxing, quiet getaway, forget the Dead when the big water flows. But if you're looking for thrills and chills (you're going to get wet), this is the place.

We began our adventure at Northern Outdoors' Resort Center in The Forks, Maine. Northern Outdoors is New England's oldest and largest commercial whitewater rafting outfitter, sitting on 100 acres of piney woods adjacent to the Kennebec River. *Outside* magazine recently named Northern Outdoors one of the nation's ten best one-stop sporting resorts, and the honor is justified; options here include hiking, backcountry bike touring, river float trips, world-class fishing, rock climbing, and more. Consider coming early to sample the opportunities or simply to relax in the pool or soak in the hot tub.

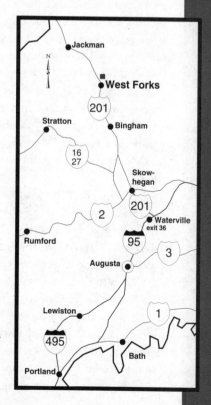

A choice of accommodations is offered, including logdominiums, each with a living room, kitchenette, and upstairs loft; lodge rooms, located in the main building; cabin tents, canvas-covered wooden platforms with screen doors, gas lighting, and

Whitewater Rafting

cots; and rustic campsites where you can pitch your own tent. The main lodge houses a restaurant, a game room, and a full-service bar—and the night before a trip is party time! Often a band plays until the wee hours, and many soon-to-be rafters can be found seeking bravado in a bottle, or two, of Sam Adams lager. So if you prefer to do your rockin' and rollin' on the river, request an overnight space away from the lodge. If you're a party animal, you'll feel right at home; just be ready for an early start in the morning.

Rafting day begins with assigning guides, handing out helmets and life jackets, and signing the obligatory disclaimers. Wetsuits are available for rent, and, we warn you, this is not the time to economize. No matter how warm the air might feel, the waters are icy, rarely breaking the fifty-degree mark.

The bumpy forty-five-minute bus ride to the put-in point leaves just enough time for last-minute jitters to build, and to hear the inevitable tales of horror. "The first chute is the worst," someone on our trip said. "A friend of a friend of mine fell out of the raft and broke her nose." "I heard someone died on The Dead this spring." (Why do we do this to ourselves?) Actually, the safety record of the whitewater rafting industry is pretty good. Rafting is statistically safer than snowmobiling, skiing, and driving a car.

Are the bugs bad? Should you take your camera? Will you need a towel? Forget it! Once you don your life jacket and climb aboard you'll be thinking of nothing but running the river.

"Paddle! Paddle! Paddle!" The guide shouted as we rode the crest of a seven-foot wave. Hold on! Hold on! Hold on! Paddle! Paddle! Paddle! Hold on! Hold on! Hold on! The pattern for riding the sixteen miles of turbulent, rushing water was quickly established.

We followed the Dead from Grand Falls to the confluence with the Kennebec at The Forks. There were brief moments of calm, enough for a peek at the scenery, but they didn't last long. Paddle! Paddle! Paddle! We made a mental note to come back when the water would be slower—much slower—to enjoy the spectacular surroundings.

Five hours later, sopping wet, hearts still thumping, raft-mates slapped high-fives back at the resort. Northern Outdoors staff members shamelessly hawked photos and videos of the river-runners, and few could resist. All the highlights of the Day on the Dead were rehashed and embellished, and everyone feasted on a well-earned steak barbecue.

We think once down The Dead is probably enough for a lifetime, but many of our tripmates disagreed. "This is my fifth time down, and I'll be back again next spring," says Cheryl, a forty-something lawyer from Newton, Massachusetts. "I can't wait to bring my mother!"

Millinocket, Maine:
Running the Rapids on the
West Branch of the Penobscot

This Crib Isn't Kid Stuff

CONTACT: Most New England whitewater rafting guides offer trips down the West Branch of the Penobscot. (See the resource list at the end of this chapter.)

HOW TO GET THERE: Individual outfitters will send directions to their locations. The West Branch is located near Millinocket. Take I-95 to Exit 56, then Route 157 west to Millinocket.

RATES: Day-long rafting trips range from $75 to $100. Overnight packages range from $130 to $190.

WHAT TO BRING: A swimsuit, sneakers, a wool or fleece sweater, a windbreaker, a change of clothing, and a towel.

KIDS: No one under 14.

SKILL LEVEL: No experience necessary.

WHEN TO GO: Most companies offer trips beginning Memorial Day weekend and run them weekends through July 4, then daily through Labor Day weekend.

Okay, it's not the fabled Colorado River trip through the Canyon. It's not the surging Salmon River in Idaho. It's not the remote Tatshenshini in Alaska. But as any East Coast water rat will tell you, a day on the Penobscot ranks with the best of them.

The West Branch of the Penobscot challenges whitewater enthusiasts with exploding Class IV to Class V rapids, and soothes them with interspersed swirling floats through spectacular northern Maine scenery. As one guide put it, "One moment you're in water so big and loud you can't even hear your own screams. The next bend brings a silence so deep, your whisper shatters it."

Alas, the Nob, as veteran rafters call it, is no secret among Maine outfitters. Several busloads pull up at put-in spots on busy weekends, and rafters wait in line to enter the water. Most outfitters drop in at the headwaters—Ripogenus Gorge, at the base of sheer, vertical eighty-foot walls. The big-volume, drop-and-fall rafting trip runs thirteen miles from Ripogenus Dam to Pockwockamus Falls. It's an awesome setting, but you won't notice much here except the stomach-in-your-throat plunge into a frothy boil of whitewater.

If you're lucky, you'll stay in the raft, and the raft will end rightside up. Most do. If not, well, that's why you're wearing that humongous flotation device, wetsuit, and helmet. First, try to grab the boat. When that fails, keep your feet and head up and try to time your intake of breath with the surges of water. Somewhere downstream, someone will pick you up.

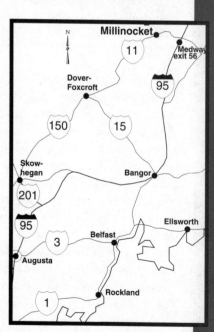

Our guides assured us that they, with our paddling help (this is a participation sport), had it all under control. What arrogance, we thought; who are we to challenge the forces of nature? Seconds later, we were thrown into a wall of water. The raft bent and buckled like a wild mustang. We paddled hard, then held on tight. (We can't figure out why they call it running a river— it was clear at this point that the river was running us.)

And this was only the beginning. Guides have

Catch 'Em While You Can

T. S. Eliot called April the cruelest month, but big-water rafting fans would beg to differ. Catch these connoisseurs-only river runs while you can.

For much of the year, Bulls Bridge Gorge on the Housatonic River is dry and dormant, due to a bypass canal that diverts water to a hydroelectric plant downstream. But come April, this barren stretch is engorged with spring runoff, creating a frenzy of wicked whitewater. The rapids at Bulls Bridge Gorge, rated Class V, are among the fiercest in New England. Want to ride the bull? Begin in Kent, Connecticut, where an eight-mile trip will take you past an old covered bridge, cascading waterfalls, and lush Connecticut countryside. Contact North American Whitewater Expeditions, Inc., Suite 140, 170 Boston Post Road, Madison, CT 06443; (800) RAPIDS-9.

While New Englanders revel in those first sun-kissed days of spring, whitewater thrill-seekers are trampling the crocuses to get to Millers River in western Massachusetts. Class III and IV rapids peak at the Funnel, while diagonal waves and holes challenge the unsuspecting. Catch Millers in April, when it's running fat and sassy. Outfitters include Zoar Outdoors, Mohawk Trail, Charlemont, MA 01339; (800) 532-7483.

The Wild West comes to Southern Vermont but twice a year. On

dubbed the first nasty plunge the Exterminator. Next we came upon Staircase, then descended Big Heater. We made it through the gorge, but Trouble lay ahead. Once past Troublemaker, we were able to relax—and look back. What we saw was a breathtaking silhouette of Mount Katahdin.

It would have been nice to dawdle here, floating in the shadows of Maine's highest peak. But the most challenging section of the river lay ahead: the infamous Class V Cribwork Rapids. We'd heard about The Crib since we signed up for this trip, and now we truly heard it: a soft, unmistakable rumble in the distance, building to a crescendo. Once through it, we wanted to do it again. (Some outfitters offer two-for-one trips; rafters can take The Crib twice in a day.) Below The Crib, we got some sightseeing in—and a few more rapids.

the last weekends in both April and September, rafters saddle up for a go at Jamaica Gorge, where the rapids are steep, drenching, and nonstop. Be warned: the Dumplings here are nothing like Grandma's. The ten-mile trip has pretty scenery, too, not that you'll notice. Contact Crab Apple Whitewater, Inc., Crab Apple Acres Inn, HC 63, Box 25, The Forks, ME 04985; (800) 553-RAFT.

If you like to take the road less traveled, you'll love the Rapid River, in the Rangeley Lake region of Maine. This six-mile run is so remote, you can only reach it by boat. Three weekends a season, the water's high with Class IV rapids, running through scenic Maine wilderness. Its steep drop will send your heart plummeting to your booties. Plan to hike back upriver to Middle Dam afterwards; it's a good way to dry off, and the only way to get out of here. This one's run exclusively by Downeast Whitewater, P.O. Box 119, Route 302, Center Conway, NH 03813; (603) 447-3002.

Rarely raftable, New Hampshire's Swift River is sweet when she runs. Swollen with snowmelt for a few days in spring, the Swift offers eight exhilarating miles of Class IV rapids, a tight, technical ride that aficionados adore. Perhaps she's so desirable because of her elusiveness; spring levels fluctuate greatly, so you have to be flexible with a date. Contact Downeast Whitewater, P.O. Box 119, Route 302, Center Conway, NH 03813; (603) 447-3002.

All outfitters celebrate the completion of the run with a hearty barbecue. We think they should also hand out buttons or bumper stickers that say THIS BODY CLIMBED MOUNT NOB.

Charlemont, Massachusetts: Tackling the Labyrinth on the Deerfield River

Hang on for the Wildest Whitewater Ride in Massachusetts

CONTACT: Zoar Outdoors, Mohawk Trail, Charlemont, MA 01339; (800) 532-7483. Zoar runs rafting trips on the Zoar Gap and Dryway sections of the Deerfield. They also offer excursions on Millers River (spring releases) in western Massachusetts, and on the West River in Vermont. Ask for their brochure, detailing release dates. In recent years, the Dryway has been released most weekends in the summer and a couple in the fall.

HOW TO GET THERE: Zoar's base camp is about 2 hours west of Boston on Route 2 (Mohawk Trail). Go 17 miles west of the rotary in Greenfield to Charlemont. Go through Charlemont Village. Zoar is on your right.

RATES: A fee of $80 per person includes guide, transportation to the river, and a barbecue lunch.

WHERE TO STAY: Zoar Outdoor offers onsite camping for $6 per person, per night, or they'll book a room for you at a local inn or motel. If you come for a weekend, consider a rafting package: on Saturday, raft Zoar Gap; on Sunday, raft the Dryway. Sleep at the rustic Charlemont Inn or the Maple House Bed & Breakfast. Package prices are $165 per person and $172 per person, respectively.

WHAT TO BRING: A swimsuit, sneakers or river sandals, long underwear, a jacket or sweater, and windbreaker or rain jacket.

KIDS: Minimum age is fourteen on the Dryway. (Gentler Zoar Gap is suitable for children age seven and up.)

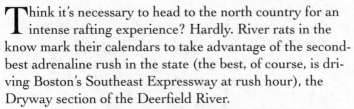

Think it's necessary to head to the north country for an intense rafting experience? Hardly. River rats in the know mark their calendars to take advantage of the second-best adrenaline rush in the state (the best, of course, is driving Boston's Southeast Expressway at rush hour), the Dryway section of the Deerfield River.

Just a couple of hours west of Boston, with the Berkshire hills as a backdrop, this river delivers thrills aplenty. While you won't have to dodge careening trucks, you'll be clutching those paddles in a death-grip as you match wits with the devilish Labyrinth. This is rubber-burning, Class IV rafting, on New England's most technical whitewater. Wimps need not apply, nor neophytes; this one's too tricky for first-timers. And it promises to get better: the New England Power Company recently signed an agreement that should result in more release dates and improved put-ins, take-outs, and portage trails.

We had a go at the Dryway with Zoar Outdoors, based in Charlemont. When the Monroe Bridge dam releases 900 to 1,100 cubic feet per second of water, rough-and-tumble types head to Zoar (or Crabapple Whitewater) to suit up and get in on the action. And they come in force; outfitters' rafts, private rafts, and kayaks galore are drawn to this mecca of whitewater mania.

After getting booties and jackets at Zoar's base camp, we went through the standard safety drill. Main message: If you fall out, float downriver, on your back, toes pointing up, so you don't get your feet stuck under a rock and drown. Cheery stuff. We were issued paddles, life vests,

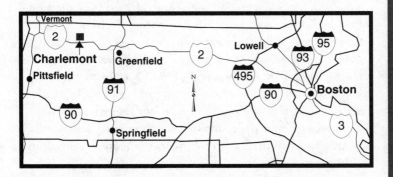

and helmets, then took a bus ride to the dam. There we met our guide, Gary Duncan, and fellow victims, er, river-runners. We'd been warned about the Dryway, but many of us had tackled the mellower (Class II to Class III) Zoar Gap section of the Deerfield with aplomb. How bad could this be?

We soon found out. Almost immediately, we encountered our first frothy challenge, Factory Rapid. Oops — lost two of our party of six. While a couple of us paddled frantically, the rest lunged at the dumpees, managing to pull them in by the scruffs of their necks after a fifty-yard float. "We're not in Kansas, anymore, Toto!" someone squealed. Anyone who'd started the trip groggy was suddenly jerked into wakefulness, and using every ounce of energy to paddle with some degree of control.

On to the aptly named Split Hair, where the river is divided by boulders and you have to navigate (pick a side, any side) through Class III water. We picked, we paddled, with Duncan shouting instructions as we galloped along on Bronco-sized waves.

"Want to have some real fun?" Duncan asked. "Surf's up!" And surf we did, sitting stationary in the trough of a rapid while vigorously paddling upriver. "Let's go surfin' now, everybody's learnin' how," someone sang as the raft filled with water. We glided downriver into an eddy, then ashore to bail out. The Beach Boys themselves had never had such a time.

After a quick snack stop (had we been paddling for an hour? it seemed like seconds), we were back in the saddle, anticipating the wickedest section of the Dryway, the Labyrinth. As we watched the other rafts go over the first rapid and disappear, we started to panic. Perhaps Duncan smelled fear. "It'll be a great run," he reassured us. "I haven't lost anybody yet — today." Well, there was no turning back now. At the crest of the first rapid, we looked down — big mistake — into a tumble of rocks and roiling water. Just before that dizzying sensation overwhelmed our innards, Duncan's voice boomed commands, and our survival instincts took over. We made it, shrieking all the way.

Exhilarated, we cruised the rest of the run, past giant boulders into deep troughs, up steep-crested waves, rapid after rapid, until the Labyrinth was conquered and we were spent.

Upstream, we found a cranny where we could wedge ourselves in and watch other rafters tackle the Labyrinth. Some barely made it. Some fell out. Some got pinned on the rocks. But at the end of the ride, everybody wore an ear-to-ear grin.

Resources

Additional Outfitters

Clarke Outdoors, 163 Route 7, West Cornwall, CT 06796; (203) 672-6365.

Crabapple Whitewater, HC 63, Box 25, The Forks, ME 04985; (800) 553-7238.

Eastern River Expeditions, P.O. Box 1173, Greenville, ME 04441; (800) 634-7238.

Magic Falls Rafting, P.O. Box 9, The Forks, ME 04985; (800) 207-RAFT.

Maine Whitewater, P.O. Box 663, Bingham, ME 04920; (800) 345-MAIN.

Moxie Outdoor Adventures, Lake Moxie Camps, The Forks, ME 04985; (800) 866-6943.

New England Whitewater Center, P.O. Box 21, Caratunk, ME 04925; (800) 766-7238.

Professional River Runners, P.O. Box 92, West Forks, ME 04985; (800) 325-3911.

Riverrunning Expeditions, 85 Main Street, Falls Village, CT 06031; 203-824-5579.

Unicorn Rafting Expeditions, P.O. Box T, Brunswick, ME 04011; (800) UNICORN.

Wilderness Expeditions, P.O. Box 41, Rockwood, ME 04478; (800) 825-WILD.

BOOKS

The Complete Whitewater Rafter. Jeff Bennett, Ragged Mountain Press.

The Whitewater Source Book. Richard Penny, Menasha Ridge Press.

Fishing

97

Greenville, Maine: Floating the Penobscot

A River of Ghosts

CONTACT: Dan Legere, Maine Guide Fly Shop, P.O. Box 1202, Greenville, ME 04441; (207) 695-2266.

HOW TO GET THERE: Take the Newport exit off I-95, then follow Route 11 to Corinna, Route 7 to Dexter, and Route 23 to Sangerville. Head toward Guilford on Route 16, then follow Routes 6 and 15 (same road) into Greenville. Maine Guide Fly Shop is in the center of town, on the right-hand side. If it is more convenient, Legere will meet you on the river; make arrangements with him.

RATES: A day-long drift-boat trip costs $250 for one or two people, and includes all equipment, transportation to and from the river, and a shore lunch.

WHAT TO BRING: Bug repellent, a hat, sunscreen, and layered clothing.

KIDS: Twelve and older.

SKILL LEVEL: All levels.

The heavy flowing waters of the Penobscot River in northern Maine run cold and powerful, roaring over polished granite sheets and water-worn boulders. Full of riffs and eddies, the river falls down in a hurry out of the deep woods, slipping in and out of the shadows of mighty Mt. Katahdin.

It is a wild river with wild fish. The salmon are native and stay in these waters year-round, which means the six-pounder that got away last spring is still here.

It is also a river of ghosts. Gray Ghosts and Black

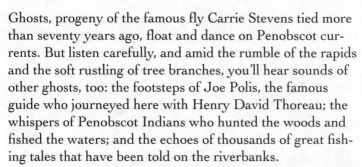

Ghosts, progeny of the famous fly Carrie Stevens tied more than seventy years ago, float and dance on Penobscot currents. But listen carefully, and amid the rumble of the rapids and the soft rustling of tree branches, you'll hear sounds of other ghosts, too: the footsteps of Joe Polis, the famous guide who journeyed here with Henry David Thoreau; the whispers of Penobscot Indians who hunted the woods and fished the waters; and the echoes of thousands of great fishing tales that have been told on the riverbanks.

There's a great advantage to knowing a river well, which is one of the reasons we hooked up with Maine guide Dan Legere, owner of the Maine Guide Fly Shop in Greenville. Legere is something of a legend; it can be argued that few people living today know the Penobscot better than he does. A lifelong Mainer, he's fished the Penobscot since he was a boy; he's returned so often that the trout have become his companions.

The Penobscot is deep, wide, and fast-flowing, making 90 percent of the fishing slots unreachable in waders. To fish it right, you need a boat. Legere floats the river in a two-person, western-style McKenzie River drift boat with an anchor rig.

We came to fish the west branch of the Penobscot more out of respect for its legendary waters than with hopes of catching big fish. On this morning, the river was wearing its late-summer, dry-season dress. It was a day of terrible fishing conditions: hot and bright; the river warm, slow, and low. There were few rapids and no tough water. Legere rowed us downstream, dropping anchor to fish a slot, then floating on.

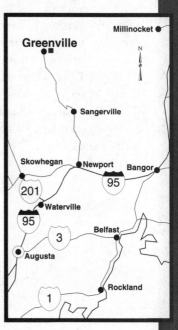

The fish were sluggish, so we talked flies. Legere had us using big, long streamers—stone flies and big wolves. He showed us the Thunder Creek tying strategy, where marabou is tied pointing frontward and then pulled back to form a bullet head. And he revealed his new secret: the Tarantula. (Every Maine guide has a few flies up his sleeve.) Legere is generous with both his equipment and his knowledge.

We floated in sun-dappled glory, dropping our flies lightly on the water, hoping for a rise. The Penobscot, of course, is not always so quiet. On an average day, two people can catch up to twenty-five salmon, running from eight to fourteen inches; ten percent of your catch is likely to measure over sixteen inches.

"One of my best days on the Penob was in mid-June, for the Hendrickson hatch," Lagere told us. "I was up on the river by myself, and caught at least twenty salmon — all over sixteen inches — in a matter of four or five hours. It was unbelievable. I remember one particular stretch, I was playing fish for literally three hours straight. It was one of the finest days I ever had."

Legere likes to tell fish stories, and after a lifetime of fishing and twenty-two years of guiding — fourteen of them on the Penobscot — he has a bunch of them.

That morning, we caught a couple of small landlocked salmon and some brook trout; we left the Penobscot with no great fish stories in our repertoire. That's okay; as any angler knows, there's a lot more to fishing than catching fish.

Note: Legere told us that the best times to drift the Penobscot are late May for streamer fly-fishing; June 5 to June 21 for mayfly hatches; and June 21 to July 20 for caddis fly hatches. Be sure to reserve a date with Lagere well in advance.

Various Maine Sites: Fly-Fishing Is Made Easy at This Traveling Classroom

Taking the Mystery Out of Muddlers and Woolly Buggers

CONTACT: Edge of Maine Flyfishing, P.O. Box 377, Coplin Plantation, ME 04982; (207) 237-2405. For reservations and directions, contact the individual school locations. They are:

Tim Pond Wilderness Camps, Box 22, Eustis, ME 04936; (207) 243-2947 (in season) or (207) 897-4056 (winter)

Lakewood Camps, Middledam, Andover, ME 04216; (207) 392-1581 or (207) 486-3200

Riverview Cottages, P.O. Box 396, Jackman, ME 04945; (207) 668-5601

Sugarloaf Ski Touring Center, Carrabassett Valley, ME 04982; (207) 237-2405.

RATES: Three-day classes, including cabin rental, meals, and instruction, cost $350 at Tim Pond Wilderness Camps, $305 at Lakewood Camps, and $295 at Riverview Cottages. Classes at Sugarloaf Ski Touring Center cost $135, instruction only.

WHAT TO BRING: All equipment is supplied, including rod, reel, line, and flies. Bring a fishing hat, bug repellent, sunglasses, rain gear, and warm clothing.

KIDS: Twelve and older with long attention spans; instructor Holding doesn't have much patience with kids.

SKILL LEVEL: All levels.

Mickey Finns and ghosts . . . nymphs and caddis flies . . . dryflies, wetflies, and mayflies. . . . It's all a mystery to you, right? All you know is you've been standing on the riverbank, spitting blackflies, sneaking up on fish you can't see, and wondering: Why all the fuss about fly-fishing?

It's time to go see Bonnie Holding, the person who can crack the code for you, open the doors and spark a passion for the sport. Once an employee of the L.L. Bean Fly Fishing School, Holding now owns and operates Edge of Maine Flyfishing, a guide service and school. We recommend her two-day learn-to-fly-fish program, a straightforward approach that demystifies the sport, untangles its complexities, and gets you on the river in a hurry.

The Location: Everyone knows that being smack in the middle of a gorgeous chunk of wilderness is at least half the reason for fishing. Why should a school be any different? You'll want to learn to fly-fish just so you can earn the right to come back to these rustic cabins nestled in the remote northern Maine woods. If you can't make it to the backwoods (or, like us, you wait too long to make reservations for the camp sessions, which fill up fast), check out her class at Sugarloaf/USA. The Carrabassett Valley is Holding's home territory; ask her and she'll show you some of the best fishing holes in the region, where you'll be able to try out your new skills after class.

And who says school has to be all work and no play? Tack on a couple of days in any of these locations and spend them hiking, canoeing, wildlife-watching, or just plain relaxing in the great outdoors.

The Knots: No need to get tangled up in tying on. Holding teaches four basic knots: the tube knot (backing to fly line); the needle knot (leader to fly line); the surgeon's knot (leader to tippet); and the Duncan Loop (fly to leader). She, of course, can tie them in a blink of an eye; you will lose the end of the line, go under instead of over, over instead of under, fumble and curse. But by the end of the day, you'll get it down.

If you've ever tied hook to line, you'll appreciate the Duncan Loop. "Learning this knot, alone, is worth the class tuition," said one participant. "It'll save me hours on the water."

The Cast: Holding is no poet. You'll hear no Norman Maclean–style prose on four-count rhythms of the line and grand circles of motion. Instead, Holding breaks fly-casting down to its simplest terms: "This is how you hold the rod; this is how you cast the rod; now, you try it."

Holding walked around and worked with each student individually. "You're bringing it back way too far. Stop it right here." "Put some power in that backcast." "Wait until your line straightens out before beginning the forward cast." "Stop your rod tip here for just a moment to let the loop unroll. Now, follow it down with your rod tip."

Snap! Snap! Not a good sound. "You just lost a four-dollar fly," she told us. (In theory, that is; in fact, we were fishing with fuzzy pieces of yarn—safe and cheap.) "You're starting your forward cast too soon. Watch your backcast, keep your eyes on it, let it unroll and then begin to bring it forward." The snapping sounds diminished. One by one, we corrected our mistakes and began to control our casts.

Eventually, we achieved it: the perfect cast, in which the rod is brought up in an effortless, graceful arc; the line floats in the air, unrolls gently (no snap), floats again, then extends fully (no spaghetti mess left in front of us); and the fly plops ever so softly, right where we want it. Ah, the rhythm, the beauty. . . . Help us, Holding; we're getting carried away!

The Bugs: We walked down to the stream and stood around while Holding told us how important it is to know fish food sources: aquatic insects (such as mayflies, stone-flies, caddis flies, and midges); terrestrial insects (spiders, beetles, crickets, grasshoppers); crustaceans (shrimp, cray-fish); minnows; and other invertebrates (leeches, snails, worms). Holding lifted rocks and gleefully pointed to an assortment of tiny, squiggly, wet things in various stages of their life cycle. We feigned interest, but most of us just wanted to get back to our casting.

The Flies: Ah, the flies. The fascinating mix of feather and fur, thread and tinsel. One of the bonuses of attending an Edge of Maine Flyfishing class is that you'll get a glimpse of, and a hand at, the art of fly-tying. Holding admits she doesn't have the patience or the interest to tie her own flies, but nonetheless, she'll teach you three basic designs. This is slow, precision work: threading and wrapping near-invisible pieces of filament, making dinky knots and wee hackles. Hackles, smackles; it's clear that for some, fly-tying is a tedious, frustrating chore. But for others, it is a passion, a consummate art.

The Mystery: Back where it belongs. When you complete the Edge of Maine Flyfishing class, the equipment, techniques, and methods of fly-fishing will hold no mystery. You'll know how to *do.* Pack your fly rod and head to a gorgeous flow of water, where the mysterious wonder and beauty of nature still exists.

Ashland, Maine: Nothing but Woods, Water, and Fish at the Libby Camps

Fly in to a Wilderness Paradise Deep in the Northern Maine Woods

The trip in was dazzling enough. We took off in a seaplane from Lucky's Landing on Pushaw Lake, just outside Bangor. Not until you've flown 1,500 feet above the northern Maine woods can you comprehend just how big this state is. We flew over a sprawling, dense wilderness, punctuated by countless glistening lakes and rivers that looked as if they were pulled like ribbons from the sky.

"Think we'll take a pass just east of Katahdin," pilot Tim Hodgkins shouted over the roar of the engine. We took an angle of ascent at which souls are said to leave the body (the contents of our stomachs almost did), flying so close to Mt. Katahdin we could feel the cold from its granite. (Okay, so the ascent wasn't that steep and we didn't get that close, but everything out here seems exaggerated.)

An hour after take-off, Hodgkins pointed down to our destination: Libby Camps on Millinocket Lake. This is not to be confused with the lake of the same name near the town of Millinocket. Libby's is way back in the backwoods, sandwiched between Baxter State Park and the Allagash Wilderness Waterway. Officially, we'd landed at Township 8, Range 9; unofficially, we were in the middle of the wilds of the northern Maine woods.

"True wilderness is what sets us apart from other places. The fishing is a bonus," said Matt Libby. We looked in

CONTACT: Libby Camps, Drawer V, Ashland, ME 04732; (207) 435-8274.

HOW TO GET THERE: Libby's is located 150 miles north of Bangor, Maine, near the Canadian border. You can drive to the camp, but you must request a detailed map; from Ashland the trip takes 1½ hours over gated, dirt logging roads. Better to fly in. Flights to camp are available from Bangor, Millinocket, and Greenville. We hired KT Aviation, located about 8 miles from Bangor International Airport (Exit 48 off I-95). Write them at Route 1, Box 1688, Bangor, ME 04401, or call (207) 945-5087.

RATES: Libby Camps offers a variety of packages. Package #1 includes a private cabin; meals; maid service; and use of a boat, motor, and canoes. It costs $105 per day, per person, double occupancy; $125 per day, single occupancy. Package #2 is the same as #1, and also includes seaplane flights out every other day, outpost overnights as desired, and a fishing license. It costs $150 per day, per person, double occupancy; $195 per day, single. Package #3 is the same as #2, plus full guide service. It costs $210 per day, per person, double occupancy; $295 per day, single. For children under twelve, the costs are $50 less a day.

WHAT TO BRING: Warm clothing, all fishing equipment, waders, a fishing hat, bug repellent, sunscreen, and a small backpack for day trips. Libby's has a selection of equipment and hand-tied flies for purchase. B.Y.O.B. if you so desire.

KIDS: Yes. Generally, families make up the bulk of the business in July and August; couples and father/son, mother/daughter guests in June and September; leaf peepers and upland bird hunters take over in October; and deer hunters in November.

SKILL LEVEL: All levels, but, as you'd expect, most guests are outdoor and/or fishing enthusiasts. Fly-fishing only on most lakes and streams; catch and release is encouraged.

ETCETERA: You don't have to be a fly-fisher to enjoy Libby Camps. They currently offer more than forty different day trips out of the lodge, including hiking, canoeing, photography, sailing, and bird-watching.

every direction, and saw nothing but woods and water.

Matt and his wife, Ellen, are the fourth generation of Libbys to own the camps. More than 100 years ago, the Libby family owned and operated Atkins Camps on an island in Millinocket Lake. In 1938, the cabins were relocated to the current site. Today, there are seven guest cabins (one original), handcrafted of peeled spruce and balsam fir, and a main lodge. The cabins vary in size, accommodating from two to ten people, and each has a private shower, a woodstove, gas lights, and a great front porch overlooking the lake.

We threw our bags down in our assigned cabin, anxious to check out the fishing, reputed to be some of the best in the East. It was almost too much: using a seaplane (Libby's is the only New England sport camp offering fly-outs on a daily basis), four-wheel drive trucks, canoes, boats, and trails, we had access to more than a half-million acres of wilderness, with countless ponds, lakes, and streams to fish, including the headwaters of the Allagash, Aroostook, and Penobscot Rivers. Orvis-endorsed guides (they spend most of seven months at the camp) were available to show us around. If this is not enough, Libby's has nine outpost cabins on remote ponds and rivers, which may be used in conjunction with package trips. It was daunting; we spent the rest of the day in jaw-dropping wonder, floating flies on nearby

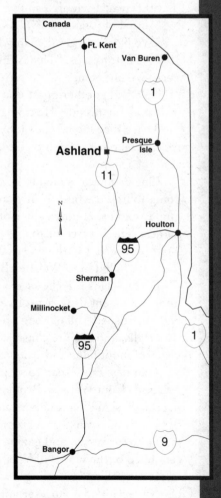

Round Pond, to fish who refused our offerings.

That evening, we gathered in the dining lodge with other guests. The cozy lodge is just what you'd expect: it's hand-crafted from forest timber; a large stone fireplace fills the center of the room; the walls are adorned with turtle shells, bear heads, antlers, and big fish. It faces west, so each evening the room is awash with the light of crimson sunsets.

We dined on comfort food—heaping servings of pork roast, potatoes and gravy, homemade applesauce, and freshly baked breads. We learned that sportsmen Teddy Roosevelt and Jack Dempsey had visited the camp, and that the award-winning show, "Cry of the Loon," produced by Mutual of Omaha's *Wild Kingdom*, was filmed here.

"We have one gentleman who's come every year since 1937," Matt told us. "This is the first year he hasn't been here. We miss him."

"We had another guest this year whose father had come in 1934," Ellen said. "He brought pictures to show us."

That's the way it is at Libby's; most of the guests are repeat customers, often the second and third generation to visit the camp.

One day, we decided to go stream fishing. "You're not going to find the best trout waters on a map," one of the guides told us. "In fact, some of them don't even have names." He directed us to one that did: Webster Brook. Matt flew us out to the end of Mantagamon Lake, and from there we hiked in to Webster Brook.

Brook? This is a classic example of New England understatement. It was a roily river, one of the prettiest we had ever fished, full of deep pools and eddies, cascading waterfalls, and granite chasms, all flanked by spectacular vistas of mountains and woods.

That day, more than forty trout were caught (and released) from Webster Brook. When the plane circled overhead, signaling time for our return to camp, we were done fishing. Sitting on a granite slab heated by the sun, listening to the water, and gazing out at the woods, we were reminded of the words of Washington Irving: "There is certainly something in angling that tends to produce a gentleness of spirit and a pure serenity of mind."

Grand Lake Stream, Maine: Roughing It in Style at Weatherby's

At This Angler's Haven, the Only Problem Is Choosing Where to Fish

Pocumcus. Wabassus. Sysladobis. They sound like things you wouldn't want to see on your medical chart, but in fact, all three are lakes surrounding Weatherby's fishing lodge. Tucked away in Maine's St. Croix valley, two hours northeast of Bangor, Weatherby's is smack in the middle of a fertile fishing ground known as the Grand Lakes region.

Take out your map of Maine, put your finger on Bangor, then slide it to the right, toward New Brunswick, Canada. You'll see few highways, but patch after patch of blue; there are more than thirty-two productive waters surrounding Weatherby's camp, making it heaven on earth for anglers. Depending on the season, the take includes smallmouth bass, landlocked salmon, Atlantic salmon, brook trout, lake trout, white perch, and pickerel.

Need more persuasion to hire a seaplane or drive seven hours out of Boston to get in on all this? How about pristine Grand Lake Stream, one of the liveliest salmon rivers in the country, where you can easily hook and release two to five salmon between dinner time and the eleven o'clock news. Time your trip from mid-May to early July, or from mid-September to mid-October for some of the best fly-fishing New England has to offer.

Or set your sights on Scraggly Lake, home of L.L. Bean's intermediate fly-fishing school. This is where Bert

CONTACT: Weatherby's, Grand Lake Stream, ME 04637; (207) 796-5558 (summer) or R.R. 1, Box 2272, Kingfield, ME 04947; (207) 237-2911 (winter). Open late April through mid-October.

HOW TO GET THERE: From Bangor, take Route 9 east to Route 1 north to Princeton. Just beyond Princeton, turn left to Grand Lake Stream. Weatherby's is about 2 hours from Bangor. Or fly in from Bangor by seaplane to Grand Lake. The cost is approximately $150 round trip.

RATES: Lodging, with breakfast, lunch-to-go, and dinner, costs $80 per adult, double occupancy per night; for kids, $50. Guide service is $125 per day. Boat/motor rental is $40 a day. A 15 percent service charge is added to your bill; guide's tip not included.

WHAT TO BRING: Fishing gear, waders, light-colored clothing, a warm jacket or sweater, rain gear, sunscreen, bug repellent, and a fishing hat. Maine fishing licenses are sold at Weatherby's. L.L. Bean spin- and bait-casting equipment is available for rent.

KIDS: Yes. This is a family fishing resort. The best way to increase the odds of other kids being present is to book in August, which is family month at the camp. The fishing action at that time is primarily smallmouth bass, white perch, and pickerel.

SKILL LEVEL: All levels and fishing techniques are appropriate. Grand Lake Stream is the only area restricted to fly-fishing.

ETCETERA: Aside from fishing, there's lake swimming (in late summer only, unless you love frigid water); or you might want to paddle to an island for a picnic and nature hike. Adjacent to the camp are basketball and tennis courts, and areas for croquet and horseshoes, but we can't vouch for these. Mainly, it'll be you, the water, the woods, and other like-minded types.

Lahr of *Field & Stream* once enjoyed "the greatest smallmouth fishing" he'd ever experienced. Smallmouth bass are in a striking frenzy in early June, but commonly hit all season long, said Ken and Charlene Sassi, owners of Weatherby's. Baitfishing for smallmouth becomes legal in late June. With so much water to choose from, you can give all your freshwater techniques and tackle a workout.

Ken told us that the land around the stream is owned by timber companies. In 1994, a company planned to sell the land for house lots, but locals and fishing enthusiasts (including the L.L. Bean people) raised enough money to buy the land to keep the stream in its natural setting.

This region is a sporting kingdom, and it's not yet fished extensively. This is all the more remarkable considering Weatherby's camp was opened in the mid-1800s.

The Sassis, lifelong Mainers, have run the place for more than twenty years. The guides they hire are local, and possessed of the wry humor Mainers are noted for. Even better, they know where the fish are biting. You don't need a guide to fish these waters, but it adds to the experience. The guides are known, too, for their skill at preparing fast, tasty lunches at waterside, perhaps featuring the catch of the day.

Guests stay in log cabins—Weatherby's has fifteen of them—decently spaced apart and quite nice by sporting camp standards. "Compared to other places, this is a five-star cabin," one guest declared. The rustic cottages were spotless, and most have full baths, electric heaters, and screened porches. Each has a fireplace and a stocked wood box, a great feature on a cool night (and that means just about every night in this part of Maine). Even the mattresses were a pleasant surprise.

The main lodge is just as you'd picture it, with a fireplace, overstuffed chairs, books, a piano, and even a televi-

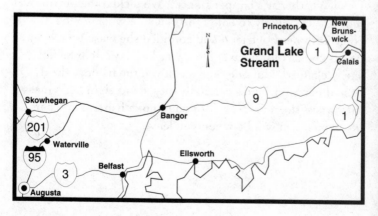

sion; but the fish story reigns supreme as the evening entertainment. The dining room is decorated with the requisite
mounted game fish, and each party has its own separate
table. The Sassis work the room with a skill few Capitol
Hill socialites could match, keeping the chat flowing among
guests. If the fish are biting and you don't make it for dinner, no problem: fishing comes first here; they'll feed you
later. Typical fare includes fish chowder, roast turkey, boiled
lobster, and fresh-baked breads and pies. Charlene cooks
dinner, Ken makes breakfast. It's B.Y.O.B. as far as liquor is
concerned.

So how's the fishing? We visited in August, not exactly
prime-time for salmon or brook trout stream fishing, but we
cast our lot in Grand Lake Stream anyway, mainly out of
curiosity. Waders on, we padded along this sandy-bottomed
stream, casting often but coming up empty.

The next day, everything was charmed. Guide Alvah
Harriman drove us to the St. Croix River, along the Canadian border. We put in his handmade canoe, with motor,
and were overwhelmed with beautiful scenery and smallmouth bass. We didn't see another human on the river, but
we did spot five or six bald eagles. And the fish! After
catching (and releasing) at least fifteen smallmouth apiece,
we lost count. Harriman knew every fishing hole. The
campfire lunch he whipped up was dandy, if not exactly
low-fat. And his coffee, complete with crushed egg shells,
would put Starbuck's to shame.

We'd had a great day, but was that just dumb luck or the
usual Weatherby's happenstance? We picked the person we
judged "least likely to enjoy the place," a woman who'd
come with her boyfriend and confided she wasn't too keen
on his choice of holidays. How was her day? "Fantastic!"
she exclaimed. Not only had she loved the fishing, she'd
bested her boyfriend's catch, twenty-six to eighteen. Guess
the Sassis' slogan is true: "If you're not a fisherman when
you come, you will be when you leave."

Manchester, Vermont: Here's How They Do It at Orvis

Experience the Mystique of the Granddaddy of All Fishing Schools

CONTACT: Orvis Fly Fishing School, Box 798, Manchester, VT 05254; (800) 235-9763. Classes run April through August; book at least two months in advance.

HOW TO GET THERE: Take Route 7 north to Manchester, Exit 4. Turn left onto Route 7A. Orvis is 0.5 mile on your left. Or take scenic Route 7A, all the way up through southern Vermont. Orvis is about 25 miles from Bennington on Route 7A.

Rates: A package that includes a three-day Vermont fishing license, lunches, use of Orvis gear, and an Orvis fly-fishing guidebook costs $395.

WHERE TO STAY: Orvis can arrange lodging at the Equinox Hotel or at other local inns and bed-and-breakfasts. Some offer special rates for Orvis students.

WHAT TO BRING: Rain gear, sunglasses, a fishing hat, and insect repellent.

KIDS: Children are welcome only on special parent-child weekends; ask for dates, and book in advance.

SKILL LEVEL: Fine for novices and those who have some experience; students are grouped according to ability.

ETCETERA: In addition to the original school in Vermont, Orvis has a saltwater fly-fishing school in Cape Cod (see "Power Fishing on the Flats of Cape Cod," page 118) and an outpost in Evergreen, Colorado.

Orvis. The name alone conjures visions of antique fishing rods, zippered vests, rivers meandering through quaint New England villages.

Taking a class at Orvis Fly Fishing School is a quintessential New England experience. The setting is picturesque Manchester Village, Vermont. Students may stay at the posh Equinox Hotel, established in 1769 by the Orvis family. The stream is the fabled Batten Kill. Even the instruction has a Yankee feel—crisp, matter-of-fact, highly knowledgeable, consistent. Rick Rishell has been director of the school since 1978.

There's definitely an Orvis mystique. That's why many people wouldn't think of going anywhere else. It's like buying a Mercedes; it has a good reputation, and you know what you're getting. Yet some complain it's too big, too commercial. (The Manchester school is part of a complex that includes a retail store and manufacturing facility.) As one student put it, "Corporate commercialism and the Zen of fly-fishing can seem an odd mix at times." Those who prefer the personal touch might be more suited to a one-on-one fishing guide experience.

But you can't argue with success. Since the school began nearly thirty years ago, Orvis has introduced thousands of people to the art of fly-fishing. Their highly refined, step-by-step teaching method has set the standard in the sport, and an Orvis endorsement is highly prized among fishing guides.

Sessions for fly-fishing enthusiasts from beginner to advanced last two-and-a-half days, Friday to Sunday or Tuesday to Thursday. Classes start out with groups of thirty or so, and are then broken up into smaller sections based on experience.

Does this school live up to its image? Here's what we found.

First, we were issued a three-day Vermont fishing license and matched up with an Orvis rod, reel, leaders, and flies. Our fellow

Class is in session. The attentive instruction at Orvis has introduced thousands of people to the art of fly-fishing.

Manchester, Vermont

students ranged in age from seventeen to seventy-five. About a third were women.

The big classroom was abuzz with anticipation. Friends, co-workers, husbands and wives, even a grandson-grandfather duo looked forward to learning the intricacies of this intriguing pastime. About six of us, novices all, were matched up with instructor Keith Abbott, then led to the trout ponds behind the Orvis store for a casting lesson. The casting ponds are manmade, mechanically aerated, and stocked with fish.

Now this was fun. Standing twenty to thirty feet apart, we casted with all the style we could muster. Our instructors demonstrated the mechanics, then worked with each of us individually to help us put the pieces together. A real plus for Orvis: You get the benefit of several instructors' insights, not just one approach. As we practiced, the guides roamed around the pond, stopping to make comments and suggestions. "You're lifting your arm way too high; let's do it together so you can see how it's supposed to feel," said instructor Tom Dick, taking a student's hand in his own. "Don't try to muscle it." With that quick tip, the student's technique improved dramatically.

Lunch is a high point at Orvis. We trooped over to the

lovely old Equinox Hotel, where a buffet meal was offered in a private dining room. Options included hot entrees, salads, sandwich fixings, and dessert, everything tasty and nicely presented. Then it was back to the classroom for lessons in knot-tying, followed by more casting practice on the pond.

At about this time, an interesting psychological phenomenon kicked in. Students had begun to feel that their casting technique should be shaping up. When the art of a perfect cast seemed elusive, frustration built; you could see it in the knit brows and frowning mugs. The instructors, having seen this a million times, tried to coax us out of it. "Hey, this is supposed to be fun," one said. Another asked, "Does that sucking-a-lemon expression make your roll cast better?"

Our second full day, Saturday, began with more casting practice on the ponds. A strong breeze challenged our new-found skills, as we now had to cast into the wind.

Next, it was back to the classroom for lessons in fly selection, entomology, and tactics; basically, how to find and identify what fish eat, and other useful things to know if you want to catch (and release, naturally) the Big One.

Finally, after lunch, we went on the field trip we'd been waiting for, a drive to the Batten Kill. Here, we had the opportunity to face actual stream conditions. While one instructor described the water conditions, the other demonstrated the proper method of casting into different spots—and promptly got his line hung up in a tree. He was embarrassed, but his foible made us novices feel better.

Sunday morning was slated for the equipment lecture, the most controversial aspect of the Orvis program. An instructor demonstrated Orvis equipment, everything from pontoon boats to line clippers, prefacing the lecture with, "This isn't a sales pitch." Some weren't convinced. "I'd call it a bit of a hard sell," one student said. Others rolled their eyes, clearly not tickled to pay for a product pitch with their tuition money. Others found it helpful and informative to have the gear described and features compared, and felt it made their buying decisions easier. A further nudge to buy is the temporary store credit card, issued to students at the beginning of the course. You don't have to pay for anything until school is over. Obviously, it's easy to get carried away spending money this way, and many students did; one fellow was decked out from hat to shoes in Orvis duds by the second day of class. For some folks, shopping is part of the experience.

And while some would agree that other manufacturers make gear as good as or better than Orvis, the retail store is a popular hangout. At least half the students in our class bought things, perhaps a sign that they're serious about fly-fishing and plan to do lots more of it.

Another reason this school could cost you more than you bargained for is Manchester itself. Antique shops, restaurants, and outlet shops will tempt you, and perhaps you'll want to extend your stay.

East Harwich, Massachusetts:
Power Fishing on the Flats of Cape Cod

The Stripers Are Back

CONTACT: Fishing the Cape, Routes 137 and 39, Harwich Commons, East Harwich, MA 02645; (508) 432-1200.

HOW TO GET THERE: Take Route 6 (Mid-Cape Highway) to Exit 11; go south on Route 137. Fishing the Cape is located 1 mile from the exit, in the Stop and Shop Plaza.

RATES: The Monomoy guided trip costs $350 per day or $225 to $250 for a half-day. Fishing the Cape also runs guided flats-fishing boat trips, which cost $175 (for up to two people); and wading trips, which cost $250 a day or $195 a half-day.

WHAT TO BRING: Fishing the Cape supplies all necessary equipment, including rods, reels, lines, and flies. Bring a change of clothes, a warm jacket, sunglasses, and a hat.

KIDS: Twelve and older.

SKILL LEVEL: All levels.

ETCETERA: If the fishing bug hits you especially hard, the Orvis Saltwater Fly Fishing School offers three-day courses featuring instruction in all aspects of saltwater fly-fishing. The school is based at the Fishing the Cape shop and presented at the Wequassett Inn, located on the waterfront in Chatham, Massachusetts. The two-and-a-half-day program is offered two times a week from May through September. Sixteen students are accepted for each session, with a four-to-one student-staff ratio. The program costs $395, which includes instruction, use of equipment, and lunch. It does not include lodging.

There are two good reasons why, if you even occasionally like to toss a hook in the water, you should check out Fishing the Cape in Harwich, Massachusetts. First, the amazingly productive fishing grounds on the southeast corner of Cape Cod are wild, raw, beautiful, and loaded with striped bass, one of the most exciting game fish in the world. Imagine fly-fishing in wide open waters, with nothing in front or in back of you but the misty merges of sky and sea. No branches to snag; no trees to roll cast around. And fish abound.

Second, while no guide can guarantee you'll hook up, these folks just don't seem to get skunked.

Fishing the Cape is the dreamchild of Bob Benson, a lifelong sportsman and something of a legend in angling circles. Benson has captured world records for blue shark taken on a fly rod and for striped bass taken on a four-pound-test leader ("more than fourteen pounds" was all the description we could get out of Benson). He created a weekly cable television show called Fishing the Cape, and when the once-threatened population of striped bass rebounded and began to thrive in the waters of southeastern Cape Cod, he set up shop under the same name. Today, Fishing the Cape is headquarters for the Orvis Saltwater Fly Fishing School, a well-stocked fishing supply store, and a guide service.

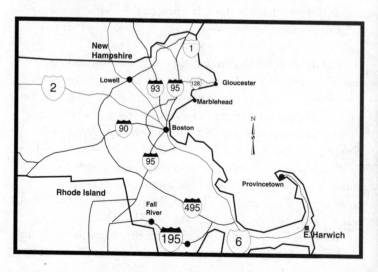

We met with Fishing the Cape's head guide, Peter Alves, early on a warm summer morning. The sun, barely above the horizon of sea, had already burned off the early fog, and was shining bright and clear. Still, it was no match for Alves's unflaggingly cheerful disposition; a definite morning person, we decided.

We were going after stripers in the spectacular waters surrounding Monomoy Island. The currents raging around the islands and beaches off the southeastern tip of the Cape create massive shoals and deep, quick-moving channels—perfect terrain for stripers. As the tide flooded, Alves explained, we'd fish the flats—areas recently vacated by hundreds of professional clammers in search of quahogs, littlenecks, and steamers. The holes they leave provide a rich soup of shrimp, eels, sandworms, and other great fish food, and the stripers move in to forage.

We started by working the east shore of Monomoy Island. The tide was out—way out—and the water lapped onto a beach studded with starfish. The water's edge was more like a mountain ridge: two feet from where it lapped the sand, it dropped straight down to a depth of ten feet. Instant vertigo, brought on by the thought of accidentally falling into the sea while wearing chest-high waders, overcame us. It would be tough to get out of the water, and easy to be stranded by a rapidly advancing tide. Anglers need to be cautious in these waters. It's one of the best arguments for going with a guide. We were glad Alves was there to keep us (literally) out of deep water.

Enough sightseeing; it was time to get set up and go fishin'. Fishing the Cape guides supply equipment for their sports to use, and in Alves's case, that included tying flies for us. It's amazing how easily striper delicacies—sand eels, minnows, squid—can be imitated with fur and feathers. Alves rigged up our lines with flies of his own design—an appealing (to the fish, too, we hoped) combination of feathers, thread, and a hint of tinsel. He paced back and forth between us, coaching a cast, changing a leader, directing a placement, and teaching us the techniques of saltwater fly-fishing.

While delicacy and gentleness are the requisite skills for freshwater stream fishing, saltwater fishing off Monomoy requires something else: power. Gusty winds had whipped up a knee-high surf where the water broke over the channel edge onto the flats. We had to punch the fly right through the wind. Freshwater casting requires the arm, the wrist; but saltwater casting uses the whole body to enable the fly to land exactly where the fish are heading.

And how does one know where the fish are heading? That's the key.

"This isn't just about dropping a line in and seeing if anything comes up," Alves said. "It's hunting, knowing where they're likely to be, spotting them, and dropping the fly in exactly the right spot, feeling them hit, playing them. It's incredibly exciting.

"And you get all this, too," he said, with a sweep of his hand.

"All this" is the incredible scope of Monomoy. It's a national wildlife refuge, home to deer, seals, and hundreds of species of birds. There is a pedestrian corridor that narrows to about twenty feet in width across North Island. Everything else is off limits. You'll see gulls, of course, including the comical fuzzballs of newly hatched herring gulls. But you'll also see a wide variety of terns and other seabirds, including transients who summer in the Arctic and fly to Tierra del Fuego for the winter.

The water is sparkling clear, dotted with thousands of acres of sandbars and channel banks. And if you're accustomed to sneaking up on trout along heavily canopied mountain streams, you'll delight in these larger-than-life sport-fishery grounds.

Actually, these waters are home to several species of sport fish—principally blues and stripers. While the voracious bluefish (thought to be the only living relative of the piranha) remained plentiful over the years, the striped bass, an anadromous fish (meaning it spawns in fresh water), underwent a period of rapid decline. Thanks to strict limits on commercial and sportfishing for stripers, and pollution control efforts in rivers along the northeastern coast of the United States, stripers are coming back in big numbers.

They were there for us. If the fishing hadn't been so darn good, we could have spent all day soaking up salt air and limitless views. But they were hitting. Alves seemed to have a sixth sense that told him where the fish were, and when we managed to cast our ultralight fly rod (into the wind) into the spot he directed, we hooked up.

We don't imagine that it's cheaper to fly-fish for stripers than to march down to the local fish store and buy some. (We caught and released, anyway; it's the unofficial rule here.) Like any outstanding guide service, Fishing the Cape is pricey, and the fish you hook into are likely to be young ones; 95 percent of the fish landed in the area are juveniles, and therefore illegal to keep. But even the babies are fighters and a challenge to land—and it's a whole lot more fun than going to the market.

Hancock, Massachusetts: A Little Bit of Montana in Massachusetts

You Can Catch a Few Trout with Fred Moran—
If You Can Stop Laughing

If Fred Moran ever decides to hang up his waders, he'll do well to consider the comedy club circuit. Fly-fish with Moran and you'll hold your rod with one hand, stomach with the other. But there's little chance he, or his sons, will give up the family business anytime soon. They're having too much fun.

"If I were a kid and were granted just one wish, this would be it," Moran said. "My wish came true. I've done what everybody wants to do—turn their hobby into a business." His passion for the sport is hard to resist, whether you join a Points North two-day fly-fishing school or hire Moran as a guide.

But nobody goes on a fishing trip strictly for belly laughs. The river has to deliver the goods, and the Deerfield, in western Massachusetts, is no slouch in that department. The eight-mile stretch from Fife Brook Dam to Route 2 is considered one of the top trout rivers in New England, with the average-size take fifteen to seventeen inches long. Every couple of trips, they nail one over twenty inches, Moran said. He's fond of calling the upper Deerfield a Western-style river, like you'd see in Montana ("Not that I've ever been to Montana," he admits). It's wide and riffling, and if you stretch your imagination, the Berkshire Hills that flank it might resemble the Rockies

CONTACT: Points North Fly Fishing Outfitters, Route 8, Adams, MA 01220; (413) 743-4030. Two-day fly-fishing classes are scheduled throughout the summer; call for dates. Guided trips are offered from April through September; each runs for four hours. Times are arranged at mutual convenience and in accordance with water levels.

HOW TO GET THERE: Class meets in front of the main lodge at Jiminy Peak ski resort. Take I-90 (the Massachusetts Turnpike) to Exit B3 crossing the state line into New York, then take New York Route 22 to Massachusetts Route 43 east. On Route 43 east, you'll see signs for Jiminy Peak.

RATES: The two-day fly-fishing school is $175; four hours of guide service (for proficient fly-fishers only) is $100 for the first person, $50 each for the second and third person. A deposit is required.

WHERE TO STAY: Points North will supply a list of inns and hotels, such as the Mountain Resort at Jiminy Peak. Tent camping is offered at Pittsfield State Forest, about 10 miles away. There are no showers, but you can use the ones at the Pittsfield YMCA for $3.

WHAT TO BRING: An eight- to nine-foot rod; line weights up to 7; felt-soled chest or hip waders; sunglasses (polarized, if possible); bug repellent; rain gear; sunscreen; a fishing hat; a Massachusetts fishing license (you can get one at their store). Points North is an Orvis dealer, and will provide equipment at no extra cost. They also provide all flies.

KIDS: Minimum age is thirteen.

SKILL LEVEL: Fly-fishing school is recommended for novices or near-beginners; guide service is recommended for fly-fishers looking to learn the Deerfield from an expert. (Note: Leave nonfishing companions at home; they host only those who are fishing.)

(albeit puny ones). You don't need to dream up the fish, however. The river is loaded with rainbow, brown, and brook trout.

If you're looking for a challenge, you may find one. Consider Moran's favorite fish story—all true, he swears, and he has witnesses: "Longest fight of my life was right here; lasted from 7:45 to 10:15 at night," he recalled. "That sucker took me into my backing [the part that's past the eighty-two feet of fly line] not once, but thirteen times! If I'd had a stiffer rod, say a graphite, and not the bamboo, he would've broke me off—he ran like crazy, a monster brown trout, over thirty inches long, thick as my thigh. . . . " Then, with the wistfulness that only a fellow fishing enthusiast can truly appreciate, "I had him a couple of times. And I lost him."

Spend a few minutes on the river with Moran, and you'll soon be spinning your own fish tales. Fishing with Points North "feels like going out with a bunch of buddies," as one student put it. Groups are usually small, the lesson usually lively, although the content is basically the same as you'd encounter at any fly-fishing school (how many ways are there to demonstrate a clinch knot?). The difference here is in style, not substance. For example, "If it happens to be a day that runs dry, we'll stay longer, tell funnier stories—anything we can think of to make it a better experience," Moran said. "So, maybe later you'll say, 'That was some beautiful water out there, some day we're gonna catch a fish on it.'"

Points North guides don't take themselves, or their sport, too seriously. Nor do they commit what Moran considers an unpardonable offense, fishing while guiding. "Some guides ask, 'Do you mind if I fish?' Whaddya gonna say? And they end up a mile down the river from you—he's fishing, you're the chump paying for it."

We spent the first day of class at a trout pond at Jiminy Peak ski resort, covering the basics and viewing a slide show featuring close-up shots of flies at various stages. This appetizing production preceded lunch at a nearby tavern. The afternoon was devoted to casting practice; then, students headed out to explore the Berkshires or check into their lodgings.

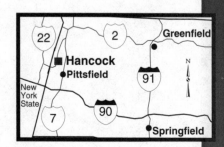

Points North doesn't offer accommodations, but

they'll supply you with a list of local options. On our own, we discovered Pittsfield State Forest, in nearby Pittsfield, an economical choice for those who like tent camping.

The second day of school we spent on a particularly beautiful stretch of the Deerfield called Carbis Bend. Here, the river scoops into the woods at a ninety-degree angle, framed by mountains. As students made cast after cast, Moran offered advice, anecdotes, and good-natured ribbing. The mood was low-key and relaxed.

Considering that people have been fly-fishing since 200 B.C. (the Macedonians are credited with inventing the sport), it's amazing that nobody's got it figured out yet. Sometimes the craziest things work. "A couple of weeks ago, we were into pocket-fuzz-sized flies," Moran recalled. "We've got a theory that when something doesn't work, go to the other extreme. So we tried a size-12 yellow humpy, a big, dust-bunny-sized fly about ¾- by ¾-inch, and damned if we didn't pull in a six-pound rainbow trout on the first cast."

By their reactions, actions, or lack of action, the fish "keep you humble, and keep you guessing," Moran said, chuckling. He's been at this since age seven; that's forty-five years of fly-fishing. "I figure I've got forty-five years to go, and maybe by then I'll call myself an advanced beginner," he said.

Wakefield, Rhode Island: Hooking Big Game Off the Coast

You'll Need Patience and Power for This Adventure

CONTACT: Captain Ed Hughes, Wakamo Park, 691 Succotash Road, Wakefield, RI 02879; (401) 783-5912.

HOW TO GET THERE: Hughes will meet you at the Snug Harbor Marina in Wakefield. Take Exit 4 off I-95 south; this will turn into Route 1. Follow Route 1 to the East Matunuck exit, to Succatash Road; turn on Gooseberry Road (at the fork). Snug Harbor Marina is 2 miles down. He will also pick up sports at Block Island.

RATES: A full day of offshore big-game fishing for up to four people costs $650.

WHAT TO BRING: Play it safe; take seasickness medicine the night before and watch what you eat for breakfast. Bring sunscreen, sunglasses, and a hat. Hughes supplies all other equipment.

KIDS: Hughes said he'll take kids ten and older. We don't see it; it's a long, tough day.

SKILL LEVEL: No experience necessary.

We were miles out in the Atlantic Ocean, surrounded by nothing but big skies and vast, open waters. The motor of our small, twenty-six-foot fishing boat had been turned off, leaving us to drift and bob up and down with the currents. An ocean of silence. It was a rare, sun-dazed, water-as-smooth-as-glass morning, and we were on the lookout for our quarry: tuna, bonito, perhaps a shark.

"There's one!" shouted Captain Ed. We saw it, too, a giant that instantly grabbed the indicator bait and pulled it under. It felt like we'd hooked a submarine—every crank on the reel required Herculean effort yet brought the sea monster only inches closer to the boat. After thirty minutes, our arms cramped from exertion, we had him—a 470-pound blue shark. On a fly rod. Eighty-pound test line.

No, this is not a Herman Melville sequel. And it's not a grossly exaggerated fish tale. It is fly-fishing for big game with Captain Ed Hughes. In angling circles, where big is always better, there is nothing to compare to this.

Ed Hughes, an Orvis-endorsed fly-fishing guide, operates out of Snug Harbor in Wakefield, Rhode Island. The twentieth century has not quite caught up to this corner of the state; it is quaint and noncommercial, still sporting the air of a working fishing community. The same could be said of Hughes. Casual and unassuming, Hughes has a knack for putting people instantly at ease. Before we left the harbor, we were like old, pat-on-the-back-buddies going out on a fishing trip.

We met Hughes early in the morning (he likes to get going by 6:30 A.M.) at his boat, the Fly Swatter, and motored for about an hour-and-a-half to our destination: the Mud Hole, a ridge in the ocean where the big fish like to hang out, about thirty-five miles offshore.

"You never know what you're going to see out here," Hughes told us. It is this unexpectedness that is the mystique and appeal of big-game fishing. This, and the sheer power and size of the prey.

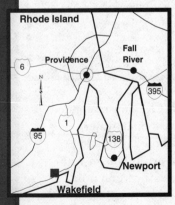

Hughes began to throw out small pieces of herring, one by one behind the boat, setting up a fish slick. The scent of blood will attract any fish in the vicinity and send them in for a feeding. Our job was to drift, and to wait. Fifteen minutes . . . thirty . . . forty-five . . . .

"Do you ever get skunked?" we asked. Hughes told us he catches fish every time he goes out. These waters are no mystery to him; a former commercial tuna fisher, he knows where to find fish. And there seems to be no science to luring them. To the freshwater fly-fisher (whose tackle box might include hundreds of flies, several rods and reels, and other paraphernalia), Hughes's no-frills equipment might appear startlingly sparse: a rod, reels, a gimbal (worn around the waist to help support the rod when a fish is on), and one fly variety—a white streamer chub fly. A frozen bucket of chub (herring pieces) completed his outfit.

Fifty minutes went by, and at last the water began to churn around us. It was a school of bonito, moving through our slick like missiles. Within minutes, they were gone, leaving our white streamers untouched.

"We've got something keeping them off," Hughes told us.

A few minutes later, a shark circled, so close we could have touched it. Another shark began to bump and bite at the boat stern. Then, one took a streamer.

Nothing can prepare you for the surge of power when a 300- to 400-pound fish hits on your fly. The fly rod arced, its tip nearly touching the water, and only brute force kept the rod from being yanked from the gimbal. Forget finesse, tactics, and techniques—it is just plain hard work and muscle that will land these massive aquatic machines. The fly rod that felt so limber and light when we started began to feel like a telephone pole—with a Volkswagen bus at the end of it. Twenty minutes of struggle went by. The shark was visible, thirty feet from the boat, when—PING!—the line snapped and he was gone. But another had hit the other line, and this one—the 470-pounder—we landed, tagged, and let go.

We continued to drift the slick, and other deep-sea beauties followed us. We saw a spectacular white marlin, rarely seen in these waters; dolphin fish; bonito. We hooked more sharks. By four o'clock, our backs were aching, our arms quivering, our bodies sore. It was starting to feel like a Jerry Lewis telethon or an all-you-can-eat buffet: too much of a good thing. We called it enough, started the engine, and left the sharks behind.

Resources

Other fly-fishing schools in New England include:

L.L. Bean Fly Fishing School, Outdoor Discovery Program, L.L. Bean retail store, Freeport, ME 04033; (800) 341-4341, Ext. 6666.

The Battenkill Anglers, R.R. 1, Box 2303, Manchester Center, VT 05255; (802) 362-3184.

Vermont Bound Outfitters & Guide Service, Route 4, Killington, VT 05751; (800) 639-3167 or (802) 773-0736.

FOR A COMPLETE LIST OF MAINE SPORTING CAMPS:

Maine Sporting Camp Association, P.O. Box 89, Jay, ME 04239.

OTHER FISHING GUIDES IN NEW ENGLAND INCLUDE:

Chuck Kashner, Four Season Angler, P.O. Box 156, Pawlet, VT 05761; (800) 682-0103.

Capt. Rusty Barry, Guided Fishing for Stripers and Blues, P.O. Box 467, Marshfield Hills, MA 02051; (617) 834-6932.

Lee Bailey, Bass Guide: Connecticut River, 19 Hamilton Street, Hartford CT 06106; (203) 951-0598.

David Dean, Strictly Trout, RFD 3, Box 800, Putney, VT 05346; (802) 869-3116.

Copper Gilkes, Inshore Fly-fishing/Spin-fishing on Martha's Vineyard, RFD Box 19, Edgartown, MA 02539; (517) 627-3909.

Streamline, P.O. Box 1218, Waitsfield, VT 05673; (802) 496-LINE.

FOR A LIST OF RHODE ISLAND FISHING GUIDES:

The Rhode Island Tourism Division, 7 Jackson Walkway, Providence, RI 02903; (800) 556-2484 or (401) 277-2601.

FOR A LIST OF MAINE FISHING GUIDES:

The Maine Professional Guide Association, P.O. Box 847, Augusta, ME 04332; (207) 785-2061, or

The Maine Publicity Bureau, P.O. Box 2300, Hallowell, ME 04347; (207) 623-0363.

FOR A LIST OF MASSACHUSETTS SALTWATER SPORTFISHING CHARTER GUIDES:

The Massachusetts Division of Marine Fisheries, 100 Cambridge Street, Boston, MA 02202; (617) 727-3193, or the sportfishing information line at (800) ASK-FISH.

FOR INFORMATION ON FISHING IN CONNECTICUT:

The State of Connecticut Department of Environmental Protection, Fisheries Division, 79 Elm Street, Hartford, CT 06106; (203) 424-3474.

FOR INFORMATION ON FISHING AND GUIDE SERVICES IN NEW HAMPSHIRE:

The New Hampshire Fish and Game Department, 2 Hazen Drive, Concord, NH 03301; (603) 271-3421.

BOOKS:

Advanced Fly Fishing Techniques. Lefty Kreh, Delta Sports.

The Complete Book of Fly Fishing. Tom McNally, Ragged Mountain Press.

A Different Angle, Fly Fishing Stories by Women. Holly Morris, Seal Press.

Fishing Fundamentals. Wade Bourne, In-Fisherman, Inc.

Fishing Vermont's Streams and Lakes. Peter F. Cammann, Backcountry Publications.

Fly Fishing Made Easy. Michael Rutter and Dave Card, Globe Pequot.

Fly Fishing in Maine. Bob Newman, Down East Books.

Fly Rodding the Coast. Ed Mitchell, Stackpole Books.
Northeast Guide to Saltwater Fishing & Boating, Second
    Edition. Vin Sparano, ed., International Marine.
The Orvis Fly-Fishing Guide. Tom Rosenbauer, Lyons &
    Burford Publishers.

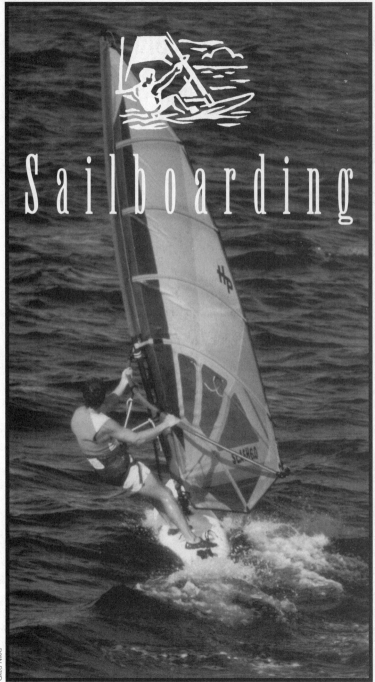

Sailboarding

Various Sites: Sailboarding Meccas

When the Wind Cranks, Carve Your Duck Jibes at These Sweet Spots

Let's make one thing perfectly clear: You can't plan a windsurfing trip. As Peter Bogucki, editor of New England Windsurfing Journal, says, "When the wind is right, you have to drop everything and go sailing."

With this sport, the wind is all that really matters. And it's a commodity that's out of your control. For many, the unpredictability is part of the kick, and for hard-core types that means keeping the board strapped to the roof of the car at all times, just in case. That said, there are some perennial hot spots in New England, where wind-junkies can usually find a fix, whether they ride short boards or long ones.

Kalmus Beach, Hyannis. Like Vienna and pastry, Paris and attitude, Kalmus and windsurfers are an inspired match. "Kalmus is arguably the windiest beach on the Cape," Bogucki says. It's also the only beach in Hyannis where windsurfing is allowed.

What drives the wind in Nantucket Sound? Unobstructed, it can build thermals (sea breezes) and pick up southwesterlies. "You get more wind and more reliable wind," Bogucki explains. If you take out a Massachusetts map and eyeball Cape Cod, you'll get the picture: it's out there, way out there, fist curled in defiance of the big water that surrounds it. So situated, Cape Cod gets whipped to a frenzy year-round, with northerlies on the bay side or southerlies via Nantucket Sound. At Kalmus, the channel sucks the wind right up into it, Bogucki says. You won't be sailing alone, but there's room for everybody here, from the never-been-on-a-board beginner to techno-types with stacks of pricey gear.

CONTACT: Sound Sailboards, 223 Barnstable Road, Hyannis, Massachusetts; (508) 771-3388. Located 1.5 miles from Kalmus Beach. Open Monday through Saturday, 9 to 5; Sunday, 9 to 1. Closed January through March. Private lessons, available May through September, cost $45 per hour, including the use of a sailboard. For additional people, add $5 each. Sign up a day or two in advance.

ON YOUR OWN/HOW TO GET THERE: The following are some of the beaches mentioned in the text.

Kalmus Beach, Hyannis, Massachusetts: Take Route 6 to Exit 6. Follow Route 132 to the airport rotary. Take Barnstable Road off the rotary, about 2 miles, to Kalmus Beach.

Chapin Beach, Dennis, Massachusetts: Take Route 3 to Route 6A; follow the signs.

Ned Point, Mattapoisett, Massachusetts: Take Exit 19 off I-95, Mattapoisett. Continue south on North Street, across Route 6 and to the water. Turn left onto Water Street, through the intersection. You are now on Ned Point Road. Follow it toward the water. The launch is gravel, not sand, so footwear is advised. Beware of rocks at low tide.

Ellacoya State Beach, Gilford, New Hampshire: From Route 93, take Exit 20 to Route 3 north. Connect with Route 11 to Lake Winnipesaukee; follow signs for Ellacoya State Beach.

WHAT TO BRING: Depends on the vagaries of the weather and your cold tolerance. Usually, you can get away with not wearing a wetsuit from July through September.

KIDS: Sure. Some kids as young as six are able to handle a sail. (Tip: Try a parent-child lesson before investing in equipment.)

SKILL LEVEL: All levels. Most windsurfing in New England is purely recreational.

"Everybody's at Kalmus, to see who can go the fastest, jump the highest, and carve the most radical duck [under the sail] jibes," says Steve Colby, owner of Sound Sailboards in Hyannis. "It's a sweet spot and a friendly gang of people who help each other out," he says, calling Hyannis a "windsurfer-friendly" town. Colby is part of the 150-member Kalmus Boardsailing Association, whose members meet

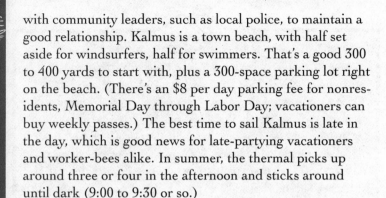
with community leaders, such as local police, to maintain a good relationship. Kalmus is a town beach, with half set aside for windsurfers, half for swimmers. That's a good 300 to 400 yards to start with, plus a 300-space parking lot right on the beach. (There's an $8 per day parking fee for nonresidents, Memorial Day through Labor Day; vacationers can buy weekly passes.) The best time to sail Kalmus is late in the day, which is good news for late-partying vacationers and worker-bees alike. In summer, the thermal picks up around three or four in the afternoon and sticks around until dark (9:00 to 9:30 or so.)

On a nice day, you can count 200 sails out catching the wind off Kalmus Beach. "Nice day" is a relative term, however: for high-performance sailors, that means twenty miles per hour and up; for beginners, under twenty is good, ten to fifteen, ideal.

Kalmus is a good place to learn, because at low tide, the water is waist deep. "When you fall—and you will—you're in plenty of water, so you're very safe," Colby says. He recommends taking a lesson, naturally (his shop offers them), noting that Kalmus draws its share of people who think this looks easy. "I've seen 'em head out on a long board—they can stand up and make it go—but they don't know how to turn around and come back." Next stop, Bermuda. Sound Sailboards has taught kids as young as five; their most-senior student was a ninety-four-year-old woman.

In summer, sailboard enthusiasts from Europe, Canada, and the southern United States (where the wind is dead that time of year) converge on Kalmus. Then they're gone, leaving fall and spring for the hard-core bunch who live for forty-mile-per-hour gales.

Phil Atkinson agrees that Kalmus Beach is the gold standard in these parts. He should know; as the operator of The Wind Hot Line, he collects wind data from computers at sixty beaches and sells the readings, current to within five minutes, via touch-tone phone. (The service costs forty dollars for twelve months, plus ninety-five cents per ten wind reports. Call (800) 765-4253.) Kalmus, and Chapin Beach in Dennis (also on Cape Cod), tend to be the windiest, he says, calling them extremely versatile beaches because they pick up good onshore and offshore winds.

"In the summertime, there is no choice—you have to go to Cape Cod," he says. The Wind Expert Has Spoken. Later in the season, he allows, other beaches may have more wind than those on the Cape, and in the fall, when the wind returns, just about anyplace can provide a good ride. During storms, naturally, the path of the storm determines which beach is windiest.

From a statistical standpoint, Kalmus reigns, but there are trade-offs. Other spots may offer less wind, but also less driving time and no parking fees. Atkinson likes Chapin Beach, on Cape Cod Bay, considering it a hidden treasure because it's smaller than Kalmus and more difficult to find. "You have to know what you're looking for," he says. At Chapin, you park on sand, not asphalt. Windwise, it's often on a par with Kalmus, he says.

Another tip from Atkinson: check out the virtually undiscovered beach at Ned Point, in Mattapoisset on the mainland side of Buzzard's Bay. Ned Point is a publicly accessible beach with good thermals, but people drive right by, autopilot set for Kalmus. "You might get less wind, and have to sail with the next-largest sail in your quiver, but you'll spend more hours on the water and less on the road if you go to Ned's," Atkinson says. It's also a good choice for early birds; the wind tends to drop rapidly after 4 P.M.

Then there's Winni. The Granite State may be better known for backpacking than boardsailing, but New Hampshire's Lake Winnipesaukee does have a following. Ellacoya State Beach, on the lake's west shore, is famous for hard-blowing northwesterlies. "Many a sailor has been humbled by the radical and uneven chop" at Ellacoya, says Michael Manna of the Granite State Boardsailing Association. The chop doesn't seem to follow any pattern, he says. You can be going with the flow, then hit a rogue wall of water. "Once you get used to it, Ellacoya becomes addictive, offering great bump-and-jump sailing," Manna says. When it's blowing hard, boat traffic is nil and windsurfers rule.

And there's Powder Point Bridge in Duxbury, Massachusetts, a grand place to learn how to short-board without being beaten to death; and Joppa Flats, at Plum Island near

Newburyport, Massachusetts. . . . The point is, when the wind cranks, be ready. New England waters are perfect for sharpening your skills, and even in the 3-H (hazy, hot, humid) doldrums of July and early August, there's bound to be some wind somewhere.

But beware of getting too good, too fast, lest you run into the catch-22 of windsurfing. As Bogucki puts it, "The better you are, the more wind you crave. The more wind you crave, the less you sail."

Resources

Additional Outfitters

CanAm Sailcraft, 48 Charles Street, Cambridge, MA 02141; (617) 661-7716.

Water Bros. Surf Shop, 39 Memorial Boulevard, Newport, RI 02840; (401) 849-4990.

The Winni Sailboarders' School & Outlet, 687 Union Avenue, Laconia, NH 03246; (603) 528-4110.

BOOKS

Advanced Windsurfing. Farrel O'Shea, Stackpole Books.
Adventure Sports Surfing. John Conway, Stackpole Books.
Start Windsurfing Right! James Coutts, U.S. Yacht Racing Union with Mosby-Year Book Inc.
Windsurfing. Ken Winner, Human Kinetics Publishers.

MAGAZINES

New England Windsurfing Journal. P.O. Box 2120, Southbury, CT 06488; (203) 264-WIND.

Scuba Diving

139

Burlington, Vermont: Wreck-Diving in Lake Champlain

Below-the-Surface Tales of Drama and Tragedy

CONTACT: Waterfront Diving Center, 214 Battery Street, Burlington, VT 05401; (802) 865-2771. This full-service shop is open year-round, offering equipment rentals, instruction, and dive trips.

HOW TO GET THERE: From I-89, take the downtown Burlington exit to Main Street. Follow Main Street toward the water to Battery Street; the dive center is at the corner of Battery and Maple Streets.

RATES: Varies; book individually with a local charter-boat captain/divemaster. Waterfront Diving will supply a list of names.

WHAT TO BRING: A ¼-inch wetsuit, a tank, a weight belt, a buoyancy compensator, a mask, fins, a snorkel, mitts, booties, a regulator, and an underwater light. (All can be rented at Waterfront Diving Center.)

KIDS: If they're certified.

SKILL LEVEL: The *General Butler*, at 40 feet, and the *Diamond Island Stone Boat*, at 25 feet, are deemed fine for all levels. The *Coal Barge* (65 feet) and the *Horse Ferry* (50 feet) are recommended for intermediate and advanced divers; the *Phoenix* (60 feet to 110 feet) is recommended for experienced divers only. For diagrams and information about each wreck in the preserve, pick up a flyer at the dive shop.

Things are rarely what they seem. Take Vermont's Lake Champlain, for instance. A casual bystander would see a long, skinny expanse of beautiful blue water, dotted with pleasure boats, a setting that embodies the phrase "fun in the sun."

Below the surface, though, Lake Champlain tells a different story, one of savage storms, harrowing escapes, and sunken ships.

Hundreds of wrecked vessels lie on the bottom of this deceptively placid-looking body of water. Many were victims of calamity in the mid-1800s, when Burlington was a major shipping port and commercial vessels plied the lake and its canals. Timber, iron ore, marble, and other hefty cargoes were transported here, mostly in wooden boats. Some ships met their tragic fate by powerful gales, some by fire, some under the crushing weight of their own cargo.

Because Champlain is a freshwater lake, these 120- to 150-year-old wrecks are amazingly well preserved, drawing divers who are willing to look, but not touch.

"A wreck is something that's frozen in time. That's what makes it so incredible," says Jonathan Eddy of Waterfront Diving in Burlington. Eddy himself has found Revolutionary War artifacts, cannons, and cannonballs as a volunteer diver on archeological research projects for the Lake Champlain Maritime Museum in Vergennes.

Five shipwrecks are part of an underwater preserve managed by the State of Vermont. These protected wreck sites—and perhaps more to come—are buoyed for divers, with lines leading to and along the wrecks.

You don't have to go far to find them. Three sunken ships—the *Horse Ferry,* the *General Butler,* and the *Coal Barge*—are right off the breakwater, at depths of 40 to 65 feet. The deepest of the five is the *Phoenix I,* a 146-foot-long steamer in 110 feet of water, a favorite of experienced divers. The *Phoenix* is eight miles off the breakwater. Even farther out is the *Diamond Island Stone Boat,* a 93-foot-long flat-bottomed cargo boat submerged about twenty-five miles south of the breakwater.

We were intrigued by the 85-foot schooner *General Butler,* whose story possesses all the elements of a good dime-store novel: howling gale,

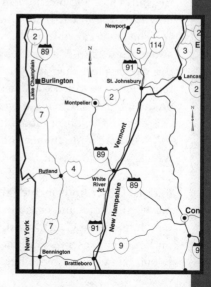

brave captain, perilous escape, heroic rescue. The wreck
was discovered in 1980. Like the other sites in the preserve,
the *General Butler* is a nonpenetration wreck, and thus not
dangerous; there's no chance of a diver going inside and getting lost or trapped.

Visibility is sometimes a problem here. Good visibility
is twenty to twenty-five feet; poor is five to ten feet; fifteen
feet is typical. What you can see is great. Most ocean shipwrecks resemble a mobile home after a tornado, but the *General Butler* is beautifully intact. And crowds aren't a problem,
even in the peak dive season (July), because only two boats
can tie up at once, one on each of the *Butler's* two buoys.

With Eddy guiding, we proceeded down the anchor
chain. (Note: you don't need a guide to dive here.) When
we got to the wreck, the bottom was stirred up a bit.
Another dive boat had just left with three or four divers.
Too bad we weren't fishing; there were bass everywhere.

As we swam over the top of the deck, we could make
out the housing of the forward mast. The ship's masts and
rigging have been removed, but her hull and cargo hold
remain. She rests on her keel, bow toward the breakwater.
Huge slabs of marble lie undisturbed in the main cargo
hold, while a rusted cookstove marks the galley. A jury-
rigged tiller bar, chained to the steering gear, reveals how
the ship's steering mechanism broke during the storm and
how the captain tried, in vain, to fix it.

The scene can only be described as surreal, imbued with a
strong sense of loss. It must have been quite a thrill to discover
this wreck, more than 100 years after it sank, suspended in
time, complete with a wooden ship's model and cookware still
on the table. These items are now on display at the Shelburne
Museum in Shelburne, about five miles from Burlington.

What are your chances of finding an undiscovered
wreck in the depths of Lake Champlain? It could happen.
"There are wrecks all over the lake, at every depth," Eddy
told us. Other finds include the delicate *O.J. Walker*, with
masts still intact and cargo in place, "more of a Hollywood
wreck, picture-perfect," Eddy said, and a candidate for the
underwater preserve. And there's the *Sarah Ellen*, submerged
in 300 feet of water, with her masts still upright, like a ghost

ship ready to sail. Alas, if you find one, it belongs to the State of Vermont or the State of New York (the state boundary line runs right up the middle of the lake).

There has been little vandalism within the preserve. Divers treat the wrecks responsibly, like the treasures they are. "We like to hope divers will be in awe of them, and be preservationists, not salvagers," Eddy said, adding, "If you've got the attitude, 'I'll take that deadeye for my fireplace mantel,' stay away."

We agree. Better to leave the watery ghosts of Vermont's past to rest in peace.

Jamestown, Rhode Island: Tropical Fish in Rhode Island?

*Few New England Divers Know It,
but Exotics Can Be Found Right Here*

CONTACT: Ocean State Scuba, 70 North Main Road, Jamestown, RI 02835; (401) 423-1662 or (800) 933-DIVE. This full-service dive shop offers boat dives at wrecks and reefs off Jamestown, day-long trips to Block Island, PADI certification courses, float-plane dives, and kayak dives. It is also a nitrox training and filling facility. Dive charter season runs from April through November. Reservations are recommended.

HOW TO GET THERE: From I-95, take Route 4 east to Route 138, Jamestown exit (Helm Street). Proceed through the first stop sign, then turn right at the bottom of the hill. Ocean State Scuba is 1.5 miles on the right.

RATES: There is no charge for group dives Saturday and Sunday mornings at 10 A.M., from July Fourth weekend through Columbus Day.

WHAT TO BRING: Full dive gear. Rental gear is available from Ocean State Scuba.

KIDS: Yes, if they're certified divers.

SKILL LEVEL: Fine for beginners.

Rhode Islanders are prone to bragging about the warmth and clarity of the Ocean State's waters, but tropical fish? Surely this fish tale was too far-fetched to be believed. Yet the myth persisted. We asked several savvy New England divers about it, and some hadn't even heard the story. None had seen the exotics with their own eyes. Time to do some undercover—er, underwater—investigating.

"It's not a joke, the fish are for real," said David Swain, owner of Ocean State Scuba in Jamestown, Rhode Island. The fish are swept northward by the Gulf Stream, Swain explained, often arriving after storms. "I'll prove it," he said, offering to take us on a dive.

The exotics seem to congregate near the Green Bridge in Newport, between King's Beach and Lands End, and on the other side of the channel, about two miles away, near Ft. Wetherill State Park in Jamestown. Here, the water is warm and calm, almost Caribbean-like. Often the exotic beauties make their guest appearance in late July or early August, sticking around as long as the weather stays warm, usually into October. (The water is warmest here in September.)

What does it cost to see them? Absolutely nothing, except air, if you join a group dive on Saturday or Sunday morning. Morning is a prime time to go, we were told, as is late in the day, because the fish tend to hide in crevasses when the sun is high overhead.

Chatting with other divers, we learned that filefish, box fish, bigeyes, blue damselfish, snappers, trumpet fish, pipe-fish, smooth trunkfish, puffers, groupers, spotfin butterfly fish, and even sea horses can be seen here! Unbelievable. If this was a scam, a lot of people were in on it.

So six of us, led by Swain, drove to a cove near Ft. Wetherill State Park. We suited up, were assigned buddies, and were off. Entry is easy here; the water is shallow for several yards. But the bottom is rocky, so you have to watch your footing. The best place to see the fish, Swain told us, is along the sides of the cove in about ten to thirty feet of water. With a full tank, depending on how hard you breathe, you could be down there a couple of hours, going slowly to maximize the chances of seeing something.

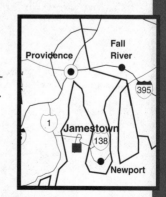

It wasn't easy. The seas were up, and visibility was very low. We had to go slowly, looking very carefully through thick strands of eelgrass and kelp. The fish that are swept here are juveniles, so they're tiny and hard to spot; fortunately, we had a dive light. Mike Dunlap, the manager of the dive shop, had warned us that this activity is akin to looking for a needle in a haystack. "The first couple of times I went out, I didn't see anything," he said. "When you're looking for a one- to two-inch fish in a sea of kelp, it teaches you to pay attention to the small stuff."

Suddenly, a tug on a fin. It was Russ, our dive buddy, pointing to a small crevasse. There, gleaming jewel-like in the murky water, was a two-inch-long spotfin butterfly fish! We stared in amazement as the tiny yellow exotic darted in and out of the undulating seaweed.

We dove on, looking for more, but to no avail. Back at the dive shop, we discovered everyone on the outing had seen tropical fish that day. Pretty cool to have a little bit of the tropics in Jamestown, Rhode Island. Now, all we needed was a steel drum band and a vat of rum punch. "Amazing," one fellow from New York muttered over and over, "Amazing. Just amazing."

A sobering note: Most of those little fish probably won't last the winter in these cold North Atlantic waters. "They'll either be fish food, or die from the cold," Swain said. However, there might be a happy ending for some: The Mystic Marinelife Aquarium in Connecticut and the New England Aquarium in Boston make regular collecting trips here, and private collectors have been known to scoop up exotics and take them home for personal enjoyment. We captured ours on film with an underwater camera, a souvenir of this intriguing adventure, and proof that this phenomenon is no fish story. Now, about that Loch Ness monster. . . .

Resources

Additional Outfitters

Aqua Diving Academy, P.O. Box 563, Portland, ME 04112;
 (207) 772-4200.
The Dive Center at The Great Outdoors Trading Company,
 41 Center Street, Rutland, VT 05701; (802) 725-9989.
Newport Diving Center, 550 Thames Street, Newport, RI
 02840; (401) 847-9293.

BOOKS

Jeppersen's Open Water Sport Diver Manual. Clinchy, Egstrom,
 Fead; Mosby-Year Book Inc.
Sport Scuba Diving in Depth. Tom Griffiths, Princeton Book Co.

Hiking

Baxter State Park, Maine: Climbing Mt. Katahdin

Wild, Raw, and Mighty:
"The Greatest Mountain" Demands Respect

CONTACT: Baxter State Park, 64 Balsam Drive, Millinocket, ME; 04462; (207) 723-5140.

HOW TO GET THERE: From I-95 north take the Medway exit, and then go west on Route 157 to Millinocket and into Baxter State Park. The park gatehouse is just north of Togue Pond, about 18 miles from Millinocket. Or, continue on I-95 to Sherman Mills, and then follow Route 11 to Patten and then Route 159 west past Shin Pond Road to the park's northern entrance.

RATES: $8 a day. There are ten campgrounds in the park; two are accessible only by trail. It's best to reserve well in advance; some campsite reservations fill up in January for the coming summer season. "You'll have no hope of getting a campsite in August unless you have a reservation," say park officials. Call or send for a packet of information and reservation forms; then send in reservation form with full fee to the above address. There are no refunds.

WHAT TO BRING: Everything; there are no stores, gas stations, electricity, water or restroom facilities in the park. Some campgrounds feature bunkhouses and simple lean-tos. Weather is unpredictable; come prepared for anything. Bug repellent is a must; black flies and mosquitos are particularly voracious here.

KIDS: Use your judgment. Consider the campgrounds and trails in the north end of the park.

SKILL LEVEL: Experienced hikers only on Mt. Katahdin.

It is an extraordinary feeling. We're perched on a narrow, serrated ridge of fractured granite, inching our way over rocks and cairns. We have two feet—maybe three—on which to move: Steep, dizzying cliffs plunge down on both sides. Stretched before us is a stunning panorama of thick forests, glacier-carved peaks, lakes, and streams. We are surrounded by an aura of wildness.

We take it slowly, one step at a time, until we reach a spot that seems impossible to negotiate. The trail drops into a sharp cleft, so steeply that it seems our legs are too short to reach. We hold our breath, stretch, but can't help imagine ourselves tumbling and falling 1,000 . . . 2,000 . . . 3,000 feet into the Great Basin.

We are on the Knife Edge, traversing the south side of Mt. Katahdin. It is the most spectacular trail in the East. It is also perilous.

"It is the most exposed place in the Northeast," says Jean Hoekwater, naturalist at Baxter State Park. "I suppose part of the attraction of hiking the Knife Edge is the danger."

More than half the people who visit Baxter State Park come to climb Mt. Katahdin, much to the chagrin of park officials and naturalists.

"The emphasis on climbing Katahdin is not doing anybody any good," laments Hoekwater. "The likelihood that visitors can do what they want on the mountain is slim; and there is so much more to see in the rest of the park."

True. Access to the mountain is restricted due to limited camping spots and parking spaces, and weather conditions. More often than not, visitors who come for the day to climb Mt. Katahdin are disappointed. They are turned away at the trailhead parking lots, or forced to adjust their route plans up the mountain. Still, most who have been in the shadows of Mt. Katahdin fall under its spell.

Mt. Katahdin, the Abenaki's name for "greatest mountain," holds a special place in the hearts of New Englanders, and an irresible, almost magnetic, pull on all who love the wilderness. Katahdin, a 5,273-foot cloud-shrouded giant of massive cliffs, steep ridges, craggy peaks, and glacial cirques, rises abruptly from a boulder-strewn floor. It is not the region's tallest summit—Mt. Washington holds that honor at 6,288 feet—but it is arguably its most dramatic.

"Katahdin is the most spectacular mountain in the East," says Mike Dickerman, author of *Off the Beaten Path*. Dickerman, a veteran peak bagger, has climbed all the high summits in the Northeast, four or five times each. "None of them match up with Katahdin," he says.

"It is the most magnificent summit this side of the Mississippi," agrees Steve Smith, veteran hiker and author of *Ponds and Lakes of the White Mountains*. "Katahdin has a feeling of expansiveness, wide open, wild spaces. It's the ruggedness of Mt. Washington, without civilization close by."

Few would argue. Mt. Katahdin lies in Baxter State

Park, surrounded by 200,000 acres of remote, northern Maine wilderness. The park was a gift of Percival Baxter, a son of a wealthy Maine family, who bequested that it "forever shall be held in its natural wild state." Park and state officials have held to the spirit of his gift; you'll find few trappings of civilization in the park. To enjoy Baxter and attempt Katahdin, it's best to come humbly and simply, with a love of nature and a willingness to make an effort to be close to it. The park's perimeter road is unpaved, narrow, and twisty, with few views. To appreciate the park, you'll have to get out and explore, hike, and camp. Modest camping facilities are offered at 10 campgrounds; two are hike-in only, and all need to be reserved well in advance.

If you set out to climb Mt. Katahdin, be ready for some of the steepest and toughest trails in the Northeast. And, be ready to change your plans: There are only three parking lots at Katahdin trailheads (at Abol Campground, Katahdin Stream Campground, and Roaring Brook Campground); they fill up fast.

One option is to park at the Roaring Brook Campground lot. From there, you can follow the Helon N. Taylor Trail to Pamola summit and across the Knife Edge to Baxter Peak. But, this route is extremely exposed to the weather, and can be very dangerous. Once at the summit, you must either return down the other side to the Abol or Katahdin parking areas (leaving you with the problem of finding a ride back to your car); make the long loop around the summit and down Chimney Pond Trail; or go back down the Knife Edge.

"This is where most people get into serious trouble," says Hoekwater. "It's foolish to think that you can go up and down the Knife Edge in one day. It's not as easy as it looks, and conditions change quickly."

The best option is to take the Chimney Pond Trail to gorgeous Chimney Pond campground; from here you'll have lots of trail options. It's hard to imagine a more beautiful setting. The pond, a color that defies description, shimmers like a sheet of glass, surrounded by towering cliffs and giant glacial cirques. "Many get to Chimney Pond and decide it's all they need or want to do," says

Hoekwater. At Chimney Pond, weather and legs permitting, you can hike Cathedral Trail, Dudley, or the Saddle Trail to the peak. The Saddle is the easiest route up and down Katahdin.

Hikers also have the option of parking at the Abol Campground, or the Katahdin Stream Campground. The Abol Trail, said to be the oldest route up the mountain, is steep and rocky, and not recommended for descent. Better to connect with the Hunt Trail on the way down, continue to the Katahdin Stream Campground, and hitch a ride back to your car.

How many times have we seen the picture of Appalachian Mountain Club through-hikers hugging the sign at the top of Mt. Katahdin? They follow the white-blazed Hunt Trail, which leaves from the parking lot at the Katahdin Stream Campground. Through-hikers can leave their backpacks at the ranger station and make the final, steep 5.2-mile ascent to the end of their journey. For this reason, the Hunt Trail is a favorite among hikers.

No matter what route you choose to climb Mt. Katahdin, the going is tough. Come prepared, and be prepared to turn around. The Abenaki Indians believed that the spirit of Pamola, the storm-bird, kept people from climbing Katahdin. The legend says that Pamola used storms, winds, and fog to keep climbers below the treeline. Even today, it's best to heed her warnings.

Pinkham Notch, New Hampshire: Hut to Hut in the Presidentials

Full Moon and Shooting Stars

CONTACT: Appalachian Mountain Club, P.O. Box 298, Route 16, Gorham, NH 03581; (603) 466-2727.

HOW TO GET THERE: Trips meet at the AMC Pinkham Notch Lodge in Gorham, New Hampshire. Take Route 16 north; the lodge is about 15 miles north of North Conway, on your right.

RATES: A three-night trip, including hut lodging, breakfasts, dinners, and guide service, costs $310.

WHAT TO BRING: AMC will send you an extensive equipment list. Generally, you'll need warm clothing; gloves; a hat; wind and rain gear; sturdy boots; high-energy snacks; two to four quarts of water; lunch for three days; sunscreen; and bug repellent. Bedding is supplied in the huts.

KIDS: Unless they're strong, active, and really into hiking, leave them home. Generally, no one under ten years of age.

SKILL LEVEL: This is a strenuous hike on Class III and IV trails. You should be in good physical condition; some backpacking and hiking experience would be useful.

The last rays of twilight mixed with moon glow, casting a pink hue on the craggy granite peaks. We were on top of 5,385-foot-high Mt. Monroe, looking at a view that went clear to the other side of heaven. We gazed, wonderstruck, as the full moon rose above the wall of mountains and a thousand stars splashed across the sky. The scene produced an odd sense of both vulnerability and infinite possibility.

This was our second night out on a four-day traverse of

the Presidential Range in the White Mountains of New Hampshire. We had joined the Appalachian Mountain Club's Moonlight Serenade hike, an excursion that would take us up seven mountain summits, including Mt. Washington, the highest peak in New England. The hike was timed to coincide with a midsummer full moon and the annual Perseid meteorite shower.

We met early the first day at the AMC's Pinkham Notch headquarters and, after equipment checks and brief instructions, drove to the trailhead at Crawford Notch. Our guides, Waverly and Sears, emphasized that the group was in control, and that the guides were there only for safety and information. Waverly led the way, and Sears brought up the rear, which allowed us to go at our own speed. This was critical; there were some who zipped up the mountain, while one almost quit on the first section of the trail.

The first mile was rugged, the rest a steady three-mile climb for an 1,800-foot elevation gain. We reached our goal, the Mitzpah Springs Hut, midafternoon. The AMC operates a system of backcountry cabins and lodges, strung along fifty-six miles of the Appalachian Trail in the White Mountain National Forest and Franconia Notch State Park in New Hampshire, and in Mount Greylock State Reservation in Massachusetts. Each hut is different, but all offer bone-weary hikers simple, warm accommodations and a hearty breakfast and dinner. The Mitzpah Springs Hut, overlooking scenic Crawford Notch, has eight coed bunkrooms; our group (three men and two women, and guides Waverly and Sears) shared one room.

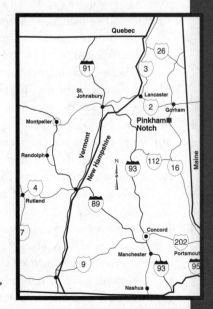

With enough daylight left, the group decided to bag another peak. We took a short, easy hike up Mt. Jackson and had just enough time to make it back for dinner. We sat with fifty or so other hikers in the communal dining room, swapping stories and filling up on hearty minestrone soup, baked fish, steamed vegetables, homemade bread, and cherry pie. We even had entertainment: AMC staff performed, as they do every night, funny skits about hut rules and hiking etiquette.

After dinner, we hiked to the top of Mt. Clinton to watch the sun set and the moon rise. It was a warm, clear night, and the cranberry bush and partridge berries glowed in the waning scarlet light. When the sun dropped below the peaks, a saw-whet owl graced us with his presence. We were awash in moonlight, eyes cast skyward in search of shooting stars. Unfortunately, Perseus was in the northeastern sky—right next to the big, full moon. We all agreed, though, that if forced to choose, we'd pick bright moonlight over faint shooting starlight.

The next day shone bright and clear: a good sign, as we'd be spending the day above the tree line. We hiked along at a steady pace, in idle conversation and in silence, drinking in the ninety-mile views, warmed by the sun and cooled by gentle mountain breezes. We began to feel the cares of nine-to-five life strip away. As we climbed, the trees became stunted and squashed, and finally disappeared. In their place were tiny alpine plants. We marveled at the ancient and fragile Diapensia plants that filled nearly every crevice, and at the red lichen that hugged cairns and jagged rocks. Mt. Eisenhower was the first bare peak we reached; from there, we stayed above the tree line, climbing the ridge to Mt. Franklin, Mt. Monroe, and up to the Lakes of the Clouds hut, where we stayed the second night. Lake of the Clouds is as lofty as it sounds. The highest, largest, and most popular AMC hut, it sits well above the tree line at 5,050 feet.

The crowning summit of Mt. Washington towered before us like a chiseled jewel. Climbing the granddaddy of New England summits was optional, but having come this far, who could resist? We stumbled and climbed over bare rocks as we traversed the exposed ridgeline. The trail sign leading to the summit gave us pause: STOP. THE AREA AHEAD HAS THE WORST WEATHER IN AMERICA. MANY HAVE DIED THERE

FROM EXPOSURE, EVEN IN THE SUMMER. TURN BACK NOW IF THE WEATHER IS BAD. We took a moment to thank the atmospheric gods for the rare weather—clear skies, warm temperatures, and soft winds—and continued to the top.

Suddenly, we were back in civilization. A mass of summit-struck hikers joined the folks who had driven the auto road or taken the cog railway to the top. Cheaters, we thought; views like these should be earned (an elitist attitude, we admit).

That night, we climbed to the top of Mt. Monroe, staying well past sunset, basking in moon glow, and witnessing three bright shooting stars. Our silent revelry was interrupted by an onslaught of twenty or more whooping, hollering, buzzing camp-counselors-in-training. We wanted it all to ourselves, of course, but we relinquished our front-row seats and returned to the hut.

The next day was our toughest: rugged, rocky terrain with thigh-killing climbs and steep, knee-crunching descents. Mt. Jefferson is massive, and it took all morning to reach its summit. Next was Mt. Adams, looming before us like a towering giant. The last 0.3 miles from the crossroads between Sam Adams and Adams was the toughest part of the hike. Who would have thought such a short distance could take so long? We scrambled over large schist boulders, being careful not to twist or turn or slip on the jumble of rocks. We finally made the steep, slow-going descent to the Madison hut. No more peak-bagging this day; we were exhausted and looking forward to a long, sound sleep. This was not to be, however; the sound and fury of lightning and thunder woke us in the middle of the night. Four thousand feet up in the clouds, in the middle of a storm—the crackling bright light bounced off the granite, and the thunder echoed around the mountain walls, leaving us spellbound and wide-eyed. Definitely worth losing sleep over.

We arose around 5:30 on our final day. The moon was setting behind Mt. Adams, and we watched as low, fluffy clouds bumped into each other and drifted over the hills in the valley below. The sun came up over the Carters and filled Pinkham Notch valley. We began our long hike down to the AMC Lodge. We left the alpine zone; the trees grew taller, the flora and greenery more dense. The smell of wet trees and moss was intense, much more noticeable after spending three days above the tree line. The trail took us along a rippling stream, through a gorgeous mountain valley. Time in the wild, scenic outdoors tends to break down inhibitions; after lunch, we skinny-dipped in the cool, clear pools of a mountain stream. By late afternoon, we reached the AMC headquarters in Pinkham Notch.

It was good to shed the packs, replace hiking boots with sneakers, and take a hot shower. (The AMC Pinkham Notch lodge has showers available for hikers.) We just hoped our spirits would continue to soar, at least for a few days, when we returned to our nine-to-five lives.

Gorham Notch: Beyond the 4,000 Club; an Extreme Hike Through the Presidentials

Note: We can't recommend this extreme hike to most hikers or backpackers. This adventure should be undertaken only by those who are in top physical condition, completely familiar with the area and terrain, and extremely well prepared. People die on Mt. Washington every year; there are deep crevasses and dramatic changes in weather and temperature that can occur in seconds. As Dan Tetreault put it, "You have to respect this place. It's very powerful and very beautiful. But if you don't respect it, bad things can happen."

You've heard it before, but it bears repeating: Before you undertake any extreme activity, be sure you're ready for it. Tetreault concedes that the Death March hike was a physical challenge and, at the end, an emotional one as well. Both he and hiking partner Bob Tafuto are experienced hikers/rock climbers/mountain bikers/downhill skiers, and both have been hiking, backpacking, and backcountry skiing the Whites for several years. Both are skilled in first aid, with enough experience in the wilderness to know how to treat common injuries and frostbite. They carried two full packs on the trip, with plenty of food and water, extra clothing, emergency blankets, and a full complement of medical supplies.

Their major piece of advice for anyone planning a strenuous mountain hike: Always have an exit plan in case something goes wrong. Know all the routes off every summit; you may have to reach help or get out quickly.

"We had friends along the route who always knew where we were, and we knew the approximate distances to all the huts, and the exit routes from the summits," Tetreault said.

What do you do when you've hiked virtually every mountain in New England? You do something off the scale: try to conquer thirteen mountain summits in one day.

You may have heard of the 4,000 Club, hikers who have bested every 4,000-foot-plus peak in New Hampshire's White Mountains. Pals Dan Tetreault and Bob Tafuto decided to go one better: take on thirteen peaks—including the biggie, Mt. Washington—at once, squeezing the challenge into sixteen hours of daylight.

This hike originated with Appalachian Mountain Club hut crewmembers, who would tackle all the summits just to keep themselves occupied. They called it the Death March.

"Living in the Mt. Washington valley, we're constantly looking at those mountains, at that ridge," said Tetreault, a resident of Center Conway, New Hampshire. "We hike it, we ski it, piece-by-piece, but we'd never done it in just one day." That idea, he said, "kind of burned a hole in my brain."

After about three months of planning, they were ready. The goal: to trek from Gorham Notch to Crawford Notch, a distance of 28.6 miles, between sunrise and sunset. Tetreault and Tafuto packed enough supplies for a day and a half, just in case, including food, water, extra clothing, rain gear, a first-aid kit, and a celebratory beverage in a plastic bottle, to be enjoyed atop Mt. Washington.

At 5:04 on a late-June morning, they set out from Dolly Copp campground in Gorham. Mother Nature gave her blessing; the day dawned with comfortable temps and sunshine that would continue all day. They hiked up the Daniel Webster trail, easily conquering Mt. Madison (5,363 feet), and arrived at the AMC's Madison Hut shortly after 8 A.M.

"We ran into some other hikers up there," Tetreault recalled. "When we told them our plan, one guy said, 'You'll never make it in a day.' We snickered. Far from discouraging us, it put a spring in our step."

Tetreault and Tafuto hustled up John Quincy Adams, then John Adams (5,798 feet), passing Thunderstorm Junction on the way to Sam Adams. Next came Mt. Jefferson, at 5,717 feet. "We were really moving, stopping to rest only at the summits," Tetreault said. At times, they ran. "We just felt good, excited, ready to get to the next peak," he explained.

Finally, between 1 and 2 P.M., they reached Mt. Washington— 6,288 feet, the highest point in New Hampshire. Time for a longer break: a change of clothes, a leisurely lunch, a chat with some friends who work at the summit. It would have been easy to stretch out in the sun, give the legs a break—but there were more mountains to climb.

Tetreault and Tafuto left Mt. Washington for Lake of the Clouds and the summits of mounts Monroe (5,385 feet), Franklin (5,028 feet), and Eisenhower (4,775), pausing momentarily to savor each summit—but not with the same zeal as at the beginning. Fatigue was setting in.

"We continued on in drone mode to Mt. Clinton," Tetreault said. They consulted maps and watches before deciding to continue the journey to mounts Jackson (4,012 feet) and Webster (3,876 feet). "We weren't skipping anymore; we were dragging." Arriving at the Mitzpah Spring Hut around dinnertime, they contemplated sitting down to eat. But they didn't. "We knew we wouldn't get up if we stopped," Tetreault said. After they bested Jackson and Webster, around 8:10 P.M., it became a race with the sun. They took a moment to gaze at the pink-tinged sky, realizing the greatest part of the challenge lay ahead: Would they make it to Crawford Notch before darkness fell?

Seriously tired by now, they made a mistake; they misjudged their distance from the Notch. "We saw a sign that said 'cliff' and we thought we were at Elephant's Head in Crawford Notch," Tetreault explains. "We waltzed out, only to find ourselves on Webster's Cliff with a mile yet to go."

The woods were getting dark. Fortunately, the trail was good, "because our feet weren't coming off the ground much!" Tetreault said. The two dragged out of the woods at Saco Lake at 9 P.M. and made a warm beer toast, "to summits conquered and those yet to reach." Despite being more tired than ever, "I had a huge feeling of accomplishment," Tetreault said, "and a big, goofy grin that didn't go away for days.

"It may have been called the Death March," he added, "but I've never felt so alive in my life."

Crawford Notch, New Hampshire: A Family Backpacking Trip in the White Mountains

Kids Lead the Way to Waterslides and Mountaintops

The key to a successful backpacking trip is careful planning. This is even more crucial when hiking with children. Seek out the advice of friends, relatives, and acquaintances who are experienced hikers; they are great resources. Read some of the books listed at the end of this chapter.

Start small, with day hikes and short overnight trips. Consider signing up for an Appalachian Mountain Club beginning backpacking workshop or trip. (You can contact the AMC at P.O. Box 298, Route 16, Gorham, NH 03581; (603) 466-2727.)

It's important to get the kids involved in the planning. Discuss possible routes; plan and shop for meals together; encourage them to help you pack.

Think safety first. Make sure someone in your group is trained in first aid procedures, and carry a well-stocked kit. Always leave a description of your proposed route with someone back home, and be aware of alternates, in case an emergency arises.

Finally, be flexible. If you're tired or the weather turns nasty, be ready to adjust your plans.

Our friends thought we were nuts. While they were packing suitcases for Disney World and cottages on the Cape, we were loading up backpacks and gathering gear for a family hike in the mountains.

We had done a fair amount of hiking *en famille*—day hikes and a couple of one-night trips. They were brief glimpses at a world of woodlands and foothills, soaring mountains, lakes and streams, cascades and waterfalls—all hidden from the highway, waiting to be savored by those who venture off the beaten path. It was enough to entice us to try something more ambitious.

Don't let anyone convince you that the hiking itself is the hardest part—trip planning is right up there on the difficulty scale. We wanted something with variety—woods, water, and high mountain views. We didn't want anything too difficult. Ideally, the trip would be a loop; we'd end up back where we parked the car, but wouldn't have to back-track on the same trails. We decided on a four-day back-pack trip through the Franconia Range in the White Mountains of New Hampshire. We would have a nine-year-old and an eleven-year-old in tow. (Figuratively speaking; we hoped they'd gleefully lead the way.)

After hours of meal planning (keeping a refrigerator stocked is difficult enough; feeding and watering a family of four for four days on the trail—remember, you have to carry it all—requires creativity bordering on genius), shuffling gear, packing, weighing, and repacking, we were ready. We began at the Class II Ethan Pond Trail, which starts at the former Willey House railroad station in Crawford Notch.

The first few hours of a hike are the toughest. The trail was harder than we thought it would be. (Ethan Pond Trail starts with a steep ascent before leveling off.) Our packs felt heavier than they had in the living room. It was less fun than we'd expected. We trudged, nudging our young, whining hikers along; we talked about the pretty trees and the gorgeous scenery (they couldn't care less); we sang; we coaxed; we ate a day's worth of snacks in two hours. We made it to Ethan Pond around lunch time, already behind schedule.

At the pond, we dropped the packs and went swimming. Now *this* was fun. We explored the area and read comments other hikers had written in the journal at the Ethan Pond Shelter. Some warned of black bears in the vicinity, so we talked about the chances of meeting one on the trail, and what we might do. "Dibs on hanging the food up tonight," Jared said, secretly hoping for an encounter. "Why can't we just stay here for the night?" both kids asked. No, no, we need to move on, we told them; we'll camp at Shoal Pond; it'll be pretty, too.

Shoal Pond, the small, blue puddle on the trail map, turned out to be a mosquito-infested swamp. We thrashed through thickets and thorns to the banks, then sank to our knees in muck. Swimming would have to wait; instead, we busied ourselves with setting up camp and preparing meals.

It is repetition that makes chores tedious; the novelty of putting up a tent, making a fire, and cooking on the small backpack stove made these tasks fun. The same is true of food. Oodles of Noodles, soup in a cup, and dried spaghetti dinners do not typically grace our table, which makes this only-on-hikes cuisine special.

We were sitting at the campfire at dusk, spooning up chocolate mousse (just add boiling water) from enamel cups, when a giant moose came out of the woods on the other side of the pond. Another emerged a little farther down, and still another entered the water just yards from us. We sat in silence. Shoal Pond may have been a disappointing swimming hole, but it proved itself a treasure nonetheless. Now we were on an adventure.

The next day, we continued on Ethan Pond Trail to beautiful Thoreau Falls, a gushing torrent that tumbles fast over smooth, water-worn boulders. It was well worth the short side-trip.

On our way back to the main trail, we bumped into a man and began the usual hiker chatter: where ya' been, where ya' going, how long ya' been out? He'd been on the trail for more than four months; he'd be out for another two. Even the kids were impressed. He left us pondering how many ways there are to live your life.

The trail climbed gradually and entered the south end of Zealand Notch, where it followed an old railroad bed. We scrambled up Zeacliff Trail, which runs along the notch walls, making for spectacular views. We reached Zealand Falls in time for lunch. "Why don't we stay here for the night?" Sadie asked. (The Appalachian Mountain Club Zealand Falls Hut is located here.) No, no, we said; we need to get to the Mt. Guyot Shelter.

This part of the hike, we underestimated. Or perhaps we were just getting tired. Leaving Zealand Falls, the trail rises fairly steeply, slabbing up Zealand Ridge. We made giant steps, sliding and scrambling, moaning and groaning. At one point, nine-year-old legs refused to go on. A much-needed break, a piece of Power Bar, and sips of Gatorade did the trick. The view at the top of Mt. Guyot was little consolation, but the promise of shelter, and thus an end to the day's hike, was enough to propel us on. We dropped our backpacks on the ground and ate dessert first—apple cobbler with raisins and dates (just add water).

We shared the campsite with a small group of hikers, and when darkness fell, they invited us on a walk up to a rocky outcropping for stargazing. Lying flat on our backs on granite sheets still warm from the sun, we gazed up at the stars pinwheeling in an ink-black sky. Stars without competition. "It's like the dome in the planetarium," someone said. "Yeah, only this is real."

The third day we took our toughest and most spectacular hike, a steady climb up Mt. Bond, and then over to the famous Bond Cliffs. We left early in the morning, fortified with oatmeal and dried fruit, hot cocoa and Tang, kids leading the way. We watched as they skipped and climbed their way up the ridge and over; they looked like tiny dolls in the expansive terrain. Above the tree line, on the craggy mountain ridge, we could see forever. More importantly, we could see where we had been, what we had traversed. By the time we reached Bond Cliffs we were in the clouds—literally and figuratively—high on sweeping views (said to be some of the prettiest in New England) and our accomplishment in getting there.

When the trail guide says "steep descent," believe it. We were on our butts most of way down the backside of the cliffs; in some spots we had to remove our packs and lower them. The kids thought it was great fun—like a giant playground. We reached the beautiful Pemigewasset Wilderness Trail by late afternoon. Here was some great swimming. We slid on granite sheets through the Pemigewasset River into deep holes and tiny rapids. Who needs a water park?

Later, we built a small campfire, and while our clothes dried, we took a sunset stroll along the river. When we returned we noticed that the wonderful outdoor aromas of pine and moss and fresh stream water had been replaced by the smell of burning rubber: Jared's shoe was on fire. We rescued it in time, the sole only slightly melted, but it left us thinking how bad it could have been if he'd had to hike out with only one shoe. Next time, we would bring extras. It also got us thinking about first aid, and how important it is to keep our training up-to-date.

The last day. One can of tuna left and seven miles to go. We vowed not to plan it so close next time, to take a little extra food even if it meant more weight.

We were wrong, by the way: it's the last few miles of a hike that are the toughest. We lightened the kids' loads and doubled ours. We were out of snacks, songs, and good humor by the time we reached the end of the trail. But we did it. Yeah! High fives. It felt like crossing the finish line. We shed our backpacks and called dibs on the first ice cream cone.

Jeffersonville, Vermont: An Inn-to-Inn Journey to Quebec and Back

This Catered Trek Offers Variety, Romance, Even Religion

"The unexpected adds an element of adventure," guide Lowell Hart told us as we embarked on a five-day hiking trip with thirteen strangers. You got that right, Lowell. Who knew that a hiking holiday could be so luxe, and, moreover, inspire poetry and romance in the souls of its participants?

Pardon us for gushing. But our hiking trips had always been of the freeze-dried food, haul the backpack, hitch-hike back to the car variety. We were (as you might be) purists. Who needs a guide when any fool can read a map and sleuth out trail blazes? But if we climbed up the mountain skeptics, we climbed down believers. If it's not against your religion to indulge in some frills with your thrills, you'll love the lush life according to Hiking Holidays.

Based in Brandon, Vermont, Hiking Holidays runs catered, inn-based trips all over the world. Our five-day trip from the Northeast Kingdom of Vermont to Quebec showcased what these folks do really well: Put together a trip that provides physical challenge, fun, and variety.

No two trips are exactly alike. The only fixed element is the inns; beyond that, the plans are flexible, depending on the group's stamina and interests, and the weather. That said, here are the highlights of our adventure, led by Lowell Hart and Bruce Acciavatti.

Hiking highlights first. We began the trip in Jeffersonville, Vermont, then piled into two vans for our first (and

CONTACT: Hiking Holidays, P.O. Box 750, Bristol, VT 05443; (802) 453-4816. The company runs hiking and walking tours in Vermont, the Berkshires (Massachusetts), and on the Maine coast, in addition to trips elsewhere in the United States, in Canada, and in Europe. Generally, their New England tours run late-May through mid-October.

HOW TO GET THERE: The Vermont-Quebec trip begins at the Sterling Ridge Inn, RR 1, Jeffersonville, Vermont 05464. From I-89 north, take Exit 10 (Waterbury/Stowe). Go north on Route 100 for 10 miles to Stowe. In Stowe, turn left on Route 108 and follow it for 18 miles. In Jeffersonville, turn right onto Route 15 east; follow it for 1.2 miles to Junction Hill Road. Turn right on Junction Hill; the inn is on the left.

RATES: Our five-day, five-night trip cost $895, including all meals, fees for museum visits, support van, and gratuities (except guides' tips).

WHAT TO BRING: Dress in lightweight layers, such as light wool and synthetics. Bring two or three pairs of comfortable, loose pants; a sweater or a fleece pullover; rain gear; good walking shoes or hiking boots; comfortable shorts; several shirts; warm socks; a swimsuit and a towel; a small day pack; a water bottle; bug repellent; sunscreen; binoculars; a camera; and sunglasses.

KIDS: Age ten and up when accompanied by an adult.

SKILL LEVEL: This hike was rated easy to moderate. A normally fit person should have no problem.

best) day of hiking. We passed the hairpin turns of Smugglers' Notch, stopping at a mountain spring (parasite-free, according to Hart) to fill our water bottles, then drove on to Stowe Ski Resort. There, we rode in a gondola to the summit of Mt. Mansfield, the highest point in Vermont.

Hiking and climbing carefully to avoid crushing the fragile alpine tundra vegetation, we made our way along the ridge of the mountain on a section of the Long Trail. Much of this was fairly challenging stuff; lots of Class V rock-scrambling, which came as a surprise to those expecting an easy first-day hike. A good test of the hiking boots, and pity for those who were breaking in new ones. But what views! Pulling on fleece jackets (in spite of ninety-degree heat in the valley), we took in a panorama that included Burlington, Lake Champlain, the Adirondacks, and nearby Smugglers' Notch and Spruce Mountain. The hike took about four hours, including breaks to bask in the sun. For lunch, we drove to a pretty rock-banked stream (part of the Lamoille River) to take off our socks and boots and plunge grateful feet into the river. Meanwhile, Hart and Acciavatti laid out lunch on a red-checked tablecloth. Bliss. We blew off plans to hike to Devil's Gulch that afternoon and headed to Canada.

In Quebec, we discovered a place that surely made everyone's list of highlights: L'Aubergine, an 1820s farm-house-cum-inn set in Quebec's Eastern Townships. Besides being friendly and funky (it's hard to be formal when cows are mooing next door and farm equipment is clattering past), the inn boasts fantastic French food. You'd never find this place on your own, but it proved to be a good base for adventures. Just outside the door is thirty-mile-long Lake Memphremagog (a good spot for post-hike and moonlight swims); country roads leading to a Ukrainian settlement (the Ukrainian Catholic church is worth a peek); Owl's Head ski mountain, for strenuous hiking; and, a drive away, Saint Benoit du Lac Abbey, where monks sing the vespers in Gregorian chant at 5 P.M.

After three nights in Quebec (two at L'Aubergine and one at a Victorian hotel, L'Auberge Waterview in Lac Brome), we headed back to Vermont, where we'd spend our final night at the Black Lantern Inn in Montgomery, "the covered bridge capitol of Vermont." (This bit of trivia would prove meaningful later in the trip.) About three miles from the inn, the guides asked if we wanted to walk along the paved, two-lane road the rest of the way. Sure, why not? Weird, though. As you trudge along the blacktop, taking in the bucolic real-Vermont scene (complete with local Here-fords), you're bound to ask yourself, "Why are we walking when there's a perfectly good set of wheels going to the same place?" Those who said to themselves, "Why, indeed; I'm hot and tired, and this is stupid," had the option of climbing back into the van when the guides made a sweep.

It's the guides' job to make sure everyone is comfortable and happy, no easy task when dealing with a dozen different personalities. As Acciavatti put it, "You can teach people about the outdoors. People skills, you can't teach; they have to come naturally." The guides' personalities can make or break a trip like this, and if they're having a great time, their enthusiasm spills over onto everyone else. Hart kept asking us, individually, "How are your legs? How are your spirits?" When asked how he was, he always had the same reply, "Awesome!"

The best was yet to come. In Montgomery, the guides piled us into vans and took us to a favorite local swimming place, Hippie Hole. Talk about a hidden treasure! A steep downward climb leads to an ice-cold mountain stream. There, giant boulders form a passageway that leads to a waterfall; we swam under the pounding cascade for the best natural hydrotherapy of our lives. Great fun; we dove, jump, swam, and played like little kids, while one member of the group perched on a boulder, writing poetry. After Hippie Hole, we tried out yet another swimming hole, this one under an old covered bridge. "I spent all of last week sleuthing out the best swimming holes around here," said Hart, who was always the first to dive off the rocks. Tough job.

That evening at dinner, we learned that more than swim-

The pause that refreshes: A no-sweat break at Hippie Hole.

ming had taken place at Swimming Hole Number Two. A couple in the group (fans of the book *The Bridges of Madison County*) had become engaged to be married on the covered bridge. That made for much wine-drinking and toasting of the happy couple as they "hiked the mountains and valleys of life together." The evening capped what was, for all of us, a trip full of unexpected pleasures.

South Egremont, Massachusetts: Symphony and Scrambling in the Berkshires

A Concert Under the Stars Is the Perfect End to a Day on the Trail

CONTACT: New England Hiking Holidays, P.O. Box 1648, North Conway, NH 03860; (603) 356-9696.

HOW TO GET THERE: The trip meets at the Weathervane Inn, Route 23, South Egremont, MA 01258; (413) 528-9580. From Boston, take I-90 (the Massachusetts Turnpike) to the Lee exit, then Route 102 to Stockbridge. Then take Route 7 south to Great Barrington, to Route 23 west.

RATES: The Tanglewood Three-Day Weekend costs $529 per person, with everything included except your bar bill.

WHAT TO BRING: They'll send a list. In general, hiking clothes and outerwear, concert clothes (slacks and sweaters are fine), a day pack, sunscreen, bug repellent, and a water bottle.

KIDS: This trip is not appropriate for children.

SKILL LEVEL: Easy to moderate.

ON YOUR OWN: For information on the Boston Symphony Orchestra at Tanglewood, call (413) 637-5165. Lawn ticket prices range from $11 to $15, depending on the performance; they're free for children under twelve. For a guide to lodging, dining, and other activities in the area, contact the Berkshire Visitor's Bureau at (800) 237-5747 or (413) 443-9186. For hiking information and trail maps, including state parks and forests and the Appalachian Trail, contact Berkshire Region Headquarters, 740 South Street, P.O. Box 1433, Pittsfield, MA 01202; (413) 442-8928.

With its gorgeous countryside, lively arts scene, and Norman Rockwellian quaintness, is it any wonder that Berkshire County is a cherished destination for overworked urbanites? Located in western Massachusetts, the region is a mere two-hour drive from both Boston and New York City.

There are lots of ways to experience the Berkshires, but the best way to savor the area is to hike it. With at least a dozen great places to hike, and about a zillion places to stay, how to plan the best getaway? Add this one to your Rolodex, overloaded active types: New England Hiking Holidays. They run guided, all-inclusive hiking trips in the Berkshires (and elsewhere) that include country inns, meals, and even concert tickets.

We joined them for a Tanglewood weekend; the brochure promised lovely hiking in the Berkshire Hills, lodging at the comfortable Weathervane Inn in South Egremont, and a Boston Symphony Orchestra concert under the stars at the Tanglewood Music Festival in Lenox. Nice. Easy to take. Perfect for those times when one's stamina level is not up to peak-bagging, and one's spirit is in need of Mother Earth's nurturance.

Guide Brenda Donnelly, an eight-year veteran with N.E.H.H., told us the average age of participants is forty-five, but that they see many older couples, as well as women traveling solo. "Lots of single women join us because they don't feel safe going into the woods alone, and don't have friends who like to do this.

"Lots of people say they like to do this because it's a nice way to meet people," she added. However, she said, "Some groups are friendlier and more cohesive than others."

Indeed, group dynamics played a big part in this experi-

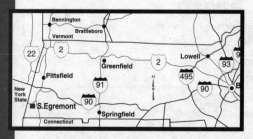

ence. We started out as strangers, straggling into the Inn and sizing each other up, then all met officially at the predinner get-acquainted chat. Then our guides, Donnelly and co-leader Dan Tetreault, told the group what to expect, and we took turns introducing ourselves and recounting past hiking experiences. The men generally played up their stamina and experience, while the women said things like, "I like to walk and enjoy the scenery." But, as Donnelly asked, winking, "Guess who usually ends up being the stronger hiker?"

Amazing to think that this group of strangers could feel like old pals in a mere twenty-four hours, but it happened.

Day one began with an easy, woodsy hike to a favorite local destination, Bartholomew's Cobble. This national natural landmark, one of two in Massachusetts (the other is Gay Head Cliffs on Martha's Vineyard) is said to be more than 500 million years old. What it looks like, essentially, is a big pile of big rocks. Birders, take note: more than 230 species have been identified here. The guided trails are lined with tulip trees and quaking aspen. We hiked to Hurlburt Hill, a boring stretch of pasture topped with a marker that reads CT on one side, MA on the other. Some folks straddled it to stand in two states at once. Then, we headed back to Colonel John Ashley House (built in 1735, it's the oldest house in Berkshire County) for a picnic on the lawn. Due to the impending concert and a blast-furnace heat wave, we made it an early day, and were back at the Inn by 3:30.

Time for a quick dip in the Weathervane's pool, or a quick beer on the porch. Then we donned dressier duds (no zip-off hiking shorts or T-shirts) and drove to the festival in a cloud of eau de bug repellent.

Is there a finer New England ritual than lying on a blanket under starry skies, listening to the symphony? It's hard to imagine one, especially while you're there, sipping wine and letting the music wash over you. The guides brought a basket filled with wine, cheese, crackers, and cherries.

Day two featured hiking on forest trails to the summit of Mt. Alander. Any beginner could handle this easy ascent; plenty of rocks and roots, with just a few short sections of steep inclines and rock scrambling. Donnelly proved herself quite knowledgeable about the trails and terrain, pointing out interesting flora such as albino Indian pipes and native wintergreen. And she offered lots of advice and encouragement to the less sure-footed among us: "This is a section where that side-step comes in mighty handy." "This might be a better way to get down."

This hike would be super for a novice, or someone wanting to get back into the activity after a long absence. But challenging, it wasn't.

On the afternoon's agenda was a hike to Bash Bish Falls, a 400-foot drop of rushing water just over the border in New York State. There are many legends associated with Bash Bish, mostly involving Indian maidens being thrown over the falls. (Some say the boulders in the pond are all former maidens, turned to stone.) A popular story is that of White Swan, a witch's daughter who was forced to leap from the cliff to her death for marrying into another tribe.

Getting to this fabled spot requires some effort, a four-mile-or-so hike on steep trails. By the time we heard the roar of water that signified the falls, we were hot, tired, and ready; we scrambled down the rocks, tore off our boots and socks, and rewarded our hard-working dawgs with a plunge into the ice-cold water. "Oohs" and "ahhs" all around. Some folks (not us), in spite of a prominent No Swimming sign, dove from the rocks into the boulder-lined, fifty-foot-deep pool. Happy with a foot bath, we headed back to the Inn.

The taxing day had a nice side effect: We seemed to gel as a group. Everyone was relaxed and jovial (after a shower and a drink) and sufficiently loose to swap off-color jokes and embarrassing anecdotes. Over the course of the weekend, we'd discovered there were musically inclined folks among us, so we asked innkeeper Vincent Murphy if there was a piano in the house. He produced one, and some old music books besides. We gamely launched into a medley of show tunes, from "My Favorite Things" to "Raindrops Keep Falling on My Head." Nicely warmed up, we were ready to segue into an Irish folk song set when the innkeepers prevailed on us to "Give it a rest, so we can get some sleep!" We complied, agreeing that once you've sung the theme from *The Poseidon Adventure* together, you're pals for life.

You can't plan these things, but when they happen, they make a group trip a really fun way to go.

Kent, Connecticut: Summits and Surprises on the Appalachian Trail

Rocky Scrambles and River Rambles in the Litchfield Hills

Frankly, a lot of "through-hikers"—adventurers who take on the whole Georgia-to-Maine Appalachian Trail (A.T.)—consider the Connecticut portion a necessary evil, something to get through as quickly as possible on the way to New Hampshire's legendary White Mountains or the ultimate milestone, Mt. Katahdin. (There, in Maine, the trail ends and hikers fall to their knees and kiss the ground in joy.)

But Connecticut, the first step into New England for Katahdin-bound hikers, deserves its due. Sprint through this section of the A.T. at your own peril—it's not as easy as you might think. "After hiking the flat stuff in New Jersey and New York, they expect more of the same here," says A.T. volunteer/trail maintainer Doug Christie. "But we've got some tricks up our sleeves." Biggest surprise: a wild-and-woolly stretch straight up the rocky face of 2,316-foot-tall Bear Mountain, the highest peak in Connecticut.

The Connecticut section of the trail extends for fifty-one miles from the New York state line at Sherman to the brook-crossing at Sage's Ravine in Salisbury, where it meets the Massachusetts border. When it's not steep, it's mostly hilly. Bad news for through-hikers hell-bent on getting to Maine, but good news for day-hikers and backpackers looking for fun and variety. And there's more to recommend it: The trail slices through an especially pretty part of the Nutmeg State, the Litchfield Hills area.

The major hiking companies haven't discovered this

CONTACT: Litchfield Hills Travel Council, P.O. Box 968, Litchfield, CT 06759; (860) 567-4506. We got advice and options from them, and set off on our own. If you'd prefer a guide, contact the area's only guide service, Pathfinders/The Great Outdoor Store, 44 Bank Street, New Milford, CT 06776; (860) 255-3801.

HOW TO GET THERE: The Litchfield Hills area is 100 miles from New York City, 130 miles from Boston.

RATES: There are no fees or parking fees along the trail. However, the Litchfield Hills area is upscale, so lodgings and restaurants don't come cheap.

WHERE TO STAY: In Kent, try Mavis Bed & Breakfast, 230 Kent-Cornwall Road; (860) 927-4334. A stay in this antique-filled Greek Revival house costs $85 per night. In Salisbury, try Armstrong Bed & Breakfast, on Ethan Allen Street; (860) 435-9964. Accommodations in this 1890 Victorian on a lake cost $80 per night. Country inns in Salisbury include the Undermountain Inn, on Route 41, and the White Hart, at the junction of Routes 41 and 44, both near the Appalachian Trail. There are several places to camp along the trail; some are set aside for group use only. For information, write to Appalachian Trail Conference, P.O. Box 807, Harper's Ferry, WV 25425.

WHAT TO BRING: The usual hiking gear, depending on season and length of hike, including lightweight wool or synthetic clothing for layering; hiking boots; rain gear; lots of water; a small flashlight; and a compass. In fall, wear bright colors (blaze orange is best); deer- and wild turkey-hunters sometimes use the trails.

KIDS: Use your own judgment. Almost anyone can handle the river walk, but the Bear Mountain hike is demanding.

SKILL LEVEL: Novices can hike the river walk; only strong hikers should take on Bear Mountain and the Undermountain Trail.

region yet. Too bad for them. This enticing chunk of Olde New England is chock-a-block with antique shops, covered bridges, and historic villages fairly oozing with colonial charm. *National Geographic Traveler* recently named Litchfield Hills one of the fifty most scenic places to drive in the United States.

But why drive it when you can hike it? The best stuff to see is along the hiking trails. And you'll see things that car-bound tourists usually don't, like wild turkeys, deer, perhaps even a bobcat. Pick a country inn or a B & B to stay in, or pick two, one at each end of your hike. Or reserve a campsite along the trail. Get your hands on a trail guide, such as the *AMC Guide to Massachusetts and Connecticut*, and pack your camera for the obligatory shots of 200-foot Kent Falls, the Cornwall Covered Bridge, and the views from Bear Mountain.

Anyone who's hiked this region has favorite sections. Here are a couple of ours, and a collection of must-sees to round out your trip.

The River Walk: Connecticut boasts the longest river walk on the 2,315-mile Appalachian Trail, and it's worth a ramble, especially off-season when you'll have it to yourself. The eight-mile walk begins at Bulls Bridge, to the south, and snakes along the Housatonic River. We joined it in Kent (not along the A.T., but worth a trip), an uncommonly pretty town with a waterfall and lots of B & Bs. Take Skiff Mountain Road to the hiker parking area; from there, you're never more than a few yards from the river. The wide, wooded trail is a perfect country tromp, with the river rolling on one side, hills undulating on the other. Along the way are remnants of stone walls and old foundations.

One area of the trail will stop you cold. Live forest gives way to a devastated stretch, where the trees are dead, limbless, toppled, as if a tornado cut a swath through them. This is the sad result of a blight that destroyed red pines around the state.

Keep going and you'll cross Route 4, which connects with blue-blazed Mohawk Trail, one mile west of Cornwall Bridge. The barn-red covered bridge is a much-photographed landmark. There's a pay phone in town, in case you need to call your innkeeper for a lift back to your car.

Bear Mountain: At the other extreme is Bear Mountain, the toughest stuff Connecticut's A.T. dishes out. Take on these rugged, rooted paths, scramble up the steep ledges, and you'll get a good workout and a minipeak to add to your bag. Bear Mountain is the highest peak within the state's boundaries. (The highest ground in the state, however, is actually on a shoulder of Mount Frissel, whose summit is in Massachusetts.)

Allow plenty of daylight to conquer the Bear. It takes five or six hours to hike the 6.7 miles of trail. The challenge and the views are ample reward.

Start your adventure at the Undermountain Trail entrance off Route 41 in Salisbury. It begins innocently enough, with a gentle slope. It gets tougher, evolving into a steady, thigh-testing climb. This wide trail was once used to transport charcoal, made here from hardwoods, to nearby blast furnaces. Take a right onto blue-blazed Paradise Lane, a loop trail that winds its way up the mountainside, past a black spruce bog, a pond, and some six-foot-wide American chestnut trees. You'll pass an unmarked border between Massachusetts and Connecticut. Paradise Lane reconnects with the A.T., leading to slopes of ledge that go straight up for a quarter-mile.

Then comes the challenge, a scramble up Bear Mountain's rocky face — 500 vertical feet. Natural handholds and toeholds make this doable, if not exactly a breeze, without equipment. Look over your shoulder for splendid views of the region, on a clear day as far as the Catskills to the west and Mt. Greylock to the north. A rocky descent will take you back to the junction where the Appalachian and Undermountain Trails converge; Undermountain Trail will take you back to the parking lot where you began.

This accomplishment calls for a celebration. How about a toast with a glass of wine, made from local grapes? DiGrazia, Haight, and Hopkins are three area vineyards whose products can be found in local package stores. Or head to Kent for a sweet treat at Stosh's Ice Cream or the Kent Coffee and Chocolate Company.

Looking for a multisport escape? Do a day of hiking and a day of fly-fishing on the Housatonic, or saddle up at Lee's Riding Stable in Litchfield, then ride through Topsmead State Forest. Or rent a kayak at Clarke Outdoors in West Cornwall. Or keep going, and see what adventures unfold along the Appalachian Trail in Massachusetts, Vermont, New Hampshire. . . .

Resources

Additional Outfitters

Berkshire Hiking Holidays, P.O. Box, 2231, Lenox, MA 01240; (800) 877-9656.

Country Walkers, P.O. Box 180, Waterbury, VT 05676-0180; (800) 464-9255.

North Wind Country Inn Hiking and Walking, P.O. Box 46, Waitsfield, VT 05673; (800) 496-5771.

Outdoor Adventures of Vermont, RR 5-2147, Bear Swamp Road, Montpelier, VT 05602; (800) 639-9208 or (802) 223-4172.

Sierra Club Outing Department, Dept. #05618, San Francisco, CA 94139; (415) 923-5630.

Stonehurst Manor, Box 1937, Route 16, North Conway, NH 03860; (800) 525-9100 or (603) 356-3271.

Walking Inn Vermont, P.O. Box 243, Ludlow, VT 05149-0243; (802) 228-8799.

Walking the World 50 Plus, P.O. Box 1186, Fort Collins, CO 80522; (800) 340-9255 or (303) 225-0500.

Walking Tours of Southern Vermont, RR 2, Box 622, Arlington, VT 05250; (800) 5-VT-WALK or (802) 375-1141.

Women's Outdoor Challenges, 40 Winn Hill Road, Sunapee, NH 03782; (603) 763-5400.

BOOKS

AMC Guide to Maine, Mount Washington, and the Presidentials. AMC Books.

AMC Maine Mountain Guide. AMC Books.

AMC Guide to Massachusetts and Connecticut. AMC Books.

The Backpacker's Handbook. Chris Townsend, Ragged Mountain Press.

Backpacking One Step at a Time. Harvey Manning, Vintage Books.

The Camper's and Backpacker's Bible. Tom Huggler, Doubleday.

The Dayhiker's Handbook. John Long and Michael Hodgson, Ragged Mountain Press.

The Essential Outdoor Gear Manual. Annie Getchell, Ragged Mountain Press.

The Essential Wilderness Navigator. David Seidman, Ragged Mountain Press.

Fifty Hikes in Vermont. The Green Mountain Club, Backcountry Publications. (Other areas covered in the Fifty Hikes series include Massachusetts, Connecticut, and the White Mountains.)

Hedgemaids and Fairy Candles. Jack Sanders, Ragged Mountain Press.

The Hiker's Guide to Maine. Tom Seymour, Falcon Press Publishing.

The Hiker's Guide to New Hampshire. Larry Pletcher, Falcon Press Publishing.

Hikes and Walks in the Berkshire Hills. Lauren R. Stevens, Berkshire House Publishers.

Kids Outdoors. Victoria Logue, Frank Logue, and Mark Carroll, Ragged Mountain Press.

Nature Hikes in the White Mountains. Robert Buchsbaum, AMC Books.

Nature Walks in Southern Vermont. Mike Mikolas, AMC Books.

Short Hikes and Ski Trips Around Pinkham Notch. AMC Books.

Simple Tent Camping. Zora and David Aiken, Ragged Mountain Press.

Walking the Appalachian Trail. Larry Luxenberg, Stackpole Books.

White Mountain Guide. AMC Books.

Horse Packing and Trail Riding

Dover-Foxcroft, Maine: Roughriding in Katahdin Iron Works

Horsing Around in the Wilds of Northern Maine

CONTACT: Pleasant River Pack Trips, P.O. Box 16, Dover-Foxcroft, ME 04426; (207) 564-3451 or (207) 564-2965.

HOW TO GET THERE: Take I-95 to Exit 39, then travel north on Routes 11 and 7 to Route 7 (toward Dover-Foxcroft). The Fox Run Riding School and farm (headquarters for Pleasant River Pack Trips) is on your left.

RATES: Two-day pack trips cost $275, including food, horses, a guide, and cabin rental. Half-day riding trips cost $55; day trips, $100.

WHAT TO BRING: Casual clothes, ankle-high boots, rain gear, a riding helmet, a warm jacket, bug repellent, sunscreen, a small pack to carry personal gear, a water bottle, a sleeping bag, and a flashlight.

KIDS: Ask about their special kids and family trips and programs.

SKILL LEVEL: All levels; wilderness pack trips are best suited to intermediate or advanced riders.

Some call it the last stand of great wilderness in the Northeast. The backwoods of northern Maine is mile after mile of dense forest, punctuated by glacial lakes, roily rivers, and jagged mountaintops—most reachable only on foot or horseback. If you plan right, you can ride all day (maybe even days) without seeing another soul. Go ahead and leave your VISA card at home, but you'd better take someone who knows where she's going and what she's doing.

We hooked up with Judy Cross, owner of Pleasant River Pack Trips of Dover-Foxcroft, Maine. Cross, a lifelong Mainer and award-winning dressage rider, specializes in backwoods riding adventures. She took her first guest out in 1980. Today, she offers a variety of Western-style riding excursions, including multiday wilderness pack trips, moonlight rides, kids' camps, and day trips out of her seventy-acre farm and stables. But her forte is putting together custom trips for experienced riders.

There were six in our group, and except for us, everyone was a veteran of Pleasant River rides. We took off for a weekend pack trip from Williamsburg Plantation in Brownsville Junction, heading along the old Allagash Railroad bed. Our plans were to follow the west branch of the Pleasant River into Katahdin Iron Works, and on to a cabin in the woods.

Katahdin Iron Works has earned its own chapter in Maine history books. It was built in the remote wilderness, along with a town and roads, in 1843. By 1884, during the height of the ironworks' operation, the village had grown to include the residences of 200 or so workers, a number of resort businesses, and the Silver Lake Hotel. People traveled from all over the state to soak in the local springs, rich in sulfur and other minerals. Today, the skeletons of a blast furnace and a charcoal kiln (and a small State Historic Site sign) are the lone remnants of the Katahdin Iron Works.

When northern Maine residents and Appalachian Trail through-hikers talk about Katahdin Iron Works (or simply "KI"), they're likely referring not just to the old town, but to the entire wilderness area: a chunk of 60,000 or so acres between Greenville and Baxter State Park, containing the last, long stretch of the Appalachian Trail before it reaches its terminus atop Mt. Katahdin. Most of it—forest, countless lakes and ponds, and a dozen or more mountaintops—is under the managed care of the Northern Maine

Woods Association, a group of logging companies.

We rode along a dirt path, weaving in and out of sight of the clear and rocky waters of the Pleasant River, the soft clip-clopping of hoofs mixing with the sound of rippling water. The horses trotted along, stirring the thick carpet of leaves. About three hours into our ride, we came upon a spur trail leading away from the river. Why not? The horses carried us to a bluff with a top-of-the-world panorama of peaks and valleys.

It was late afternoon by the time we reached the cabin, tucked away in a thicket of pines, ferns, and mosses on the banks of Silver Lake. It was, as Thoreau described the northern Maine woods, "all mossy and moosey." In fact, a moose clambered into the woods at the sound of our arrival.

After five hours in the saddle, it felt good to dismount. We put the horses out for the night in a makeshift rope corral strung between trees behind the cabin.

That evening, we watched the sun set and the moose return (though it may not have been the same one), and we luxuriated in the calm and quiet of the wilds. Funny, we thought, how quiet does not mean silent. We were surrounded by a symphony: the cries of loons; the sounds of crickets and toads; the soft scampering of small animals; the occasional snorts of our horses. For an urbanite, this would be as strange a land as any across the seas.

Despite the remoteness of our location, Cross told us she craves even more solitude. "I remember when I first started out. We just packed the horses and took off. We camped wherever we liked," she reminisced. Today, campers must reserve and pay for sites within the area. She hopes to reserve a site in the Hermitage area, location of the last stand of virgin pines in Maine, for a future pack trip.

The last day of our trip, we mounted the horses and climbed the 2,998-foot summit of Saddleback Mountain. That's one of the nice things about horseback trips—you get to see a lot more territory than you would if you were on foot. We traveled twenty-five to thirty miles a day, much of it over rough terrain. Not even on the best day could a hiker manage that mileage.

Still, it was just a peek at this vast vestige of wilderness.

Bethel, Maine: Llama Trekking in Western Mountains

Gentle Beasts of Burden Carry the Load
While You Savor the Scenery

CONTACT: Telemark Inn Wilderness Lodge, RFD #2, Box 800, Bethel, ME 04217; (207) 836-2703.

HOW TO GET THERE: Take Exit 11 (Gray) off the Maine Turnpike; follow Route 26 to Route 2 north, continue for 4 miles then turn left on Flat Road; go 2.6 miles and turn right; at 0.6 miles take another right. Now, watch for the Telemark Inn sign.

RATES: Three-day llama trek costs $395 per adult; $295/child. Most guests choose to stay at the Inn the night before the trek: Room rates are $90 per room/double occupancy; $75 single; $25 per additional person in room. Telemark also offers day treks ($75/adult; $50/child); two-day weekend packages ($229/adult; $149/child); and a six-day combo mountains and lakes trip ($895/adult; $695/child). Guided hiking, canoeing, and mountain biking trips: $25 to $75, depending on activity, location, and group size.

WHAT TO BRING: Sleeping bag; warm clothes; swimsuit; hiking boots; sunscreen; water bottle; bug repellent.

KIDS: Yes, all ages. Family treks are scheduled primarily during July and August. Everyone should avoid June, blackfly season.

SKILL LEVEL: All levels; hiking activities are tailored to the specific requests of the group.

C an we ride them?" asked Charlotte, our wide-eyed, eight-year-old traveling companion.

"No, they're not like horses; you don't ride them," we tell her.

"So, what do they do?" inquired Sadie, the ten-year-old in the group.

The llamas will carry all our stuff, we explained. No forty-pound backpacks for us. We'll hike unencumbered, in style and comfort.

"Cool," they say.

Yeah, real cool, we think. There is, perhaps, no easier way to explore the mountains than with a llama in tow. These sure-footed members of the camel family are gentle, easy to handle, and able to carry between sixty and 100 pounds of gear.

"Aren't they cute?" the girls gushed.

Yep, they're cute: shaggy, polite creatures with big banana peel ears and dark, soulful eyes. What more would you want in a hiking partner?

We're at the Telemark Inn in Bethel, Maine, beginning a family llama trek that will take us to some of the prettiest areas in the Northeast mountains. The Inn itself is a pleasure. Built as a turn-of-the-century Adirondack-style lodge, it sits at the base of Caribou Mountain, surrounded by

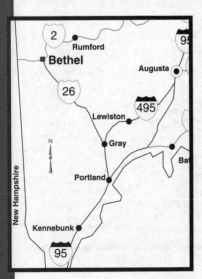

White Mountain National Forest. If Leon Blanchard returned, he'd still recognize the place. Blanchard, founder of the Prudential Insurance Company, built the lodge in 1900 as a family retreat. Not much has changed since; which, of course, is its charm. Inside it's all wood and stone, with shelves made from twisted tree trunks, and a soaring mineral stone fireplace. Outside is a hushed forest of beech and pine, with hidden ponds and streams.

Although we were only a few minutes from the ever-growing resort town of Bethel, here we were alone. No one else ventured up the long, dirt, dead-end road leading to the Telemark.

We met owner Steve Crone, and his family of llamas, at the Inn's customary wine and cheese get-together the night before our trip. Crone, who seemed more at ease with llamas than people, has run treks in New England since 1985, offering one- to six-day trips, and custom-designed pack adventures. Ours would be Telemark's most popular, a three-day, two-night trek. The llamas, of course, were the hit of the party. It took no time at all to warm to these lovable creatures and to learn why they've been called the perfect pack animal. Llamas have been used for more than 4,000 years to transport goods across South America's rugged Andes. They are surprisingly sturdy, require minimal care in camp, and leave no more trace of their visit to the wilderness than do deer or elk. Adapted to mountain travel, the llama's unique padded foot does not tear up the trail like other animals. Sounded great, but, we wanted to know: "Do they spit like their camel cousins?" Only if they feel threatened or provoked, we are told.

We headed out from the Inn the next morning, our gear loaded in saddlebags strapped to the backs of our woolly hiking companions. Llamas are willing and able hikers, so the instructions were minimal. Just give them a little tug when you want them to go. The pace was slow and easy; the trail ascended gently into the foothills. As we moved deeper into the sun-dappled forest, the sounds and light became muted. We heard the muffled thud of our own footsteps, an occasional snort from our four-legged pals, and the distant rumble of water. We planned to explore the Evans Notch region of the White Mountain National Forest, sticking to low-volume, secluded trails—staying away from the more-traveled Presidential Range area.

"We try to show the group as much wilderness as possible," Crone explained.

We were alone all day, traipsing the floor of the Evans Notch valley, stopping for a ritual toe test in an icy cold mountain stream, pausing to savor the scenery, or clamoring up a jumble of rocks for a view of the surrounding mountainside. We reached our base camp on the rocky banks of the Wild River by late afternoon. This is when we really began to appreciate our shaggy friends. Folding tables and chairs were unpacked from the llamas' saddlebags, along with such niceties as linens, sparkling water, wine—and meals unlike any we've ever had in camp. While we savored the last of the sun's warming rays, and the kids skipped rocks on the water, our guides set up tents and prepared a gourmet dinner.

Lest we'd forgotten we were in Maine—the blackflies swarmed and mosquitoes joined us for dinner, and a dense fog moved in quickly, draping us in a thick, silent cocoon. We went to sleep to the fog-amplified sound of water over rocks.

As the next two days slipped by, the relaxation and unburdening that comes with solitude and beautiful surroundings began to set in. We had several choices for daily activities: swimming in nearby ponds and river pools; hiking to mountain summits; talking to the llamas; relaxing at camp. One day we opted for an ambitious hike (without the llamas) to an overlook with sweeping vistas of East Royce, Ames, Speckled, and Caribou mountains—and expansive valleys punctuated with ponds and rivers. Our last morning we trekked a portion of the Caribou Trail, to pretty 25-foot Kees Falls before heading back to the Inn.

The ease of the trip, beauty of the surroundings, and surprising companionship of the llamas made this getaway more restful than expected. And, what did the kids think? "Awesome!" they exclaimed, as each pulled out a clump of brown and white wool from their jeans pockets. Soft, warm souvenirs of the trek. "Can we get a llama?"

Peterborough, New Hampshire: Fall Foliage Weekend in Monadnock Foothills

Walk, Trot, and Canter Your Way Through the Woodlands

There was nothing subtle about the landscape that stretched before us: the woodlands were aflame with riotous color, a broad palette of fire-engine reds, lemon yellows, Granny Smith greens, and touches of fuchsia, magenta, and scarlet. We were standing next to our mounts, at the end of a trail overlooking the foothills of Mt. Monadnock. The horses' occasional snorts produced a rising steam—warm air in the cooling fall temperatures. It smelled earthy; a combination of the horses' oaty breath and the dense, damp carpet of fallen leaves and pine needles.

We were on a fall foliage riding weekend, exploring rural southern New Hampshire on horseback. The bold landscape we viewed from the ridge was a loud exception to the otherwise quiet and calm vistas of gentle hills and valleys, colonial villages, and quaint towns. This is a land of white-steepled churches, village greens, and lichen-flecked stone walls.

The weekend began Friday evening with a champagne get-together at Honey Lane Farm, in Peterborough, New Hampshire. There were four riders in the group; two more people came for the weekend, but spent it in other activities.

Aline and Al Coutu, owners of Honey Lane Farm, take great care in evaluating riders' abilities and matching them with appropriate horses and trail rides. Guests are asked to fill out riding-experience forms prior to arrival, and additional evaluation is done on site. Generally, beginners—and

CONTACT: Honey Lane Farm, RFD 2, P.O. Box 127, Peterborough, NH 03458; (603) 563-8078 in New Hampshire, or (800) 897-8080 out of state.

HOW TO GET THERE: Follow Route 101 into Peterborough, to Route 137 south. Turn left onto Goldmine Road, then take a left at the fork. You'll see the Honey Lane Farm sign and driveway on your right.

RATES: A fall foliage weekend costs $345 per person, double occupancy, including a Friday night champagne get-together, two nights lodging, five meals, lessons, and riding. Optional massage therapy (reserve in advance) costs $30 per half-hour, $48 per hour. An all-inclusive five-night inn-to-inn trip costs $995 per person, double occupancy ($1,195 during peak foliage weeks). Five- and seven-day "Heart of New England" programs, on which you stay at Honey Lane Farm, cost $1,195 per person, double occupancy.

WHAT TO BRING: Riding breeches, chaps, or comfortable pants; high boots or paddock boots (no tennis shoes); a riding helmet (this is a must—if you don't have one, you can purchase one from the store on the premises, or borrow one from a riding friend); a bathing suit; rain gear (not a poncho); a belt pack for carrying personal items; insect repellent; and sunglasses.

KIDS: Weekend and inn-to-inn trips are not appropriate for children. Ask about kids' programs, which run throughout the summer.

SKILL LEVEL: Beginners through all levels are welcome on weekend programs and some inn-to-inn jaunts. Intermediate and strong experienced riders only on five- and seven-day "Heart of New England" trips.

experienced riders looking for a take-it-easy getaway—are drawn to the weekend holidays. Advanced beginners through experienced riders can be found on Honey Lane's five-day inn-to-inn holidays or its seven-day programs. Strong, experienced riders may include two days of long-distance trekking. Whatever your ability or your schedule, Honey Lane probably has something to suit you.

After a hearty country-style breakfast on Saturday

morning, we headed to the indoor riding arena. Our instructors were Tiffany and Caroline, two young, accomplished riders from England working at Honey Lane for the summer. The Honey Lane folks like to teach; it was clear that this was going to be a learning vacation, whether we liked it or not. First, we were instructed in the farm's grooming and tacking procedures. Next came a thorough lesson on the proper procedures of cooling down the horses and putting them away at the end of the day; then a few words on trail-riding etiquette. By this time, we were chomping at the bit to climb in the saddle. At last, we were asked to tack up our horses and ride, one behind the other, around the arena. Caroline offered instruction and pointers as we walked, trotted, and cantered to her commands.

In the afternoon, they let us out. We wove our way through country trails behind the farm, then onto a series of dirt paths and old carriage roads that took us through deep virgin woodlands. We walked and trotted until we reached a beautiful green pasture. At last, a chance to let the horses go. We cantered across the pasture and into a rolling field of grass. It felt like we were flying.

We returned to Honey Lane late in the afternoon. The farm, situated on nearly 100 acres, features a spacious

HONEY LANE FARM

You can lead a horse to water. Riders and their mounts enjoying the day on a Honey Lane Farm ride.

lodge, an indoor arena, and a stable of thirty or more horses. The lodge is decorated in English country style (lots of horse prints and fox-hunting pictures), with a dining deck and a viewing deck overlooking the hunt course. There's also a pool, a Jacuzzi, and the optional services of a massage therapist (by appointment). Al does all the cooking: big, hearty breakfasts of French toast and sausages, and a Saturday-night steak barbecue.

There's something about the feel of a horse beneath you, its rhythm coursing through your body like a cold drink on a hot, hot day. It's addictive; we couldn't wait to get back in the saddle on Sunday.

The next morning's three-hour trail ride took us up a craggy hill for an unexpected and dramatic view of highland rivers and lakes, mountaintops and valleys ablaze with fall color. We rode dirt paths into the woods and along stone fences and estate ruins, back to the inn.

The weekend ended with lunch on Sunday—way too short. The brochure describes it as two nights, one-and-a-half days of riding. It didn't feel like one-and-a-half days days of riding (and, in fact, it wasn't). We think they should include a Sunday afternoon jaunt, too. We also missed riding into the quaint villages and historic towns of this region, as promised in the brochure.

Then again, perhaps they plan it so you feel you haven't had quite enough; when it came time to say good-bye, we were all talking about returning.

Woodstock, Vermont: Inn-to-Inn Thoroughbred Riding

Experienced Equestrians Will Love This Top-Notch, High-Class Tromp

CONTACT: Kedron Valley Stables, P.O. Box 368, South Woodstock, VT 05071; (800) 225-6301 or (802) 457-1480.

HOW TO GET THERE: From Exit 1 off of I-89 in White River Junction, take Route 4 west to Woodstock. Pick up Route 106 at the Woodstock Inn and travel south for 5 miles. The stables are on your right.

RATES: A five-day inn-to-inn ride costs $1,350 per person for a double, $1,400 for a single; foliage season rates are $1,550 for a double and $1,750 for a single, including all meals, lodging at inns, guide service, horse, tack, gratuities, and luggage transfers. Weekend inn-to-inn trips cost $465 for a double, $495 for a single.

WHAT TO BRING: Casual, comfortable attire (no jeans); breeches or chaps; boots; gloves; a light jacket or sweater; an approved hard hat with harness; lightweight luggage (no heavy, oversized pieces); bug repellent; sunscreen; a bathing suit; and a small pack for carrying personal items.

KIDS: These trips are not appropriate for children.

SKILL LEVEL: You must be an intermediate to advanced rider in good riding shape for multiday, inn-to-inn trips. Beginners should ask about Kedron Valley riding clinics.

The equestrians had spent the summer morning trotting across the Vermont countryside. Stretched before them was an expansive landscape of wooded corridors, mountain ridges, and valleys crisscrossed with meandering rivers.

"Shall I call ahead for a masseur to meet us at the inn?" the guide inquired.

Oh, yeah, you can get used to that kind of treatment in a hurry.

If you're a horse-lover, nothing is likely to make you feel more indulged than an inn-to-inn vacation with Kedron Valley Stables, located in South Woodstock, Vermont. Kedron treats its guests like royalty. You'll spend your days mounted on the warm, silky back of a thoroughbred, riding the valleys and crests of the Green Mountains; evenings, you'll relax in charming country inns, pampered by gracious innkeepers. Throw in a wrangler to guide you on the trail, and another to take care of your horse, and it starts to seem downright hedonistic. Our equestrian researchers, experienced horsewomen Judy Eitler and Minna Casser, couldn't wait to saddle up.

Their equestrian background proved essential. The Kedron Valley inn-to-inn ride required long hours in the saddle — up to six hours a day — often over rough, steep terrain. "This trip is for intermediate to advanced riders only," Casser said. "It also helps to be in good riding shape. Still, you'd better throw in a bottle of ibuprofen; you're likely to need it."

Their four-day trip began at the Kedron Valley Inn, where guests are paired with four-legged companions. Eitler and Casser had asked to bring their own horses, but were discouraged. Not good, they thought; they had visions of getting stuck on a trail-riding horse with no energy, tagging along nose-to-tail in a herd-bound line. However, in just a few hours, they fell in love with their very spirited mounts.

Paul Kendall, owner of Kedron Valley Stables, was chief wrangler and guide of the trek. Kendall has a passion for horses that borders on obsession, coddling them like grandchildren, regaling guests with stories of their past deeds and accomplishments. He wants you to know and love them all like he does. Kendall owns (as opposed to leases) the horses used for the inn-to-inn excursions, and is able to suit all types of riders. (One timid rider was given a veteran trail horse, who took very good care of her.)

There was no easing into the saddle on this trip. After meeting their mounts, the riders took off for the tangle of trails and back roads leading into the Green Mountains. They climbed steep woodland paths that brought them, time after time, to splendid ridgeline views. From the peaks, they rode back into the valleys, across a pastoral utopia of rolling fields and farmlands. The ride went along at a good clip, with some long gallops from time to time. By lunchtime, some of the riders were already saddlesore—thus, the call ahead for a masseur.

By five o'clock, seven hours and twenty miles later, the riders reached their destination: the Echo Lake Inn, in Ludlow, Vermont. This is usually when the grunt work of horsemanship begins: walk, untack, lift, carry, brush, water, feed . . . when all you want is a cold drink and a soft chair. Enter wrangler number two. Dick Sweet, Kendall's assistant, is in charge of tending to the horses, while the riders, well, find cold drinks and soft chairs.

Grumpy ol' Sweet delighted in giving the riders a little grief; he was like a spouse who's cranky by nature, but still looks out for your welfare and pleasure. Underneath the gruff, he lived up to his name and took good, sweet care of the horses and the riders.

The charming Echo Lake Inn was a welcome sight at the end of a long day in the saddle. The riders dispersed, some to enjoy cocktails and hot hors d'oeuvres on the wraparound porch; some to the hot tub and pool; some to the masseur's table. They convened later for drinks, dinner, and horse tales.

The next morning began bright and hot. Eitler and Casser started the day with a swim in the warm waters of tiny Echo Lake. Then, more glorious riding, through pastures and small towns and down country lanes. The riders

Horse Packing and Trail Riding

had by now become friends, bound by a common interest. There were eight in the group (Kedron will take up to twelve): Eitler and Casser, a woman from Scotland, three women from Pennsylvania, and a father and daughter from New Jersey.

One afternoon, the riders came across a fallen tree covered with oyster mushrooms. Two of them jumped down and picked enough to fill their saddle bags. That night, at the Weathersfield Inn, the chef sautéed them in a sublime mix of garlic, fresh herbs, and olive oil.

The gracious and elegant Weathersfield is an eighteenth-century inn nestled at the base of Hawks Mountain. It has ten guest rooms, each with a private bath (eight with fireplaces), and all furnished with period antiques; and seven public rooms, one with a 4,000-volume library of interesting and rare books. Outside are twenty-one acres to explore, and a verandah and porch overlooking English perennial gardens. It was an intimate, delightful haven after a day on the trail.

Day three, and the trip had gone without a hitch (so to speak). It was time for the horses to remind the now-confident riders that they are unpredictable animals who will sometimes do what they darn well please. After several hours on the trail, the party came upon a stream, tumbling clear and cold from the mountains. Ah, what a perfect place for a dunking, Eitler's mount must have thought. The horse took a bath in the river, splashing and rolling on her side, taking Eitler with her.

The other riders would have to wait to freshen up at the Juniper Inn, in Windsor, Vermont, where they would spend the last night of the trek. This lovely, stately mansion, with its very proper, if somewhat crisp, innkeepers, has a museum quality to it. Eitler and Casser said they couldn't find fault with its appearance—immaculate and imposing, with fine antique furnishings, formal gardens, and manicured lawns. Yet it seemed a bit too formal, too reserved. If they hadn't been so tired, it might have been difficult to relax in such a cool, stuffy atmosphere.

The final day, the group rode the back roads, ever so slowly (no one was anxious to return), to Kedron Valley Stables, completing their eighty-five-mile journey. Spoiled rotten.

Waitsfield, Vermont: An Icelandic Tolt in Mad River Valley

Smooth-as-Silk Riding on the Horses of the Vikings

CONTACT: Icelandic Horse Farm, P.O. Box 577, Waitsfield, VT 05673; (802) 496-7141.

HOW TO GET THERE: Take I-89 to Waterbury, then take Route 100 south to Waitsfield. Turn on Bridge Street; go over the covered bridge and bear left onto Joslin Hill Road. At the top of Joslin Hill Road, turn right onto Common Road. A half-mile down, you will come to four corners; go straight through. The farm is on your left.

RATES: The two-day, two-night weekend trek costs $385, including lodging, all meals, guides, and gratuities.

WHAT TO BRING: Riding breeches, chaps, or comfortable sport pants; sturdy boots; a warm jacket; rain gear; a swimsuit; sunscreen; riding gloves; a water bottle; a belt pack for personal items; and a riding helmet (you can borrow one if necessary).

KIDS: Eight and older, but use your own judgment; trips include 5 or more hours of riding each day—a long time in the saddle.

SKILL LEVEL: All levels are welcome on the weekend tolt trips. Multiday inn-to-inn trips are for experienced riders only.

An Icelandic sure doesn't look like much. Compact and muscular, with a mangy coat and a thick, fuzzy tail, it resembles a big, shaggy dog or a giant teddy bear. Yet the Icelandic horse, one of the purest breeds on earth, is one of the world's premier equine athletes.

There are just a handful of Icelandic horse stables in the country, and only one in New England: the Icelandic Horse Farm in Waitsfield, Vermont. Here, owner Karen Winhold offers visitors a chance to ride the mount of the Vikings, and to discover for themselves why these funny-looking animals have such a dedicated and enthusiastic following.

Ours was a weekend getaway, including two nights at the nearby West Hill House B & B, and two days exploring the beautiful Mad River Valley atop an Icelandic. (Winhold also offers half- and full-day rides, as well as five- and six-day inn-to-inn treks, year-round.)

We had heard the legend of the Icelandic before we arrived. When the Vikings came to Iceland nearly 1,000 years ago, they brought with them their finest horses. From then on, the people of Iceland mandated that no horses would be imported to their nation, a mandate that remains in force today, preserving the traits and traditions that have long since disappeared in most European horses. Riding an Icelandic is said to be a unique, unforgettable experience.

Good thing we knew a little before arrival. When we showed up at the stable, we were quickly assigned horses— no introductions, no description of the day's ride, no friendly chatter. We wondered: Should we bring rain gear? How

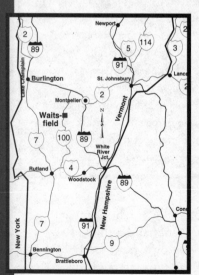

about water bottles? What do we need to know about riding these horses? But there was no time for answers; before we knew it, we were trotting with the herd, a motley crew of ten diverse riders. It felt like a big group, more so because of the wide range of abilities and experience—from nervous novices to seasoned pros, and even a frightened nine-year-old. Didn't seem to matter. We were off.

Perhaps the owners knew the horses would take care of

us. They were friendly, even-tempered animals, not at all finicky. Or perhaps the owners have adopted the very casual style of the Icelandics: mount from the left or the right; sink into the deep depression of the horse's back; relax and let your legs hang loose. We were not as laissez-faire. In fact, we were clutching the reins and hanging on for dear life as we walked, tolted, and cantered our way down the back roads.

It was quite a ride. We traveled through woods, up and down steep hills, over fallen trees, and along rocky stream beds. At one point, we crossed a marshy area, carried by our sturdy, unflappable four-legged companions through chest-high muck and mud. Wide open spaces posed a problem for a couple of riders in our group. The nine-year-old's horse liked to canter, and she did not; and Winhold's horse literally ran away with her. Oh no! Stampede, we thought, as she took off; we all pulled back our reins, hoping to restrain the herd. Fortunately, the rest of the horses remained calm. Winhold dismounted and walked her horse to our lunch destination.

"It's just unbelievable that a horse that is so friendly and easygoing in the pasture can be so spirited, powerful, and willing on the trail," said one rider. It is this unique mix of traits that makes the Icelandic so lovable: a disposition that will win you over, and a spirit and repertoire of smooth gaits that will (literally) carry you away. By the end of the day, despite rough riding, mud, runaway horses, and our reserved hosts, we were quite attached to our fuzzy friends and the Icelandic horse experience.

The staff from the stable met us and untacked the horses, hosed them down, fed them, then put them in the pasture across from the West Hill House. Dotty Kyle and Eric Brattstrom, the congenial, chatty innkeepers, more than made up for the lack of chumminess we encountered at the farm. Their 1860s Vermont farmhouse sits on nine quiet acres, and has five private-bath guest rooms. We had dinner by candlelight, family style, in the English antique dining room. The next morning we feasted on coffee cake, fruit and homemade granola, waffles, and soufflé.

The second day, we were a bit more confident and

relaxed in the saddle, and had extra opportunities to experience the unusual gaits of the Icelandic. Among them is the magnificent tolt, a four-beat running walk in which the horse makes a lateral move, leaving one hoof on the ground. Smooth as silk. It's said that an Icelandic at tolt can outrun a cantering thoroughbred, but we hardly noticed how fast we were moving—at least, not until one member of our group lost his saddle and executed a flying dismount. The little girl fell off, too. Fortunately, there were no injuries, and these mishaps didn't slow us down much. We tolted across the magnificent landscape of the Mad River Valley, through green valleys, quiet meadows, and forests cut by rivers and streams. After five hours in the saddle, we returned to the farm and handed over the reins. We received not so much as a good-bye or a thank-you from our hosts at the farm. (In fact, it seemed like they were in a hurry to get rid of us.) But it didn't matter. We'd return for the scenery—and for the extraordinary sensation of riding an Icelandic.

Resources

Additional Outfitters

Acadia National Park, Park Info. Center, Hull's Cove, Route 3, Bar Harbor, ME 04609; (207) 288-3338.

Attitash, Route 302, Bartlett, NH 03812; (603) 374-2368.

Chebacco Ranch, Route 153, South Effingham, NH 03882; (603) 522-3211.

Diamond A Ranch, 975 Hartford Turnpike, Dayville, CT 06241; (203) 770-3000.

Edson Hill Manor, 1500 Edson Hill Road, Stowe, VT 05672; (802) 253-8954.

Loon Mountain Park, RR 1, Box 41, Lincoln, NH 03251; (603) 745-8111.

Mountain Top Inn and Resort, Mountaintop Road, Chittenden, VT 05737; (802) 445-2100 or (802) 483-2311.

Nestlenook Farm, Dinsmore Road, Jackson, NH 03846; (603) 383-0845.

Northeast Kingdom Llama Expeditions, 152 Heath Brook Road, Groton, VT 05046; (802) 584-3198.

Northern Outdoors, P.O. Box 100, Route 201, The Forks, ME 04985; (207) 663-4466.

Northern Vermont Llama Company, RD 1, P.O. Box 544, Waterville, VT 05492; (802) 644-2257.

Ridge Valley Stables, Route 140, Grafton, MA 01519; (508) 859-3038.

Waterville Valley Resort, P.O. Box 252, Waterville Valley, NH 03215; (800) GO-VALLEY or (603) 236-8311.

Wilderness Expeditions, The Birches Resort, P.O. Box 41-N, Rockwood, ME 04478; (800) 825-WILD.

Bicycle Touring

Bucksport, Maine: Camping and Cruising the Coast of Maine

Even Teens (Gasp!) Have an Awesome Adventure on This Acadia Escape

On the second morning of a five-day tour with Backroads, an essential truth was revealed: this trip was as much about good food and friendship as about bike travel.

Backroads has a reputation as a purveyor of very cushy bicycle trips in lush locales such as the wine country in France, but our trip, a family camping bike tour of Down East Maine, was more Burley than Burgundy.

"Teenagers? Biking? Camping? Ugh. Doesn't sound very relaxing to me," a friend offered prior to our departure. Ah, but it was fun, and lively. Traveling with kids in the outdoors demands a what-the-hell, let's-go-for-it, devil-may-care attitude. Amid youthful exuberance, the playful inner child escapes from even the most buttoned-down adults.

Our group was big, twenty bikers and three guides, including kids from tot to teen. Two families came, separately, with tandem bikes and little tykes who trailered behind them in Burleys. "We've done this before, and we love it," said one couple, whose four-year-old daughter was a veteran, traveling happily in a trailer filled with books, dolls, and teddy bears.

At the other end of the spectrum were the teens, who wasted no time checking each other out and deciding who to hang with for the five-day adventure. Those who weren't compatible in cycling ability reconvened off the road, at beach stops, and in the evening at the campgrounds, for Frisbee, swimming, and volleyball. With all the kids in our

CONTACT: Backroads, 1516 5th Street, Suite L101, Berkeley, CA 94710; (800) GO-ACTIVE or (510) 527-1555. Backroads offers bike vacations around the world. Currently, they run the Maine/Penobscot Bay camping trip seven times per season; two trips are designated as family trips.

HOW TO GET THERE: Our trip met in Bucksport, Maine, at the Jed Prouty Motor Inn. Take Exit 30 off I-95 in Augusta. Follow Route 3 to Belfast. In Belfast, take Route 1 north to Bucksport. Turn left at the T-intersection at the end of the second bridge; the hotel is less than a mile on the left.

RATES: The trip, including most meals, all boat and campground fees, and one night's lodging at an inn, costs $698 per adult; 40 percent off for children six and under; 20 percent off for children seven through twelve; and 10 percent off for thirteen- through sixteen-year-olds. Van transfer is $50; bike rental is $109. A deposit is required.

WHAT TO BRING: Your own bike, if it has at least twelve speeds and is in excellent mechanical condition; a helmet; padded bike shorts; T-shirts; a windbreaker; a warm jacket or shell; rain gear; long bike pants; casual clothing for camping; cycling gloves; a sleeping bag; sunglasses; sunscreen; and insect repellent.

KIDS: Yes.

SKILL LEVEL: All levels. There are three alternate bike routes each day, ranging from easy to ambitious. The shortest routes are 15 to 20 miles, including van shuttles; the longest, 30 to 50 miles with longer options.

midst, it took no time to get acquainted; kids are instant ice-breakers and gave us something to talk about.

The guides weren't much older than some of the teens — Sandy, Allison, and Ken were all under thirty, tanned, and capable. Ken had ridden as a sponsored cyclist on a race team for a major bike manufacturer. He made a good riding mate for the long-tour types, those who could breeze through fifty or sixty miles and still have energy left for optional tours.

This trip was ambitious in scope, taking us from Acadia

National Park on Mt. Desert Island to Ellsworth to Blue Hill to Castine to Camden, then, by shuttle, back to the starting point. During each day's "Route Rap," the guides described three route options, from short (sixteen miles) to long (around sixty-one miles). Always, one of the guides drove the Backroads van to give lifts to cyclists needing a break or opting for a shorter route; one rode "pack" (with the group, carrying first-aid supplies and tools); and one rode "sweep," bringing up the rear.

The downside to biking Down East: the scenery is so splendid it's easy to lose yourself and momentarily forget to pedal. Day one, we rode the park loop at Acadia National Park. This enchanting ride takes you along a natural rock seawall hugging the ocean, past towering cliffs, and through valleys dense with spruce. At times the road seemed to climb forever. As we ground our way up the long hills, we exchanged brief conversation and found our pace with others of similar ability. Our camaraderie seemed to rise with the grade of the hills, as we reached each crest together and whooped in celebration. Descending, we hunkered down and gripped the bars firmly. On one stretch, the winding downgrade was flanked by a guardrail marking a sheer cliff that fell straight down to pounding surf. We soared along the asphalt ribbon, leaning into the curves, salt-tinged air whistling past our ears.

At noon, we rendezvoused at Sand Beach, a quarter-mile crescent famed for its always ice-cold water. "We're going in, aren't we?" challenged seventeen-year-old Amanda, egging on a few hardy folks to join her. Adults who might have admonished, "Are you sure you want to do that?" gave in to impulse and ran shrieking into the frigid Atlantic.

That afternoon, after using the coin-operated shower

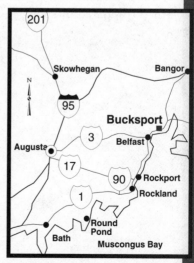

behind the general store, we dug into hors d'oeuvres and wine with gusto.

Our familiarity grew, and friendships blossomed, as we pedaled. We grew accustomed, too, to the bountiful meals prepared by our guides, such as grilled fish and chicken and, later in the week, a Mexican feast complete with sangria. Some of us added our own regional touch to that meal, with mussels we gathered from the bay.

All trips seem to play out in memory as a series of vignettes. A memorable scene from this one: Parent and teenager set off for some time alone, then realize neither of us has a map, nor any idea of where to find the rest of the group; an unplanned but ultimately hilarious adventure. More snippets: A chubby toddler bolts from her trailer to a swing-set in Blue Hill town park. Older kids race to the stony beach off Weymouth Point and jump into the drink, biking clothes and all. The delicious feeling of sinking into bed at Blue Hill Farm, and being awakened next morning by the bleating of goats. The boat trip from Castine to Camden, past stony isles covered with basking harbor seals. A lobster bake around a cozy fire on our last night camping together.

We'd experienced a rarity: a vacation that could be enjoyed by parents, teenagers, and toddlers alike. What's not to like about a trip that offers fabulous scenery, good food (prepared by someone else), and super cycling?

Jamaica, Vermont: Pedaling the Back Roads

Taking the Road Less Traveled Reveals the Best of Vermont

CONTACT: Bike Vermont Inc., P.O. Box 207, Woodstock, VT 05091; (800) 257-2226. The company offers two-, three-, five-, and six-day tours in Vermont and the Connecticut River Valley.

HOW TO GET THERE: Our tour was based at the Three Mountain Inn on Route 30 in Jamaica. To get there, follow I-91 to Brattleboro (Exit 2); follow signs to Route 30, then head north to Jamaica.

RATES: The tour costs $285 per person, including all dinners and breakfasts, use of a bike helmet, and all gratuities except guides' tips. Bike rental is $35.

WHAT TO BRING: If you bring your own hybrid or mountain bike, it should be in excellent condition, recently tuned, and have twelve or more gears. Ideally, it should have wide, smooth tires such as the Avocet Cross Mountain tire. Beyond that, bring bright-colored, loose-fitting clothing suitable for layering (wool and polypropylene are appropriate), including bike shorts; sweat pants; a windbreaker; a sweater; wool socks; a hat; and rain gear. You'll also need casual clothes for dinner, cycling gloves, a swimsuit, a camera, a water bottle, sunglasses, sunscreen, a fanny pack, and a bike lock.

KIDS: Bicycling children over age ten are welcome.

SKILL LEVEL: All levels. (Saturday's mileage is 40, 45, or 47 miles; Sunday's mileage is 20 or 22 miles.)

What good is a bike tour through gorgeous countryside if you're flying by too fast to see anything? Some bike trips feel more like the Tour de Frantic than a vacation, with competitive bikers snapping on their helmets, setting their jaws, and muscling forward in grueling endurance mode.

Fun for some. But we wanted antique shops, general stores, white-steepled churches, cheese factories. We wanted Vermont.

Bike Vermont seemed like a logical choice. They've been in business for twenty years, and their brochure makes much of stopping along the way to sample local products, photograph a village, relax along a river. "No awards are given for finishing first," they say. The goal is for each rider to get to know the area. They also emphasize riding at your own pace. "If you want to cruise solo, we won't bug you," said Bike Vermont's Merna Flood. These folks are supportive but unobtrusive.

We chose Bike Vermont's weekend escape to the Three Mountain Inn in Jamaica, Vermont. Perhaps "Jamaica" rang our tourist bells. (In fact, we learned later that the town was probably named after the tropical island by an international trader.) Maybe it was the promise of two waterfalls. Maybe it was the cheese factory. The town is located in the southern part of the state, not far from Manchester, and the tour promised unpaved back roads threading through rural countryside.

The Three Mountain Inn, on the town common, has a well-deserved reputation for its fine food. Innkeepers Charles and Elaine Murray, escapees from New York City, have restored the 1790s colonial to cozy comfort. We suspect it's even cozier in winter; the complex has nine fireplaces. Stratton and Bromley ski areas are just minutes away.

At the post-dinner group

meeting, we discovered most of the riders were of similar mind: stressed-out city folk, looking to relax and see the sights. We'd cover plenty of turf. Saturday's route was 40.2 miles (including an optional but must-do side trip to Hamilton Falls), while Sunday's trip covered twenty miles. A support van would sweep the route, guides Rich Wolf and Sadie Drumm told us.

On day one, we cruised through six quaint villages, rarely sharing the road with an automobile. Sights along the way played like a Green Mountain State travelogue: farmlands (even a llama farm) with immaculate out-buildings; ponds; forests; a covered bridge; a general store; antique shops; maple sugar shacks; well-tended gardens; and the Grafton Village Cheese Factory. The restored village of Grafton, about nineteen miles into the ride, houses art galleries, the requisite olde tavern, and several handsome homes. We picked up lunch at the Grafton General Store and were lingering at an antique shop when a thunderstorm hit. So we hung around for an hour and bought a bench, making it one of the more expensive rainstorms we've ever encountered. We even stopped at a church rummage sale, something we'd never take the time to do back home.

We wrapped up the ride with a stop at Hamilton Falls, a

KITTY FORD SHEAR

A road less traveled. A cyclist emerges from a covered bridge at Bartonsville, Vermont.

pretty cascade with three crystalline pools. The guides offered to transport our bikes back to the inn so we could hike back, about a four-mile walk along the West River on an old railroad bed. We happily accepted. We'd wanted Vermont villages; now, we were maxing out on cows and countryside.

We awoke the next day with tight muscles and sore saddles. Those famed Vermont rolling hills had been more numerous than we'd realized. Today's ride would be completely different: a cruise to Stratton Mountain ski area. As mountain roads do, this one went up, steadily but gradually. Along the way, we passed mini-Stonehenge, a 100-foot-long arrangement of stones piled into patterns, precariously balanced. No one seems to know who's responsible for this attraction.

We conquered three hills, then checked out the Swiss Village at the ski resort, incongruous in July. Heading back, we took a hard turn toward Pikes Falls, a gentle waterfall with good picnic spots and a swimming hole.

Both days, many of the roads we toured were unpaved, giving us a glimpse of Vermont few tourists see, even on a touring bike. Even better, we felt free to putz, never under pressure to hurry. And we got a taste of those rolling hills that Vermonters like to brag about to "flatlanders." Even better, we got a taste of Vermont.

Martha's Vineyard and Nantucket, Massachusetts: Cape Cod Island-Hopping

Injury, Rough Seas, Rain: Can This Bike Trip Be Saved?

Nantucket. Martha's Vineyard. Sooner or later, every New Englander is drawn to these sister islands south of Cape Cod.

Nantucket, nicknamed the Gray Lady for the fog that often envelops her, is as picturesque as a place has a right to be, with cobblestone streets, stately sea captains' homes, and glorious beaches. A strong sense of history and preservationism prevails. Martha's Vineyard is the more cosmopolitan of the two. Closer to the mainland, it draws more tourists, and a goodly share of celebrities and politicians, to its winding back roads and windswept beaches. Farmland, fishing villages, and gingerbread cottages await the visitor to this intriguing island.

Visiting the islands is an essential part of the New England experience. The question is, how? We discovered an outfitter that runs a splendid island-hopping tour: BIKEriders.

Run by Eileen Holland and Lorenzo De Monaco, BIKEriders specializes in smallish groups (sixteen or less), so they're able to book small, elegant inns and intimate restaurants for their cyclists. This isn't for the camping-and-youth-hostels crowd; you have to spend a little more to sample the islands' best indulgences. A high level of service is part of the deal, so bikers can focus on fun, not logistics. The trip is rated beginner-to-moderate (their rating), with daily mileage an easy fifteen to thirty-five miles of flat to gently rolling terrain.

CONTACT: BIKEriders, Inc., P.O. Box 254, Boston, MA 02113; (800) 473-7040. The company runs bike trips in New England, Canada, and Italy. The island escape trip currently runs four times a season, June through mid-September.

HOW TO GET THERE: It varies, but typically, bikers on the Martha's Vineyard/Nantucket Five-Day Escape take the Hy-Line ferry from Hyannis, on the south coast of Cape Cod, to Martha's Vineyard. From Boston, take Route 3 south to the rotary in Sagamore. Cross Sagamore Bridge to Route 6. Follow Route 6 to Hyannis; at the end of the ramp, take a right on Route 132. At the rotary, take Barnstable Road and follow the signs for the Hy-Line to the Ocean Street docks. Other ferries leave from Woods Hole and New Bedford. Also, there are direct flights from Boston and New York. BIKEriders can arrange air tickets if necessary.

RATES: A five-day trip, including ferry service between islands, a harbor cruise, all breakfasts, all dinners but one, a picnic lunch, and van shuttle, costs $860 per person. Bike rental is $80; helmet use is free.

WHAT TO BRING: Your bike, if it has at least twelve speeds and is in excellent mechanical condition (otherwise, you can rent one); a helmet; padded bicycle shorts; T-shirts; bicycle gloves; biking shoes or other rigid-soled shoes; a windbreaker; sunglasses; wool or polypropylene underwear; long biking pants for colder weather; and sunscreen.

KIDS: These trips are not appropriate for young children, but may be okay for well-mannered biking teens; talk to the BIKEriders staff in advance.

SKILL LEVEL: This trip is fine for beginners, with 15- to 35-mile routes and support van rides provided if necessary. Some aerobic fitness is good. BIKEriders will provide a pretour training schedule.

Lugging a bike from island to island, ferry boat to ferry boat, may not seem like a big deal until you try it for a couple of days. Traveling with a bike group removes a lot of the hassle factor that can eat up precious time and pleasure on a vacation.

Our five-day island escape began on a Sunday in June. Almost immediately, we hit a snag in our plans: the ferry we'd planned to take from Hyannis was canceled due to the grounding of the *QEII*. (How often does that happen? Not a good omen.) With a couple of phone calls, we booked on another line, and were happily Vineyard-bound.

BIKEriders guides transported us to our lodgings, the Victorian Inn, smack in the center of Edgartown, a bustling waterfront town. Decked out in lush Victoriana, the inn was a cozy oasis amid the action (read: swells of summer visitors).

Our warm-up bike ride was a 12.8-mile round trip to Oak Bluffs, on a bicycle path along the ocean. The ride was flat and easy, especially with the wind at our backs, propelling us toward the colony of colorfully painted cottages. We explored the area, marveling that it was once the site of a tent city for fervent Methodists who gathered here from around the country for spiritual rejuvenation. Heading back to Edgartown, we could've used some divine intervention. Those brisk breezes were now headwinds. We were doing the Sisyphus thing—rolling one step forward, two steps back. Rescue came, without us so much as making a phone call, in the form of De Monaco in the BIKEriders minivan. This kind of service prevailed throughout the trip.

Dinner at Savoir Faire: Steamed mussels. Caesar salad. Grilled lobster. Chocolate torte. We ordered off the menu, rather than being limited to a choice of two entrees, as is the case with many packaged trips. This is one of the reasons we love active vacations: you can eat yourself silly and know you'll work it off the next day. Savoir Faire earns its reputation as one of the best places to dine on the island. Our group of eight (including the two guides), who ranged in age from teen to fifties, sat at two tiny tables and enjoyed good conversa-

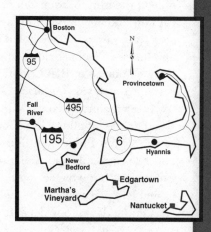

tion in the festive room. Everyone was in great spirits, anticipating a week of good weather, good food, and great riding.

Then, things started going wrong. On our first full day biking the Vineyard, half the group went to Gay Head, the other (our half) to the fishing village of Menemsha. The much-photographed fishing docks on Menemsha harbor are situated at the bottom of a hill. Upon reaching Menemsha, we heard a scream, and saw one of our party sprawled on the road. One of us was put in charge of the group, while Holland joined the injured woman in an ambulance. She had broken both wrists and sprained a shoulder, injuries not conducive to continuing a bike tour. She and her husband headed to the mainland.

More misery: it started to drizzle, and would continue to do so for the next two days. We opted for a minivan ride to Chicama Winery for a tour and tastings. While there, we toasted the health of our departed tourmate. Then we had dinner in Oak Bluffs at Jimmy Seas, whose satisfied diners have included a couple named Clinton.

The next day, we took a quick ferry ride to tiny Chappaquiddick Island with its infamous bridge, then pedaled around a bit before our departure for Nantucket. Bad weather here usually means rough seas, so some of us took motion sickness medication prior to the ferry crossing. Those who didn't were sorry.

Wet and grateful, we reached Nantucket. We walked a mile in the rain to Four Chimneys Inn, an antique-filled sea captain's home. Good thing it was comfortable, because, soaked to our skins, we holed up in our rooms with books and hot tea. No bike riding that afternoon. For dinner, we were on our own. BIKEriders supplied us with a list of restaurants in varying price ranges.

Over the next two days, in spite of less-than-ideal weather, we hit all the hot spots: Siasconset ("Sconset") Beach, Brant Point Lighthouse, Madaket, Jetty's Beach, and Nantucket Town. A planned lobster boat cruise was rained out, but we went with the theme, anyway, dining at a casual fish place called the Lobster Trap.

On the day of our departure, naturally, the weather

cleared up. Despite the unrelenting drizzle and resulting change of plans—mainly, a lot less biking than we'd hoped—we'd had a fine time, seeking shelter in nooks and crannies of Nantucket that we might've breezed past had the weather been better.

Had we arranged this trip ourselves, without the convenience of a minivan-at-the-ready and congenial guides with insider knowledge, the whole trip might have dissolved into misery. Perhaps that's an added bonus of traveling group-style: you stay on your best behavior, and are less likely to whine or sulk!

Mt. Washington, New Hampshire: Cycle to the Clouds

*It's Steep, Steep, Steep, Sub-Zero at the Top,
and Bikers Can't Wait to Climb It*

CONTACT: Mt. Washington Auto Road Bicycle Hillclimb, P.O. Box 278, Gorham, N.H. 03581; (603) 466-3988. The race is held annually in late August; contact the above address to register at least two months in advance.

HOW TO GET THERE: Meet at the Mt. Washington Auto Road entrance, off Route 16 in Gorham, N.H.

RATES: Entry fee is $40.

WHAT TO BRING: Expect it to be fairly windy and pretty cold up top. Most racers wear a cotton T-shirt; polypropylene layer; racing jersey; arm warmers; tights; gloves; biking shoes or booties; racing gloves; helmet. Essentially, you're dressing for the last mile-and-a-half.

KIDS: Age 17 and up.

SKILL LEVEL: You don't need to be a bike racer but you'd better have some solid experience in tackling hills.

You've seen the THIS CAR CLIMBED MT. WASHINGTON bumper stickers. How about earning one for your touring bike?

One day a year, the Mt. Washington Auto Road opens to cyclists willing to take on the challenge of pedaling up the highest peak in the Northeast. Not only do you ride—you race—straight up the mountain. The Mt. Washington Auto Road Bicycle Hillclimb or "Cycle to the Clouds" race is a benefit for Tin Mountain Conservation Center, a nonprofit environmental education organization. Anyone can enter, but beware: steepness and severe weather at the top make this one of the toughest bike races in America.

How tough? The seven-and-a-half-mile-plus ride, on smooth gravel and pavement, gains 4,727 feet in elevation. Average grade is twelve percent, but there are extended sections at eighteen percent, and the last 100 yards are a killer, gravity-defying twenty-two-percent grade. As for a course description, racer Jim Graham put it like this: "It's just one hill; you go up until there's no more 'up' left. There are no flat spots, no easy sections, and no places where you can rest."

Then there's the weather. Mt. Washington has the dubious distinction of having the world's worst. The highest wind observed on the Earth's surface was recorded here: 231 miles per hour. Located at the confluence of three different weather systems, there can be snow, hurricane-force winds, and below-zero temperatures any day of the year — even in late August, when the race is held. Amazingly, this event has been cancelled due to weather just twice since it began nearly twenty-five years ago. Temperatures at the summit over the past decade of races have ranged from fifty-six degrees to twenty-eight degrees with rime ice and thirty-five mile-per-hour winds. The race traditionally took place the Sunday after Labor Day, but, after weather cancellations in 1994 and 1995, the date was moved back to August to give riders a better shot at bearable conditions.

"It's a great race," said Joe Bucchiaglia of Willow Grove, Pennsylvania, 1995's top finisher. He's done the Hillclimb five times, and each time, he's startled anew at how imposing Mt. Washington is. "You look up at that mountain, and it's huge. You think, 'No way.' But once you're on that hill, you just feel good." Bucchiaglia's family can relate to his extreme avocation; his sister, father, brother-in-law, brother, and brother's girlfriend have all done the race. "Even if you don't win, you feel great when you reach the top, it's such an accomplishment," Bucchiaglia added, crediting his own super showing to a combination of hard training ("My specialty is hills.") and positive energy. Riding hills is a maximum workout, and takes a lot of mental strength, he says, but there's a reward at the end. "You look down, and you know you've done it."

Four hundred cyclists compete in this ultimate uphill challenge. All but twenty are selected on a first-come, first-served basis; an elite group is made up of Hillclimb veterans and other highly credentialed racers. But you need not be a professional racer to take on this knee-popper. "Ninety percent of the participants are just guys and gals who ride their bikes a lot and like a challenge," said Suzy Engler at Tin Mountain Conservation Center. "To do something this grueling, you have to be pretty crazy, too." Lots of people are; last year, more than 600 hopefuls vied for the 400 slots. Mark this one on your calendar now, and contact the committee no later than June to register.

Entrants pay forty dollars and are asked to raise funds through pledges. All the proceeds go to the Conservation Center, and the top fundraiser gets a pair of airline tickets. Bikers come from as far away as England, Canada, and the western U.S. to test their mettle. The top five finishers in categories from junior (age seventeen is the minimum) to senior grand master (age sixty-five and up) in men's and women's divisions win medals. The men's record of fifty-seven minutes, forty-one seconds was set in 1980 by Dale Stetina. Stetina's time will be tough to beat; he's a former U.S. National Cycling Champion and Olympic Team member. The women's record of one hour, fourteen minutes, twenty-three seconds was set by Murrie Green of Colchester, Vermont, in 1982. Torturous as it is to get to the top of Mt. Washington, don't plan on careening back down on your bike; this is a one-way race. You'll need a lift back down. And don't count on a big welcoming committee to greet you at the summit. This isn't much of a spectator event. As Engler noted: "There's only so much room at the top, and the top is miserable." Remember, even if it's fifty-some degrees and pleasant on the bottom, the summit is like another planet. Best strategy for spectators is to hike part way up the mountain to find a good vantage point.

This race, obviously, is not for Sunday-around-the-park cyclists. If you don't have thighs of steel and lungs like bellows, you'll never tame this beast. As racer Scott Wells said, "In the end, the mountain always wins. But without challenge, life would be a little less worth it."

Happy Trails: A Self-Guided Bike Path Sampler

Cycling along New England's designated bike trails is a great way to see the sights and get some exercise. Cruise these paths and say hello to scenery, good-bye to gridlock.

Within the wilderness of Maine's Acadia National Park on Mount Desert Island lies a network of fifty miles of carriage roads. These wide paths crisscrossing the interior of the island are designated for bicyclists, hikers, and horseback riders. The paths are flanked by stone retaining walls and crossed by thirteen hand-cut stone bridges. Call Acadia National Park: (207) 288-3338.

Surely the best way to tour New Hampshire's Franconia Notch is by bike. The paved eight-mile bike path begins at Echo Lake, the northernmost landmark in Franconia Notch State Park. Mostly downhill, the ride winds through some of the most beautiful scenery in the White Mountains. The path ends at the Flume Visitors' Center. Call the New Hampshire Division of Parks and Recreation, Trails Bureau: (603) 271-3254.

The Stowe Recreation Path in Stowe, Vermont, meanders over the West Branch River on eleven gracefully arched bridges. Limited to bikers and walkers, the 5.5-mile path links several village landmarks, with scenic views of the river and Mt. Mansfield, Vermont's loftiest peak. The greenway starts in the village behind the Community Church and ends on Brook Road. Call the Stowe Area Association: (802) 253-7321.

Massachusetts boasts more than 200 miles of designated bike trails. A couple of standouts: the Paul Dudley White–Charles River Bike Path, a 17.7-mile loop. This lively ride runs from the Museum of Science on the Cambridge side of the Charles River, crosses to the Boston side of the river and runs through the Esplanade to Watertown Square, then hops back across the Charles to Cambridge, returning to the Museum of Science. Lots of local color (and lots of fellow bikers, joggers, walkers, and skaters) on this loop.

The Cape Cod National Seashore has terrific bike trails, especially Province Lands Trail in Provincetown. This paved eight-mile trail winds through forests and around ponds, bogs, and spectacular sand dunes. Trail maps are available at the visitors centers in

Eastham and Provincetown. Call the Massachusetts Office of Travel and Tourism: (617) 727-3201.

Rhode Island's East Bay Bicycle Path is a 14.5-mile trail exclusively for cyclists and walkers. The paved pathway winds from Providence to Bristol, leading to several parks, Brickyard Pond, and the historic Loof carousel.

You'll share the road with cars, but not many, on Block Island, a biker's paradise. This eleven-square-mile island off Rhode Island's coast offers windswept country roads and bucolic scenery. Stop in at the chamber of commerce for a map marked with best roads for biking or pick one up at one of the many bike rental shops. Call the Rhode Island Tourism Division: (800) 556-2484 or (401) 277-2601.

Resources

Additional Outfitters

Bicycle Holidays, RD 3, Box 2934-CB, Middlebury, VT 05733; (802) 388-BIKE.

Country Inns Along the Trail, RR 3, Box 3115, Brandon, VT 05733; (802) 247-3300.

Cycle-Inn Vermont, P.O. Box 243, Ludlow, VT 05149; (802) 228-8799.

Green Mountain Bicycles, Route 100, P.O. Box 253, Rochester, VT 05767; (802) 767-4464.

Mountain Road Tours, 132 Peterborough Street, Jaffrey, NH 03452; (800) 636-8707 or (603) 532-8707.

Vermont Bicycle Touring, Box 711, Bristol, VT 05443; (800) 245-3868.

BOOKS

The Essential Touring Cyclist. Richard A. Lovett, Ragged Mountain Press.

Greg LeMond's Complete Book of Bicycling. Greg LeMond and Kent Gordis, Perigee Books.

Short Bike Rides in Connecticut. Edwin Mullen and Jane Griffith, Globe Pequot Press.

The Best Bike Rides in New England. Paul Thomas, Globe Pequot Books.

Twenty-Five Bicycle Tours in Vermont. John S. Freidin, Backcountry Publications.

Mountain Biking

222

Limerick, Maine:
10,000 Acres of World-Class Riding

Mud, Bogs, and Steeps — Way Off the Beaten Path

CONTACT: Backcountry Excursions, RFD 2, Box 365, Limerick, ME 04048; (207) 625-8189.

HOW TO GET THERE: Parsonsfield, Backcountry's base, is in the southwest corner of Maine, just over the New Hampshire border. You probably won't find it on a map. Backcountry will send very specific directions (involving back roads too numerous to mention here). Take Route 16 north to Ossipee, New Hampshire, then Route 25 east toward Portland, Maine. Take Route 160 south; from there, you'll need the written directions from Backcountry.

RATES: The standard two-day, two-night package costs $100 per person and includes lodging; two breakfasts; two lunches; trail snacks; and the use of showers, hot tub, and kitchen facilities. Ask about special rates and programs; Backcountry is always open to suggestions.

WHAT TO BRING: A mountain bike if you have one (if not, Backcountry has them for rent), a helmet, biking gloves, a swimsuit, and biking shoes or athletic shoes (avoid bulky hiking boots and shoes with bottom ridges — they get stuck on pedals with toe clips).

KIDS: All ages; if parents want to split up, smaller, nonriding children can do other activities in the area.

SKILL LEVEL: All levels, but you'd better be in shape; probably best appreciated by experienced riders.

Better not whine, moan, bellyache, whimper, squawk, or gripe when you go see Cliff Kroelick at Backcountry Excursions. No crybabies are allowed in this Maine playground for fat-tire cyclists. But the no-fear, mud-in-your-face crowd will think they've died and gone to bikers' heaven (or is it hell?)

Tucked away in the woods and hills of the southwest corner of Maine, Backcountry Excursions offers more than sixty miles of trails, way off the beaten path in a 10,000-acre timber preserve. It is the baby and brainchild of forty-something Kroelick, who runs this still-small operation single-handedly out of his home.

Lucky us, we inadvertently timed our visit to coincide with Dirt Camp, a gathering of six boys ranging in age from thirteen to fifteen—a mass of raging hormones and popping adrenal glands. We began with a few tips on technique from Kroelick, who instructed us as we circled around his backyard. "Get up off the seat." "Downshift now; again; again. Now, shift up; again. Up off your seat." Within a short time, we went from, "Okay, how do you drive this thing?" to "Let's go, we're ready."

It was time for the warm-up ride, or, as Kroelick called it, "our wake-up call." Fifteen minutes later, we were sucking for air, sizzling from heat, and dripping with sweat as we grunted our way up a gravity-challenging road. Mud. Bogs. Logs. Boulders. Another climb. Slapping rose thorns. Another climb. Relief came at the banks of a shallow, clear creek.

While some of the teenagers practiced their jumps, bumps, and aerials, the sane ones among us cooled down.

Actually, we were starting to have fun. Kroelick's love of the outdoors and his enthusiasm for seeing it over the handlebars works like a potion; his passion is contagious. And this is beautiful country—wild woods, rolling hills, rambling streams, blueberry fields forever. By the time you've reached the top of the summit or the bottom of the valley, you've earned the scenic reward that awaits.

You don't have to be an experienced mountain biker to enjoy Backcountry Excursions. While most of the terrain is for intermediate to advanced riders, beginners will find miles of lovely, gently rolling roads. All rides are guided by Kroelick; it's too easy to get lost on your own. Depending on interests and abilities, guests usually go out for two-and-a-half-hour rides in the morning and the afternoon. If that isn't enough grinding and bumping for you, you can play in Backcountry's new Rock and Log Palace, a 3,500-square-foot technical terrain garden.

And there's more to Backcountry than mountain biking. Guests can go canoeing or tubing on nearby Little Ossipee River or spend an afternoon antiquing in the surrounding towns and villages. We headed to Long Pond, a shallow, sandy lake perfect for swimming, about fifteen minutes away.

Staying at Backcountry is like visiting an out-of-town friend. Accommodations are simple and casual; there are two modest bedrooms on the ground floor of the house and cots in a yurt in the backyard. You're also free to pitch your own tent wherever you like. Meals consist of wholesome, high-energy food: lunch is fresh veggies and fruits, nut butter, falafel burgers, and hummus; breakfast may be homemade granola or blueberry waffles. Dinners are pot-luck; bring a dish to share. Everyone pitches in with cooking chores and clean-up. (Wouldn't you know it? That's about the time fatigue hit the younger guests.) No excuses accepted; every-one helps out here. After dinner and an evening soak in the wood-fired hot tub, we crawled into our sleeping bags.

The next day we set out to tackle the much-talked-about Cedar and Wiggin Mountain loop, seventeen miles of world-class biking. Backcountry Excursions calls it the "most variety of terrain on any single trail in the U.S." Gut Buster, Stream Bed Bopper, Yikes, and Downhill Flight are some of the aptly named sections of this trail.

So what if some of us didn't make it to the tippy-top of Cedar Mountain? So what if our arms felt like dead grapevines and our legs were a quivering mess?

No fear. We'll be back.

Mount Snow, Vermont: Learn from the Pros

On the Fast Track to Single Track

CONTACT: Mount Snow Mountain Bike Center, Mount Snow, VT 05356; (800) 245-SNOW. In addition to the general mountain bike clinics, Mount Snow offers several special-interest sessions, including women's weekends, inn-to-inn tours, family weekends, wilderness overnight weekends, and fall foliage tours.

HOW TO GET THERE: From I-91, take Exit 2 to Route 9 west. Go 20 miles to Wilmington, then turn right on Route 100 north. It's 9 miles to Mount Snow.

RATES: The weekend school costs $145; $165 with bike rental.

WHERE TO STAY: Mount Snow is located in Vermont's scenic Deerfield Valley. You can camp in one of several state parks or in Green Mountain National Forest. There are also country inns, B & Bs, lodges, and condominiums for rent. We stayed at the lovely Mountaineer Inn, P.O. Box 140, Handel Road, West Dover, VT 05356; (802) 464-5404. The Mountaineer is located at the base of Mount Snow in a twenty-five-acre meadow bordered by two brooks and a nature path. For complete lodging and camping options, call Mount Snow Vacation Services, (800) 245-SNOW.

WHAT TO BRING: Casual clothes; a swimsuit; biking shoes or athletic shoes (no ridges on the soles—they get stuck in pedals with toe clips); a water bottle; and a small pack for carrying personal items.

KIDS: Twelve and up on general mountain bike weekend clinics. Ask about special family weekends.

SKILL LEVEL: All levels, but you should be in good physical condition.

Riding a bike; how tough can it be? We hopped on with confidence, stuck our toes in the clips, and took off down a rocky, twisted single track, over a log—yikes!—over the handlebars. By the end of the long, torturous day, bodies battered and egos bruised, we had to admit: There's a lot more to mountain biking than we thought.

You know the saying, "It's like riding a bike—once you learn, you never forget"? Well, fat-tire pedaling is not the same kind of biking you learned when you were five.

"It's difficult to convince people that they need two full days of instruction just to ride a bike," said Meri Spicer, a marketing manager for the Mount Snow Mountain Bike Center. "But it's the best way to get started in the sport."

Quick, where was the first mountain biking school established? If you guessed one of the obvious locations, like Colorado, New Mexico, or Utah, you're wrong. In 1988, Mount Snow, in hilly Vermont, entered the very young mountain bike market with the country's first school. It continues to offer innovative techniques and programs, and instructors from around the world come here to learn how to teach.

We decided to do our bodies a favor by signing up for one of Mount Snow's weekend mountain biking clinics. Besides, we had to see if this school was all it was cracked up to be.

We met our classmates—three women, mid-twenties to mid-forties, and a sixty-five-year-old man—and our instructor, Bob Svec, at breakfast the first morning. Svec grinds moguls in the winter (he's a ski instructor at Mount Snow) and bike gears in the warmer months. After introductions and bike and equipment hand-outs, we headed for the parking lot. Yes, the parking lot; not very scenic, but it's where we learned our first maneuvers. "Let's see you do some figure-eight turns," Svec said. "Slow down. Slower. Keep it in low gear." Piece of cake, until he

squeezed the figure-eight, forcing us to make tighter and tighter turns. Everyone has a favorite side; it's easier to turn right for some, left for others. The chocolate side, we call it. We noticed that Svec was sweet on both sides.

During the second drill we begin to learn about the three basic mountain biking body positions: up and in front of the seat; up and in back of the seat; and horizontal on the pedals, off the seat. Who would have thought it was so technical?

Svec drew a line in the sand and asked us to "hop" over it. No problem. As we biked over the line, he offered instruction, "Lighten up your front wheel, bring your torso and body up and over the seat. Lift the bars. Now, shift forward and pedal harder to get your rear tire over." Say what? All this to get over a line in the sand? He replaced the line with a stick, and then with a bigger stick. Ahhh . . . SPLAT! The gentleman in our group took his first tumble. He was all right, and climbed back on to try it again. By the time we got to a smallish log, we were learning that all this tech talk about position and balance really does mean something.

But enough drills; we were ready for the real stuff, and headed out to do some off-road biking. We followed a dirt path, climbing a few hills and avoiding most of the rocks. Twenty minutes later, we found ourselves on a rock-strewn, narrow section of single track. "You can do this," Svec encouraged us. One by one, we gave it a whirl. Svec ran alongside our bikes, offering instructions, holding our seats for balance, catching us before we tumbled down or took off too fast. We felt like kids who just had the training wheels taken off their bikes.

Hairpin turn next. Ahhh . . . SPLAT! Tumble number two. The gentleman wasn't the only one to fall. Staying on (single) track was not so easy.

Stream crossing next. Ahhh . . . SPLAT! But some of us were starting to put it together—little jumps over the sticks, smooth sailing across the gravel, all the way up the hill without stopping, across the river without falling. And we were starting to give our fellow classmate (Ahhh . . . SPLAT!) a lot of room—and credit. We were surprised when he returned after lunch. (Lunch, by the way, was great: an all-you-can-eat barbecue on the deck overlooking Mount Snow's 3,600-foot summit and the scenic Deerfield Valley.)

In the afternoon, we tried our newly acquired skills on Mount Snow's midmountain intermediate course. You have to be a mountain biker to even consider calling this a course. To most, it's a big ravine full of rocks and boulders, something you'd definitely want to go around, not through. But through it we went, down one side and up the other. It required all our positions, balance, and a lot of muscle. Look out! Ahhh . . . SPLAT! (The gentleman was beginning to look a bit disheveled. "Like a piece of meat," one participant colorfully stated.) Who were we to talk? No one got out of this drill without a little coloring (black and blue). We were feeling pretty proud of ourselves, until an intermediate class whizzed by, dropped into the ravine and climbed up the other side like they were on a conveyor belt.

The last ride of the day took us down a steep section of dirt road (not single track). We practiced standing horizontally on our pedals and controlling our descent, in preparation for the next section, a steeper single track through a very dense stand of trees. "There's going to be about fifteen feet of moderate grade, and then there's some rocks before it gets a little steeper. . . . " Svec was walking us through it. Who was listening? We were getting chicken skin just looking at the incline, imagining a high-speed, head-on collision with an oak tree. "Just psyche yourself up for it," Svec told us. Half of the group went for it. The other half skirted around the perimeter on a bail-out trail.

The first day ended with a pool party, at which most of the beginner class hogged the hot tub.

Were we better the next day? You betcha'. (Though Mr. Ahhh . . . SPLAT! didn't show up.) We stuck to most of the same trails but pedaled them with a lot more confidence, a lot more speed, and less stop and go. And by the end of the day, we were whizzing by the new beginner group—down and up the ravine like we were on a conveyor belt.

Marlboro, Vermont: A Green Mountain Endurance Builder for Experienced Riders Only

Neither Rain nor Sleet nor Gale-Force Winds Will Stop These Folks from Biking

CONTACT: Bike the Light Fantastic, 195 Goodenough Road, Brattleboro, VT 05301; (802) 257-2612.

HOW TO GET THERE: Each tour begins at a different location. We met at the Whetstone Inn in Marlboro. Take Route 9 west from Exit 2 on I-91 (Brattleboro). Follow the signs to Marlboro (about 9 miles from I-91). The Whetstone is in the center of town, on your right.

RATES: Our trip cost $280 per person, including lodging, meals, and guides.

WHAT TO BRING: A mountain bike, a helmet, bike shorts, riding gloves, rain gear, a warm jacket, sunglasses, sunscreen, bug repellent, a water bottle, and a small pack for personal items.

KIDS: Not unless they're older, and avid cyclists.

SKILL LEVEL: The folks here say no mountain biking experience is really necessary as long as you're in good shape, but we suggest you have at least basic skills; this trip is demanding.

If you make your living riding the back roads up and down the mountains of New England, you're likely to have a different view of things than the rest of us. "Ho-hum, just another 500-foot elevation climb," he who rides all day, most days, must think. Meanwhile, the rest of us are likely to grunt and groan, our thighs screaming, our lungs bursting.

Snatches of our initial conversation with John Ferrara, co-owner (with Suzan Sutton) of Bike the Light Fantastic, in Brattleboro, Vermont, came back to us as we mashed the pedals to make another steep climb. "Best if you have some experience with mountain biking . . . good physical condition . . . hilly . . . spirited riding. . . ." We should have listened more carefully. Ferrara, we decided, is a master of understatement. Or perhaps this is a poignant example of the theory of relativity.

We prayed the terrain would level out, that around the next switchback there'd be a thank-God gradual descent. Of course, it didn't, and there wasn't. If we wanted flat and smooth, we should have signed up for a tour in Kansas. Instead, we were on one of Bike Fantastic's riding weekends, a two-day dirt-road tour of south-central Vermont.

The first day was miserable. "Haven't seen it rain like this for fifteen years," said the proprietor of a small general store when we rushed inside, leaving puddles on the floor. We had stopped for lunch and a drying-out, and watched as the storm grew fiercer. Sheets of rain poured off the roof, forming a waterfall in front of the store windows. But mountain bikers are a rugged bunch; why let a little rain stop us? We still had at least another ten miles back to the inn. We were on the Sunset Lake Ride, a 25.7-mile loop of country roads, dirt paths, jeep tracks, and single track. (Yes, you read that right: 25.7 miles of off-road mountain biking; that's a lot.) It's a tough up-and-down ride in the best of weather, and we were battling winds and torrential rains, pedaling on washed-out trails that a four-wheel-drive truck would get stuck in. It was beginning to feel like survival school.

Of course, the folks at Bike the Light Fantastic can't control the weather, and they certainly didn't make us ride. In fact, they made it as pleasant and safe as they possibly could. There were three guides (Sutton, Ferrara, and their friend Jerry) and four guests,

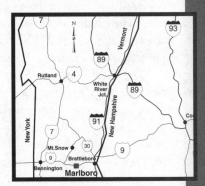

so there was always someone to help and encourage us along, or take us back if we'd had enough. They were also in radio contact with a van driver. Two people in the group had already called for rescue (after about the third uphill climb, before it started to pour); they were on their way back to the inn. The rest of the group decided to suck it up and pedal back. Halfway up the last few climbs, we dismounted; burnt out, we pushed the bikes up the hill. Everyone, that is, except Sutton and a woman named Myra. This was Myra's third mountain biking trip in as many months; the other two were in the Rockies. She was in her late fifties and clearly in another league; she rode circles around us all day. Later we asked her how this trip compared to biking out West. "The riding is not as technical, but endurancewise, this is as tough as, if not tougher than, anything I've done," she said.

That evening, we licked our wounds and refueled our bodies at the Whetstone Inn in Marlboro, Vermont, our base for the weekend. The Whetstone was built some 200 years ago as a tavern and stage stop. It's not fancy, and the innkeeper was a bit gruff (we heard him snap at one guest who "crossed the line" into the private kitchen, looking for a cup of coffee), but it was adequate. We collapsed into bed early. If there is a God, we thought, the rain will stop, the sun will shine, and the hills will flatten tomorrow.

Two out of three isn't bad. The next day we rode under clear blue skies. Sutton told us there are 7,366 miles of unpaved roads in Vermont (and only 6,530 miles of paved roads). Mountain biking the back roads, farm lanes, old stage routes, abandoned pathways, and logging trails opens up an otherwise hidden world of lush forests, meadows, ponds, lakes, streams, and waterfalls. It is clear that Sutton and Ferrara are not foreigners in this land; they know their way around.

The trails were no easier the second day, but the rewards were greater: stunning vistas, raging rivers (all the more so because of the rain), lush meadows, mountain ponds, tumbling waterfalls—and solitude. Lew Dietz wrote of adventure in *A Touch of Wildness:* "It is not so much the pain we seek, but the honing of the spirit."

Spirited riding . . . perhaps that's what Ferrara meant.

Various Sites: Pounding the Slopes

When the Snow Melts, New England Ski Resorts Turn into Mountain Biking Meccas

CONTACT: For more information, write or call the particular location you're interested in.

Sugarloaf/USA, RR 1 Box 5000, Carrabassett Valley, ME 04947; (800) THE-LOAF.

Sunday River Mountain Bike Park, P.O. Box 450, Bethel, ME 04217; (800) 543-2SKI.

Loon Mountain Park, Kancamagus Highway, Lincoln, NH 03251; (603) 745-8111.

Killington Mountain Bike Center, Killington Resort, Killington, VT 05751; (800) 372-2007 or (802) 422-6232.

RATES: Each resort has a number of mountain biking packages. Generally, bike rentals cost $20 to $35 a day. Lift tickets, to carry you and your bike up the mountain, cost around $25. Weekend packages, including rentals, trail and lift passes, and lodging, run from $85 to $125 per person.

WHAT TO BRING: A backpack for carrying snacks, lunches, etc.; a water bottle; and bug repellent. Padded bike shorts are nice.

KIDS: Yes, if they can ride a bike.

SKILL LEVEL: All levels.

If you want to skip the lung-bursting, tortuous uphill climbs and go directly to the exhilarating plunge down, check out New England's ski resorts. Come summer, these winter parks turn into fat-tire paradises. Chairlifts are outfitted with special bike-carrying racks; ski stores turn into bike rental shops; spandex replaces fleece.

But don't think the black diamonds get any easier to tackle when the snow melts. Rocks, boulders, sticks, tree stumps, roots . . . it's amazing what lurks under a five-foot base of snow. Moguls? Yep, they're still there: rock piles to jump, trees to avoid, all at a speed that will squash bugs against your sunglasses and leave you gasping for air. And you thought going downhill was the easy part!

At Sugarloaf/USA, bikers can ride all day without ever touching hardtop. The fifty-three-mile mountain bike park incorporates Sugarloaf's Nordic ski network and some of its alpine trails. The park, nestled between Sugarloaf, Crocker, and Bigelow Mountains, covers more than 7,000 acres. Maps, tours, and shuttle drop-off and pick-up service are available from the Sugarloaf Bike Shop.

We love the views and solitude here. You can meander through tall stands of spruce and birch, take in unparalleled views of towering peaks, swim in a secluded pond or stream—even see a moose, if you're lucky. How tough are the trails? That's up to you. But even on the beginner routes, you ride hills and get muddy.

Get a map and go it alone, or take a guided ride. (Half-day excursions lasting three hours, and full-day trips, from 9 A.M. to 3 P.M., are offered.)

You'll need a full-suspension bike and padded shorts to scream downhill at Sunday River's Mountain Bike Park. You'll maneuver through thirty-five miles of ruts, rocks, and roots on a single track, or coast along on the dirt service roads. With or without a guide, riders have access to a variety of terrain, with the western mountains of Maine as a backdrop.

When you've met the challenge at the park, explore the back roads through rolling farm country, atop mountain ridgelines, or along lazy rivers. Or sign up for one of Sunday River's High Mountain Adventures and combine mountain biking with other activities, such as hiking, canoeing, kayaking, and fly-fishing.

Experienced riders can take the gondola up to Loon Mountain's 3,000-foot summit. How good do you have to be to make it safely back to the base lodge? The bike shop manager responded by pointing to a set of steep stairs leading to the lower level of the store.

"If you can take your bike up and down those stairs without even giving it a second thought, then you can consider it. Otherwise, don't even think about going up there," he said. Loon's thrills-and-chills single track trails require technical expertise and a daredevil, go-for-it attitude.

At the base, it calms down, and riders of all abilities can pedal more than thirty-five kilometers of cross-country trails. You can cruise along the east branch of the Pemigewassett River, in and out of scenic woods, and on back roads.

We like Loon's special Franconia Notch bike tour. They'll bus you and your bike to Echo Lake, the northernmost landmark of Franconia Notch State Park. The thirteen-mile ride back — mostly downhill — is on a paved bike path that winds through some of the most beautiful scenery in the White Mountains. The trail back to Loon takes about an hour-and-a-half, but you can spend a day at it.

Across from Echo Lake is the trailhead to Artist's Bluff. Hide your bike in the bushes and hike to the top of the bluff, which overlooks Echo Lake and Cannon Mountain to one side and the jagged, spiraling peaks of Franconia to the other.

Back on the bike path, you'll ride by the New England Ski Museum, at the base of Cannon Mountain; Profile Lake; and the best viewing spot for eyeing the Old Man of the Mountains. Farther down, you'll bike to The Basin, an interesting river formation and a great place for a picnic. The bike path ends at the famous Flume, a natural gorge extending 800 feet, with towering granite walls. (Admission to the Flume is about $6 per person.) You'll follow Route 3 and then the Kancamagus Highway back to Loon.

At the Killington ski area, you and your bike can ride the one-and-a-quarter-mile-long chairlift to the 4,241-foot summit. On a clear day, you'll have panoramic views of five states and Canada. Take a moment to enjoy them when you first get off the chair; you'll soon be hanging on for dear life, dodging stumps, skidding across dirt, and bunny-hopping over rock pits. Even the "easy way down" trail is challenging: single-track uphill climbs and long, gravel work-road descents.

Beginners should consider Killington's two-hour tour of the mountain, with instruction on riding and bike handling and exposure to varied terrain.

Resources

Additional Outfitters

Adventure Guides of Vermont, P.O. Box 3, North Ferrisburg, VT 05473; (802) 425-6211.

Attitash/Bear Peak, Route 302, Bartlett, NH 03812; (603) 374-2368.

Balsams Grand Resort, Dixville Notch, NH 03576; (800) 255-0600, or (800) 255-0800 in New Hampshire.

Bolton Valley Mountain Bike and Adventure Center, P.O. Box 10, Bolton, VT 05477; (800) 451-3220 or (802) 434-2131.

Bretton Woods Summer Park, Route 302, Bretton Woods, NH 03575.

Catamount Family Center, 421 Governor Chittenden Road, Williston, VT 05495; (802) 879-6001.

Cortina Inn, HCR-34, Killington, VT 05751; (802) 773-3331 or (800) 451-6108.

Craftsbury Center, Box 31, Craftsbury Common, VT 05827; (800) 729-7751 or (802) 586-2514.

Great Glen Falls, P.O. Box 300, Gorham, NH 03581; (603) 466-2333.

Mountain Bike Touring Center, Hyde Away Inn, Route 17, Waitsfield, VT 05673; (800) 777-4933 or (802) 496-2322.

Waterville Valley Resort, P.O. Box 252, Waterville Valley, NH 03215; (800) GO-VALLEY.

BOOKS

Fat Tire Rider. Kennedy, Kloser, and Samer; Vitesse Press.

Mountain Bike! William Nealy, Menasha Ridge Press.

Mountain Bike New Hampshire. Stuart Johnstone, Active Publications.

The Mountain Biker's Guide to Northern New England. Paul Angiolillo, Falcon Press.

Twenty-Five Mountain Bike Tours in Massachusetts. Robert S. Morse, Backcountry Publications.

Twenty-Five Mountain Bike Tours in Vermont. William S. Busher, Backcountry Press.

Vermont Mountain Biking: The Best Back Road and Trail Rides in Southern Vermont. Dick Mansfield, Acorn Publishing.

Resources

Rock Climbing and Caving

North Conway, New Hampshire: Kids on the Rocks

Youngsters Learn the Ropes in This Introductory Climbing Course

CONTACT: Eastern Mountain Sports Climbing School, P.O. Box 514, North Conway, NH 03860; (603) 356-5433. EMS Climbing School offers a variety of courses, including basic and intermediate rock lessons, three- and four-day programs, learn-to-lead programs, self-rescue, direct aid, alpine climbs, top-rope/single pitch management, and guided expeditions. The kids' classes are offered four times a month from April through October, and are limited to a maximum of five students.

HOW TO GET THERE: Take Route 16 to North Conway. EMS Climbing School operates out of the Eastern Slope Inn, in the center of town. You can't miss it.

RATES: The intro course costs $65 per child.

WHAT TO BRING: Comfortable clothing, a small backpack for personal items, a light lunch, and a water bottle. EMS supplies all equipment.

KIDS: Children's classes are for seven- to twelve-year-olds; adolescent courses are for those twelve to fifteen.

PARENTS: For safety reasons, parents are not allowed to watch the class. But this is North Conway, home to outlet shops, boutiques, restaurants, golf courses, hiking trails, scenic train rides, and more. Grown-ups will have no trouble finding fun in this town.

SKILL LEVEL: All levels.

Be careful." "Get down from there!" "Watch your step." "Don't go any higher." A family stroll in the forest can turn parents into safety guards. Rocks, boulders, logs, trees—what child can resist monkeying around in such an inviting playground?

Parents, forget about keeping kids down to earth. Instead, tap that natural energy and enthusiasm and sign them up for Eastern Mountain Sports' Children's Introduction to Climbing course. The day-long program, designed for kids ages seven to twelve, was introduced in 1992, and participation is soaring. "It's been unbelievable," said EMS Climbing School manager Joe Lentini. "Kids are getting into climbing like they never have before."

Sadie, our ten-year-old volunteer, joined Buddy and Gee Gee, a brother-sister team from Vermont, at EMS headquarters in North Conway, New Hampshire. After being fitted for harnesses, helmets, and shoes, the three kids and instructor Paul Allen Cail drove out to nearby White Horse Ledge. Faced with the towering 1,200-foot granite slab, the peanut gallery said, "Holy Cow! We're not going up that, are we?" But after a short hike to the bottom of the ledge, and lots of reassurances, the kids were ready to begin.

The lesson started with basic safety rules, a look at the equipment, and knot tying. In the time it would take most adults to adjust their helmet straps, these three kids were in and out of their swami belts several times and were tying retraced figure eights and keeper knots with their eyes closed.

To ensure safety, the kids were hooked to a top-rope that ran from a belayer on the ground, up through a mounted anchor, and back down to the climber. They began to crawl and climb their way along the bottom of the slab.

"Take a fall," Cail instructed Sadie. "I want you to see how it feels."

Tentatively, she let go of her grip and took a soft, subtle slide before the rope caught her. "Wow, that's it?" she said. "I didn't even fall."

They each gave it a try, and, held by the rope, learned to trust their moves. They made several different ascents, gaining confidence, agility, and speed. By lunchtime, they were ready for bigger and tougher mountains. "This is easy stuff," Gee Gee said. "Yeah, we want some hard climbs!" her two buddies chimed in. Cail, who's been climbing for almost twenty years, and frequently teaches the kids' program, knew this was coming. The morning was designed to be a confidence-builder; the afternoon would be spent on Satan's Climb.

Three pairs of wide eyes peered up at a very vertical chunk of granite. "Paul, you have to go up first and show us how to do it," Buddy said. "No way," Cail quipped. "It scares me to death!"

Cail did go first, jamming his hands and feet into a tiny crack, crawling around a corner ledge, and finally lifting himself up to the ridge. He placed protection hardware along the route. "Who's next?" he asked when he got back down on the ground, ready to belay.

Sadie scrambled up first, slipping and sliding, grunting and groaning, heaving and huffing, and never giving up. Cail, on belay, coached her from the ground. "Stretch a little, Sadie." "Look for a hold to your left." "You're doing great." Gee Gee and Buddy cheered her on. She made it! The quick rappel down left her laughing and begging to go up again.

Gee Gee followed the same path, and with lots of encouragement reached the top. She was glad to get her feet back on the ground.

A reluctant Buddy went last. Halfway up he began to have doubts. "He's got Elvis Presley legs," Sadie whispered. Buddy was shaking and hugging the rock for dear life.

"Do you play checkers, Buddy?" Cail asked.

"This ain't no time to talk about checkers," Buddy yelled down.

Cail was trying to get him to plan his next couple of moves. It didn't work. But coaxing and guidance did, and Buddy slowly inched his way up until he reached the top. Cheers all around.

"So, isn't it great?" "How do you like it?" the girls shouted to Buddy.

Still on top of the ledge, catching his breath and gathering his courage, he yelled down, "I hate it!"

Guess rock climbing isn't for everyone, after all.

North Conway, New Hampshire: Learning to Lead on White Mountain Ledges

Attitude and Altitude Don't Mix on This Mountain Adventure

CONTACT: Mountain Guides Alliance, Box 266, North Conway, NH 03860; (603) 356-5310. The Alliance is a referral agency representing independent guides. Michael Jewell can also be reached at (603) 356-7738.

HOW TO GET THERE: Guides make individual arrangements. Usually, they meet at the Ragged Mountain Equipment store, 3 miles north of North Conway on Route 16.

RATES: One-day rates, per person, are $165 for a private lesson, $125 for a group of two, and $110 for a group of three. Discounts are offered for three days or more of instruction.

WHAT TO BRING: A small backpack for personal items, a light lunch, and water. Wear comfortable clothing. Alliance guides supply all technical equipment, including shoes, harnesses, ropes, helmets, and hardware.

KIDS: Yes. Classes are designed to suit individual needs.

SKILL LEVEL: All skill levels.

We were ascending Funhouse, a 5.7 climb up the side of a jagged granite cliff. Odd name for a route that stretches muscles into tight coils and relentlessly tests mental endurance. Someone has a perverse sense of humor, we thought. We renamed the route Mean Streak.

The lead climber was just about to attempt a long run-out when our instructor asked, softly, "Did you say you have an eight-month-old daughter?"

Zing! A simple question that spoke volumes. The climber had forgotten to place an important piece of protection.

This is the kind of quiet, patient, and serious care you get when you go out with a guide from the Mountain Guides Alliance. The Alliance represents a group of professional New England guides who provide instruction in rock climbing, ice climbing, and safe leadership on guided climbs. Their credentials are mighty: all guides have more than sixteen years of experience, with extensive knowledge of weather and climbing conditions, and they are considered to be some of the best climbers in the region. They are also some of the best teachers. Mention Mountain Guides Alliance to someone who's done a little climbing, and the response is predictable: "Oh, the serious guides. I'm not good enough to climb with them yet." Those who've been around more know better. The Mountain Guides Alliance will teach and guide anyone, from novice to expert. If a true love of the outdoors and an awe of the untamed and wild has a grip on your soul, you're well-suited to climbing with an Alliance teacher.

If you want to climb a mountain just to say you've done it, however, forget the Alliance. Macho attitudes are not allowed. These instructors take a Zenlike approach to climbing, emphasizing body movement, balance, and grace, as well as the ethereal and emotional benefits of ascending rock.

"This group is still in touch with the basic tenets of climbing," said Jonathan Wagman after his first guided climb with the Alliance. "They teach the simplistic beauty of rock climbing, the introspective opportunity to be an individual. Not to climb harder and longer, but to learn a sport you can continue throughout your life."

We booked a one-day lead assessment course with the Alliance. Our first exercise was a pretrip phone interview with instructor Michael Jewell. He wanted to know our level of experience, how many days we'd been climbing, how much formal teaching we'd had, where we were in our climbing career, and, most importantly, what we wanted to get from the day. "What do you want to walk away with?" he asked. Just walking away would be good, we quipped, but then we talked at length about our goals and climbing aspirations.

Jewell began climbing in 1977, and has climbed extensively throughout the United States. Asked why he climbs, he replied, "It is better than anything else in life." His passion for climbing and for teaching is instantly apparent.

We met Jewell in North Conway, New Hampshire, and drove to Funhouse, just a few minutes away. Jewell bouldered to the top of the climb and rappelled down to watch our lead. He developed this system of prussiking (using mechanical ascending devices) along the leader rope to allow him to be side-by-side with the student, but not on the same rope. The student is safe, but on her/his own.

He followed us step by step, watching our placements, offering support, and asking questions. "Which way do you think this will pull?" "How much force do you think this piece will have to hold if you fall from where you are?" As we groped and stretched, wedged and jammed, stemmed and slipped our way upward, Jewell—and the mountain— constantly reminded us of efficient body movements and tested our problem-solving skills.

"Remember, lead climbing is a dynamic dance requiring a complete awareness of the system," Jewell said as we placed belaying devices and then grappled up the steep pitch.

Despite the physical and mental challenges (or perhaps because of them), we were exhilarated by the end of the climb. Afterward, Jewell went over his observations and finished with a comprehensive review of his assessment and recommendations. We closed the day at a practice wall, once again reviewing the basics of lead climbing and going over our individual strengths and weaknesses.

Jewell contends that "the desire to climb is inherent in everyone." One thing is for sure: If you don't have it at the beginning of the day, you'll surely possess it at the end.

Manchester, Vermont: Spelunking Spectacular Morris Cave

Here's a Trip That Gives New Meaning to "Stuck Between a Rock and a Hard Place"

CONTACT: Green Mountain Adventures, P.O. Box 1711, Manchester Center, VT 05255; (802) 362-1202. Green Mountain Guides are wilderness EMTs trained in first aid. Cave guides are members of the National Speleological Society and promote safe, minimal-impact caving practices. Green Mountain Adventures also runs trips to other caves in New England, as well as rafting, canoeing, hiking, and combination trips. Winter camping in New Hampshire's Presidentials is a specialty.

HOW TO GET THERE: Morris Cave is in Dorset Mountain in Manchester, Vermont. The trip meets at Wild World on Route 7A in Manchester; you'll drive to the cave from there.

RATES: The excursion, including transportation from local lodgings, lunch, gear, and a guide, costs $85 for one person, $125 for two, $195 for a group of four, and $25 for each additional person.

WHAT TO BRING: They'll provide a jumpsuit and other caving gear; bring clothes for layering underneath it, such as a polypropylene turtleneck, a fleece shell (preferably hooded, to protect your hair), and a T-shirt. Plan on getting filthy. Bring garden gloves, knee pads (inexpensive ones are fine), tennis shoes, and a change of clothing. Also, bring a flashlight with fresh alkaline batteries, and four extra AA batteries for a headlamp, which they provide.

KIDS: Age twelve and up, depending on the child.

SKILL LEVEL: This is a fairly intense caving experience, best for experienced cavers.

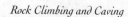

Winnie the Pooh getting stuck in the honey pot. Alice in Wonderland going down the rabbit hole. These are the images likely to go through one's head when stuck inside a cave. How do we know? We'll get to that.

Spectacular. That's how spelunkers refer to Morris Cave, Vermont's most popular, most visited cave, and the largest in New England. It is an all-marble labyrinth with 1,845 feet of explored passage, 240 of them under water. Its most extraordinary feature is a crystal-clear lake.

Morris Cave was once thought to be several short caves, but in 1963, Ron Morris dug out some clay in the entrance, thus revealing the cave's true size.

But don't let the overall dimensions fool you: Morris Cave has some fiendishly tight passages, so skinny that a warning should be posted by the entrance: "Abandon hope, all ye husky, big-boned, or voluptuous ones who enter here."

The cave is located in an abandoned lime quarry a few miles north of Manchester. Cavers park roadside, then walk about five minutes to the entrance.

Knowing that New England caving is a damp, muddy affair, we dressed for the occasion in neoprene Farmer John–style wetsuits, polypropylene turtlenecks, and, on top, coveralls lent us by Green Mountain Adventures guides Charlie Cummings and Matt Moses. We also donned knee pads (the inline-skating type) and neoprene paddling gloves. We strapped on helmets with headlamps, provided by the guides.

Cummings ran through the basics of safe, low-impact caving. Then, in we went, one guide in the lead, the other at the rear. Michelle Mato, a guide in training, rounded out our group of six.

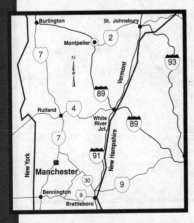

First, some simple climbing, then a long, slow slide down a gravelly tunnel. We moved down a passage called the Cobble Crawl to the first tricky spot, called the Wet Pinch. Wet, indeed—the guides bailed fifteen big buckets of water from this tiny tunnel. This gave us a chance to get oriented to the cave. It takes some time to get used to the eerie sensation of pitch-blackness. As one caver said, "You know it's dark when you can hold up your hand directly in front of your eyes and you can't even see it."

When the water level in the Wet Pinch was sufficiently low, we squeezed through, sopping up the remaining wetness with our bodies. Next came the Tight Pinch, whose name is an understatement. Hands over head, Cummings made the passage. Then it was our turn. Following Charlie's lead, I wriggled in on my back, head and hands leading the way. When my chest got to the lowest point in the chamber, I pushed forward, and . . . nothing happened. I was stuck.

Cummings pulled on my arms. Moses pushed on my feet. I wondered exactly what they could do if I was truly stuck. Jaws of Life? Dynamite? Neither a comforting option. Poor Charlie was trapped inside the next room. I wondered how long it would take before we'd tire of bat-flesh and start eating each other. "We'll get you out of here, no problem," Moses said. "Just relax, you're doing great. No problem." Uh-oh. This guy was protesting way too much; I was in worse trouble than I thought. That's when the odd assortment of storybook characters—Pooh, Alice—sprang to mind. I thought I was supposed to see a white light and a Godlike figure when the end was near, or at least my life flashing before my eyes. I made a mental note: If I ever get out of here, I'm going to ease up on the Disney flicks. In fact, if I ever get out of here, I'm going to give up a lot of bad habits. Just as I was about to make a foxhole conversion, and lots of totally unkeepable promises to God, I was out, push-pulled millimeter by millimeter to freedom.

The guides, all the while, had been totally composed and reassuring, as if they'd been through all this before. Turns out, they had. Apparently, I wasn't the first hapless soul to get stuck in the Pinch; it's a fairly common thing. Perhaps there should be some maximum size posted here, like on the rides at Disney World.

We reached the Bat Room, the largest space we'd encountered (part of the cave's main chamber), and stopped for a lunch of souped-up granola bars. We signed the cave register and explored a bit on our own. We focused our headlamps on the walls and saw bats in hibernation, stuck to the slippery, silty surface as if they were Velcroed in place. The blackish bats contrasted sharply with the milky marble of the cave's walls. We were careful not to awaken them; the guides had explained that if the bats expended energy, they might not survive the winter.

Next, we rappelled down a trail leading to the Lake Room, named for its small, crystal-clear lake. It is in the lowest part of the cave's main chamber.

Someone whistled. The Lake Room is a breathtaking sight. Oops—we found it hard to discern what was water and what wasn't, and almost stepped in. Not a good idea, since the lake is at least ninety feet deep. A false bottom is beginning to form on the lake; its surface is dotted with a crystalline formation that will eventually cover the water entirely, making it appear to be solid ground. Stepping on this stuff and breaking through is the leading cause of deaths in caving, Moses said.

Where does "getting stuck in a tight spot forever" rank on the danger list? We weren't about to find out. This time, coming back through the Tight Pinch, we dug it out a bit, perhaps making it easier for the next oversized spelunker to wriggle through.

Soon, we were outside the cave, squinting in the sunlight. We were dirty and disheveled (we'd discover the bruises later, after we washed the dirt off), but none the worse for wear. All things considered, it was worth the trip. We recommend this one to experienced cavers—it might be just the incentive to drop a few pounds.

Bennington, Vermont: Caving 101

Spelunking With Gumby

CONTACT: Green Mountain Adventures, P.O. Box 1711, Manchester Center, VT 05255; (802) 362-1202. For more information on GMA, see the "Spelunking Spectacular Morris Cave" entry, page 245.

HOW TO GET THERE: This trip meets at GMA's base camp in Sandgate, Vermont. To get there, take Route 7 to Exit 3, then head west on Route 313 to Sandgate Road. Follow Sandgate Road until you see the Green Mountain Adventures sign on the left; proceed up the hill to the cabin.

RATES: The trip, including transportation from local lodgings, lunch, gear, and a guide, costs $85 for one person, $125 for two, $195 for a group of four, and $25 for each additional person.

WHERE TO STAY: The GMA base camp is located on 11,500 acres at the base of Bear Mountain in Sandgate, Vermont. Guests can camp at primitive sites there, or stay at nearby inns, such as the casual Evergreen Inn in Sandgate, the pretty West Mountain Inn in Arlington, or the poshest local choice, the Arlington Inn.

WHAT TO BRING: They'll provide a jumpsuit; bring clothes for layering underneath it, such as a polypropylene turtleneck, a fleece shell (preferably hooded, to protect your hair), and a T-shirt. Plan on getting filthy. Bring garden gloves, knee pads (inexpensive ones are fine), tennis shoes, and a change of clothing. Also, bring a flashlight with fresh alkaline batteries, and four extra AA batteries, which they'll provide.

KIDS: Matt Moses of GMA says they've brought Scout Troops through this cave, but use your own judgment.

SKILL LEVEL: All levels.

It seemed like an omen. The cat that slept with us at the Evergreen Inn was named Indy, for Indiana Jones. We were going caving, to be led by cave maniac (and discoverer of seven caves) Greg Roscoe.

Everett Cave, at Mount Anthony on the property of the University of Southern Vermont, isn't exactly a secret. But of the forty explorable caves in Vermont, this is one of the better ones for virgin cavers. And it's the stuff of local legends. Some say Everett Cave was a stop on the Underground Railroad; some believe gunpowder was stored in the cave during the Revolutionary War. So we set off with Matt Moses, owner of Green Mountain Adventures and coordinator of the trip; Dan, his intern; and the aforementioned cave guide, Greg Roscoe.

We hiked up to the cave and donned auto mechanic's jumpsuits (complete with sewn-on name badges), helmets with headlamps, gloves, and knee pads. Underneath, we wore polypropylene and fleece. Even though it was ninety degrees outside, it's always forty-five degrees in a cave. While we outfitted ourselves, Roscoe smelled a cave and started picking away at a pile of rocks.

Filled with anticipation, we entered Everett Cave. What a disappointment! Local college kids have discovered that the cave makes a dandy beer cooler, and cans and graffiti adorn the opening. Fortunately, collegiate brewheads aren't the most intrepid souls. Deeper into the cave, there's no litter, just eerie surroundings, gray and bony like a dinosaur's skin. Our nostrils filled with a peculiar, earthy, not unpleasant smell that Roscoe said is the scent of decaying rock. Was this the odor he was sniffing out in the rock clump? "Nope. Caves smell different on the outside," he said.

One of three caves on the mountain, Everett Cave is composed of calcite and gray marble and covered with a film of grayish, silty mud. Roscoe described how caves are formed, pointing out "soda straws" (thin tubes of calcite protruding from the ceiling) and "breakdown" (pieces of rock that have crumbled from the cave over time). We half listened, simultaneously wondering, "Where do we go next?" It isn't obvious; this isn't Flintstone country, with one big room leading to the next.

We noticed a long, muddy rope dangling from a hole in the wall. Soon, we were holding onto it while locating footholds in the rock, mentally preparing for a belly slide into the next section of the cave. (Belly crawling is a big part of the caving experience.) One by one, the group flopped into a dark room about the size of a closet.

Then things got really exciting. "There's likely to be some water in here," Roscoe said, pointing to an opening that looked about two hand-spans wide. "I'll check." We were incredulous. Roscoe is a lumberjack of a guy, with a fifty-inch chest (by his own estimate). No way would he fit through a hole smaller than his head, we thought.

Well, Santa fits into chimneys, right? Faster than you can say, "On Donner! On Dasher!," Roscoe squeezed, twisted, and contorted his body into the opening. With a plop and a splash, he hit a few inches of water on the bottom. "There's water in here, all right, more than I thought. But I'll soak it up for you guys," he reassured us. Uh-huh.

"Who's coming next?" he asked from the other side. Nobody. Even the mountain guide, Matt, and intern Dan hung back. "I don't think so," said Dan. Hey, aren't eighteen-year-olds supposed to be fearless and indestructible? That's how intense this is. If you're claustrophobic, but don't know it, you'll find out here.

Logically, I knew I'd fit — Roscoe did, and he was by far the biggest of our bunch. It's the mental game that kicks in here: it's a tight squeeze, it's full of gray water teeming with who knows what, and it's damned dark. (Headlamps are useless here; to get your head through the hole, you have to take the helmet off and drag it behind you.) "Sorry, folks, I can't do this," said one of the group.

I had a brief spell of doubt. "This is crazy," I said aloud. "Why would I want to do this?" "C'mon. You can make it," urged Roscoe. I looked back at the opening behind me, looked ahead at the too-small, watery passage, then plunged in, trying to keep my nose above the water, damp clay streaming through my hair. "She's a player!" Moses shouted. "She did it!" So this is what it feels like to travel through the womb. An impossible gooey squeeze, then you're out.

Roscoe was sitting cross-legged, moving his head from side to side to light up the tiny room with his headlamp. "Isn't this awesome? Almost nobody gets back here," he whispered. It was. Here the cave formations were untouched by human hands. "Twinkle" (water droplets) on the walls of the cave made the room glitter like a 70s disco ball. We explored the nooks and crannies, then proceeded to the end of the tour, getting to each section by way of small, jagged openings. These looked fairly hairy, but Roscoe went first, describing his strategy: "I start head-first on my belly, lean over to the right, then twist onto my back. . . ." Amazingly, it works. The main thing to remember is, don't panic. If you do, you'll end up thrashing around and getting hurt, Roscoe said. He should know: he's been caving since age six (he's in his forties now) and has never been badly hurt. "Nothing that wouldn't heal," he said. But then, this guy's Gumby.

Having gone this far, I was feeling great, proud, ready for membership in the Clan of the Cave People. Then it hit me: the only way out is the way we came in, through that godforsaken puddle, out that perilous pinching hole. But now it was no big mystery, and on the Other Side, the guys who hadn't made the journey (wimps!) said, as we emerged squinting into the daylight, "Hey!"

Resources

Additional Outfitters

Alain Comeau, Mountain Guides Alliance, Box 266, North Conway, NH 03860; (603) 356-5310 or (207) 935-3843.

Hulbert Outdoor Center, RR 1, Box 91 A, Fairlee, VT 05045; (802) 333-9840.

International Mountain Climbing School, P.O. Box 1666, North Conway, NH 03860.

Mahoosuc Guide Service, Bear River Road, Newry, ME 04261; (207) 824-2073.

Mountain Hawk, P.O. Box 81, Jericho Center, VT 05465; (802) 899-3617.

Northern Pack and Paddle, P.O. Box 624, Woodstock, VT 05091; (802) 457-1409.

Peak Concepts, P.O. Box 338, Jeffersonville, VT 05464; (802) 644-5385.

Ian Turnbull, Mountain Guides Alliance, Box 266, North Conway, NH 03860; (603) 356-5310 or (603) 466-3949.

Kurt Winkler, Mountain Guides Alliance, Box 266, North Conway, NH 03860; (603) 356-5310 or (207) 935-3853.

Women's Outdoor Challenges, 40 Winn Hill Road, Sunapee, NH 03782; (603) 763-5400.

Commercial Caves and Chasms

The Flume Gorge, Franconia Notch State Park, I-93, Franconia Notch, NH 03580; (603) 745-8391.

Lost River Gorge, Route 112, North Woodstock, NH 03262; (603) 745-8031.

Polar Caves Park, Tenney Mountain Highway, Plymouth, NH 03265; (603) 536-1888.

Purgatory Chasm State Park, Purgatory Road, Sutton, MA 01590; (508) 234-3733.

BOOKS

Boston Rocks. Larry LaForge, ed., MIT Outing Club.

Climbing Rock and Ice. Jerry Cinnamon, Ragged Mountain
  Press.

"How to Rock Climb" series (including *Rock Climb!; Climbing Anchors; Sport and Face Climbing; Big Walls;* and *Knots
  for Climbers*). Chockstone Press.

Learning to Rock Climb. Michael Loughman, Sierra Club.

Mountaineering: The Freedom of the Hills. Don Graydon, ed.,
  The Mountaineers.

NOLS Wilderness Mountaineering. Phil Powers, Stackpole
  Books.

Rock Climbing Basics. Turlough Johnson, Stackpole Books.

Wilderness Exploration

Rockland, Maine:
Survival School on Hurricane Island

Life Reduced to the Raw, Rugged Basics

CONTACT: Hurricane Island Outward Bound School, P.O. Box 429, Rockland, ME 04841; (207) 594-1401.

HOW TO GET THERE: Bases in Maine are in Rockland, Newry, Greenville, Hurricane Island, Burnt Island, and Cross Island. We met at the Outward Bound headquarters in Rockland. Take I-95 north to Route 295 north in Portland, which will run back into I-95 north of the city. Then take the coastal Route 1 exit in Brunswick. Follow Route 1 into Rockland; at the second set of lights, turn right onto Route 73. Go about a mile, then turn left on Mechanic Street; the office is near the end of the harbor on the right.

RATES: Outward Bound offers a wide range of courses, including mountaineering, backpacking, wilderness leadership, canoeing, sea kayaking, and dogsledding. Courses run from eight to eighty-four days. Costs range from $795 to $7,100. The eight-day sailing course costs $795.

WHAT TO BRING: Outward Bound will send a very detailed and specific list. Generally, you'll need warm clothing, a hat, gloves, a warm jacket, athletic shoes, and a swimsuit.

KIDS: Courses for children fourteen and up are offered.

SKILL LEVEL: They say no experience is necessary, but you'd better be mentally prepared and in excellent physical condition (they suggest beginning a training program before the course).

T his was not fun. We were sleeping on the wet ground, dressed in foul-weather gear, hats, and gloves, while the dark skies continued to release endless torrents of cold, miserable rain. Shipwrecked on a tiny island in the northern waters off Maine, hungry, bone weary, sleep deprived, mentally and emotionally taxed, we were ready to mutiny. "I can't take this anymore," one woman cried. We murmured words of encouragement, little lies that none of us believed anymore, and huddled closer.

"I can't believe I paid money for this," someone said. "Yeah, well, this is my vacation, the only one I'll get this year," another lamented.

We were on an eight-day adult sailing program offered by the Hurricane Island Outward Bound School. The shipwreck exercise was five days into the survival course; the second day out we began counting the minutes until we'd be free to go home.

There were eight students (a rare combination of seven women and one man) and two instructors. After introductions at Outward Bound headquarters in Rockland, Maine (see map on page 69), we formed a circle and each promised to "commit" to the completion of the course. We were reminded of this promise throughout the long eight days, and would rue making it.

"I hope you encounter some bad weather," one of the leaders said before we boarded the boat. "It's the hardships that you'll remember the most." She got her wish.

For five days and nights, gray, leaden skies wet our bodies and dampened our spirits. To top it off, there was no wind. The sails remained wrapped around the masts while we rowed the heavy wooden boat through choppy Atlantic waters. We heave-hoed big, fat logs (they called them oars) until our shoulders ached and our hands cramped. We felt like shackled slaves, going nowhere.

"Where do we sleep?" we asked our instructors the first night out. "What do you think? What do we have that will work?" David, one of our instructors, replied.

We didn't remember packing any tents. Silly us; who needs tents when you have oars? We laid them lengthwise over the boat's seats, and voilà!—our beds for the night. We slept like packed sardines, foot to head to foot. Or didn't sleep; we were required to take turns keeping "watch" through the night, part of the Outward Bound curriculum of sleep deprivation.

The Outward Bound concept was developed by Kurt Hahn, a German exiled to Great Britain for criticizing Hitler. He was intrigued by what he saw as a pattern: when shipwrecked at sea, older men tended to survive longer than younger ones. He concluded that inner strength and mental attitude are at least as important as physical strength. In 1941, he created a training program for British seamen who were "outward bound" (heading out to sea). In 1961, the first Outward Bound school was established in the United States. Today there are five schools and two Outward Bound administrative centers.

Introspection and self-assessment are a big part of the Outward Bound program. Each night, we had a group "debriefing." Everyone was required to participate in this touchy-feely sharing: "What was your best moment today?" "How did it make you feel?" "Where does this fit into your life?" Don't feel like talking? Too bad; no one is dismissed until everyone shares.

The morning "run and dip" is also an Outward Bound requirement. We were expected to be out of our longjohns and foul-weather gear and into our swimsuits and sneakers by five A.M. ("Not 5:02," David, consulting his watch, politely scolded.) We'd disembark on the nearest ground (sometimes trudging through knee-high muck to get there), and jog over boulders and rocks or around short stretches of pebbly beach. Then, we'd "dip" in icy Maine waters that would make even the most ardent Polar Bear Club member proud.

The first dip was a shock. "We just want to assess your swimming abilities," our instructors explained. "Just jump in and make a lap around the boat." The arctic plunge sucked the breath out of us and froze shut our vital organs. A millisecond . . . a second . . . who knows? It felt like forever before we recovered and began thrashing our way through the frigid water. The dip escalated into aerial jumps. By the second day, our morning jog ended on a cliff overlooking the deep, black waters of the Atlantic.

"I can't do it," pleaded one of our classmates. She'd been standing at the edge, shaking and crying, for a long time. "Yes you can," the instructors said, adding, "The rest of the group can't get changed until you jump." We stood shivering, hoping she'd either jump or refuse and climb down. She jumped. Inner strength? Peer pressure? We wondered if she felt good for having done it, or just merely resigned, seeing no other way out.

We learned quickly not to expect much from our instructors. Most of the answers to our concerns and questions were covered with three basic replies: "No." "What do you think?" "What does that tell you about yourself?" We began to consult each other for help and support.

We also began to relish small things that might have gone unnoticed, and would certainly have been unappreciated, only days before: a temporary stop in the rain; a warm drink; a dinner of freshly caught mussels; a view, albeit cloud-shrouded, of distant islands.

Nevertheless, by the time we reached Hurricane Island on the sixth day of our expedition, three in our group asked to be taken home. They were gently coaxed out of it with promises that things would be different on the island. And they were. We slept in platform shelters, which by now seemed deluxe; we ate in a communal dining room; and the sun came out. That's not to say the physical and emotional demands and challenges disappeared. One morning we learned rock climbing techniques, then grappled our way up and down vertical slopes of granite. "Try the Tarzan climb," David suggested to one of our classmates. He struggled, stretched, slid, and struggled again until it was clear that there was no way to make this climb without the aid of a rope. "Sing us a song, and we'll throw you the rope," David called up. What could he do but sing and be saved. What next? Barking for dinner? Dancing for toilet paper?

It's all a metaphor for life, of course. Working together, finding inner strength, overcoming fears. Though it was not clear while it was happening, we were crossing invisible thresholds; ultimately, adventure became revelation.

Irritating, rugged, and uncomfortable as it was, we often find ourselves reflecting on our time with Outward Bound and drawing from the experience. It's tough, after completing an Outward Bound course, to complain about the little discomforts of daily living, and even big problems somehow seem surmountable.

Wilderness Exploration

Various Sites: Traipsing Through the Unknown for Fun and Fitness

Hate Asking for Directions? Orienteering Is the Sport for You

CONTACT: For a listing of upcoming events, call the New England Orienteering Club's hotline at (617) 648-1155. For Vermont events, contact the Green Mountain Orienteering Club, c/o Jim Howley, 41 Mackintosh Avenue, South Burlington, VT 05403; (802) 862-3170. In winter, Green Mountain Orienteering runs Ski-O events—orienteering on cross-country skis.

HOW TO GET THERE: These events are held all over New England, at city and state parks, cross-country ski areas, and on private lands. The clubs will provide directions to each event.

RATES: For recreational (local) meets, registration fees are nominal, usually around $4 per person. Compass rental is extra. Maps and informal instruction are included.

WHAT TO BRING: Dress for the weather in whatever you'd wear for hiking. Light layers are best. Wear long pants, because you'll do some trekking through the brush, and athletic shoes or hiking boots. You'll also need a compass.

KIDS: Yes, at recreational events.

SKILL LEVEL: Beginners are welcome at local recreational events. Courses are set up for all skill levels.

L ook, I see it! I see it!" squealed eight-year-old Charlotte, running to the orange-and-white marker behind a
chunk of granite. "I found the control!"

It's a typical scene in recreational orienteering, a sport
that began in Sweden in the early 1900s as a military exercise. It hit the United States in the 1940s and has a passionate following among New Englanders who like to exercise
their brains as well as their bodies. Call it the thinking person's road race, or a map-reader's marathon.

"Nobody understands orienteering," said Jim Howley of
the Green Mountain Orienteering Club. "They think it
requires a slide rule or calculator." Essentially, it's pretty
simple: You find your way through unknown terrain by
using a map and a compass. The goal is to find the quickest
path (not necessarily the shortest distance) between two
points, and to get there, pronto. Requirements are a love of
the outdoors, a little stamina, and some creative thinking.

Orienteering is a two-tier sport. There are local meets
run by orienteering clubs and open to everybody from tots
to elders. These events typically attract 75 to 120 participants. Then there's the competitive side, with regional meets
sanctioned by the U.S. Orienteering Federation, offering
complicated courses and attracting 250 or more orienteers.

There's a drawback to the serious side, said Bob Dangel
of the New England Orienteering Club: "The more competitive you become in this sport, the less you see of the woods!
You become more beady-eyed and miss the snowy owls
along the way. You get really focused."

Beginners' courses are typically a mile long, with six to ten
controls (markers) set along trails and roads so novices can't
get lost. Orienteers follow contour lines, ridge lines, gullies,
bodies of water, stone walls, and other features, all detailed on
specially made topographic maps. Clue sheets tip off participants to, say, which side of a stone wall a flag is on. Then,
you're off and running. Starts go off at different times, every
couple of minutes, so you lose sight of other participants.
"You're not supposed to follow each other; you're on the
honor system," Howley said. Nobody cheats. "You always
think the other person's going the wrong way anyway."

We joined the Up North Orienteering Club for an event

in Durham, New Hampshire. We met at the edge of College Woods at the University of New Hampshire for our start.

"Get ready to start," said the official with the stopwatch. "Ready, go!" Confidently, we'd opted for an intermediate-level course. After copying the controls on our map from the master map, we had planned our strategy. Jogging through the woods, we found the trail we were looking for, crossed the river that was just where the map said it would be, and discovered our first control. Charlotte went wild.

At each flag, or control, there's a punch that looks like a clothespin with needles sticking from it. We punched our score card, danced a celebratory jig, and trotted off to do it again, using land navigation to find the next coded control. As you go, you wonder: Are we going the right way? Are we where we think we are? At the eighth control, we had a decision to make. Should we take a trail that went south of where we wanted to go, or one that veered north, or should we bushwhack through the woods, off the trail, following compass bearings? Charlotte chose the latter approach, and we followed the compass, ending up exactly where we wanted to be. From there, we sprinted to the finish, a small band of people cheering us on.

What if we'd gotten lost? "We don't really use the word 'lost,' but people get 'misoriented' easily," Howley told us. Events have a three-hour time limit; if you haven't finished in that time, they'll come and get you. The club takes down your car's license number when you register for an event, so they can make sure you're gone—not missing in the woods—if you leave without checking out. Most people head directly to the board at the event's end, to check their time and see where they finished. (We came in third in our group.)

If anything, this kind of sleuthing sharpens your land navigation abilities, making orienteering an ideal activity for hikers, hunters, cross-country skiers, Scouts, and anyone who spends time in the wilderness and hates getting lost. And it's fun. "It's great to tune in to the woods, explore beautiful territory, and be thinking hard at the same time," a first-time participant said. "It's a strategy game."

For adventurous folks who like matching their wits

against the woods and the wiles of the course-setters, to try orienteering is to love it. Even small-fry get in on the act. "Little kids eat this up," Howley said. Those too young to read maps can follow a string course. Brightly colored ribbon is strung along the ground from one flag to the next. Instead of a punch, a cartoon-character sticker awaits each child, to be attached to the score card. "You always hear the squeal fifty yards away," Howley said. As in any treasure hunt, the fun is in the finding.

Freeport, Maine: Learn Outdoor Survival Skills in the Maine Woods

Lost in the Wilderness? Don't Panic, Give Up the Macho Thing, and Start Gathering Litter

CONTACT: L.L. Bean Outdoor Discovery Program, Freeport, ME 04033; (800) 341-4341, ext. 6666.

HOW TO GET THERE: The course meets at Fogg House in Freeport, Maine. To get there, take I-95 to Exit 19, Freeport/Desert Road. Take a left onto Desert Road; Fogg House is the first house on the left.

RATES: A fee of $150 includes a survival kit, a book, and lunches.

WHAT TO BRING: A wide-mouth water bottle and snacks; a fanny pack or day pack; a whistle; cold-weather boots; clothing to be layered (such as synthetic long underwear, pile or fleece pants and top, wind pants and jacket); mittens or gloves; wool or pile hat; work gloves (for handling brush); a notebook and a pencil; and snowshoes, if you own a pair.

KIDS: Minimum age twelve (this is flexible).

SKILL LEVEL: Fine for beginners.

Sign up for a Northwoods survival skills workshop with Master Maine Guide Ray Reitze and you'll learn an amazing amount of practical stuff, like how to build a bark shelter, how to create pure water, and how to identify edible plants. These are essential things to know if you spend any time in the wilderness.

But there's a spiritual side to all this as well. Reitze's programs are inspired by the teachings of Joe Muse, a Micmac elder Reitze calls "the grandfather." Muse traveled with the Iroquois, Blackfoot, Sioux, and Cree, learning wilderness skills he passed on to Reitze, beginning when Reitze was eight years old. Now, Reitze is passing along the ways of the elders through L.L. Bean's Outdoor Skills School and other venues. His courses are enormously popular. "People are reaching out, looking for a way back to the ancient ways," he said.

Reitze espouses a back-to-basics, nonconsumerist way of life based on the Native American philosophy of being "totally connected to the Earth and part of the whole." In many ways, he lives it, residing with his wife Nancy in an eight-sided dwelling without electricity or plumbing, existing primarily on food they grow or catch.

"The grandfather taught me we should never take a life without asking permission and giving thanks. Along with the tree people, the plant people, birds, and animals, we are connected to the circle of life," Reitze said, adding, "If you go back to the Earth, you'll find yourself."

The L.L. Bean course meets down the road from Bean's sprawling Freeport, Maine, headquarters, in a big field surrounded by woods. There is a small pond on the property. Reitze began with the basic four—shelter, water, fire, and food—noting that this is their order of importance for human survival. "You can get by without food for two or three days, even a week," he told the group. "But there is food everywhere in the forest, and you can always set up a snare to catch a partridge or a grouse."

Though he has gone into the wilderness many times with nothing but the clothes on his back, Reitze stresses the importance of carrying a safety

Wilderness Exploration

kit. Contents should include waterproof matches in a water-proof container, fishing line, fifty feet of strong cord (to make snares and/or secure a lean-to), iodine tablets (for water purification), a compass, and materials to make a solar still. Never heard of a solar still? Reitze demonstrated how to make one, using a length of surgical tubing, a piece of plastic, green plant material, and a folding cup. With a little sunshine to promote condensation, you can create a quart of pure water per day in summer, or a pint in winter.

Nearly as important as food and water is shelter. Using materials found in the forest, you can create a cozy lair out of debris. "A debris hut is by far the warmest and most comfortable shelter you can make," Reitze said. Using "litter," the stuff on the ground in a deciduous forest, you can build a hut that looks like a beached whale but will keep you toasty when the mercury drops. A two-foot-thick shelter takes three or four hours to build and will keep you warm to twelve degrees Fahrenheit; pile on a couple more feet of leaves and debris and you'll survive temperatures as low as forty below zero. "You worm your way in, then slowly plug up the cracks and go to sleep," Reitze explained. "It's like a giant sleeping bag."

A bark shelter takes less time to build. Big pieces of bark from dead trees (birch is best by far; cedar, fir, and spruce also work) serve as shingles on a lean-to made from tree branches. After you shingle the shelter, you lay green boughs on top to make sure your roof doesn't blow off. This one isn't so warm, so you need to build a fire nearby, and keep the woodpile close so you can keep feeding the fire when you lay down, Reitze explained.

Speaking of fire, most people are too impatient to build a good one, Reitze said. In a survival situation, he said, "People get nervous and try to rush it. You've got to start out with hair-fine tinder and very small, fine twigs." The trick is to build it slow.

Fear and panic are your worst enemies in the wilderness. When most people get lost, they keep walking, and they walk in a circle, he said. Right-handed people walk to the right, left-handed people go left, over and over, until things start looking familiar. "They're just burning their energy and going nowhere. It gets too late to build a fire or a shelter, and they panic and run." This has happened to folks who have been good woodsmen all their lives, he added.

"People think, 'I can't get lost.' They can," he warned. Men are the worst, he said. In the woods, as on the highway, they never want to admit they're lost. "That macho attitude will ruin you every time. You can't go against Mother Nature, you have to go with her. Women understand this a lot better."

What if you do get lost? "Ask yourself, 'Can I find my way out?' If not, tell yourself, 'This is home tonight.' Home is wherever you lay down. Make a shelter, make a fire. Tell yourself, 'Tomorrow, I'll figure out what I did wrong,' and find food and water," he said.

"There's nothing in the wild that will hurt you except another man," Reitze told us. Deep in the woods, that's seldom an issue. A thick debris hut can save your life, as can a nice, smoky fire. Build them and stay put, Reitze advised. Rescuers will see the smoke from the air.

Should you find yourself stranded in the wilderness, remember that food is everywhere. Even a pine tree can provide the makings of a decent meal. "The inner bark is edible, like pasta, if you boil it in water," Reitze told us. The resin-flavored result won't compete with trattoria fare, but it's not bad. Steep some pine needles for a vitamin C–packed cup of tea. At the right time of year, pine pollen and inner bark can be pounded into flour. Mix with white ash, which works like baking powder, to make an ash cake. Voilà—dessert. "Munch it down; it's not bad," Reitze said, offering a sample around. "The pine makes it sweet."

All these skills (except the solar still; the U.S. Army gets credit for that) were taught to Reitze by the Micmac grandfather. These practices are universal to native people around the world, Reitze said. "When we discover them, we learn to look at the earth differently."

Warren, Vermont: Bushwhacking the Backcountry

Who Needs Hiking Trails When You've Got a Guide (and a Bottle of Bug Spray?)

CONTACT: Adventure Guides of Vermont, P.O. Box 3, North Ferrisburgh, VT 05473; (800) 425-TRIP or (802) 425-6211. In addition to bushwhacking, Adventure Guides can arrange other Vermont adventures, including multiday, multiactivity trips with lodging and rental gear.

HOW TO GET THERE: These are custom-designed trips, so Adventure Guides will determine where you will meet your guide, and they will provide directions. We hiked in the Granville Reservation area, off Route 100, south of Warren. Montpelier is about 15 miles to the northeast.

RATES: A half-day bushwhack trip costs $60 per person; a full-day trip, $85. Prices may vary, depending on the guide.

WHAT TO BRING: Hiking clothes, boots, a day pack, bug repellent, and a water bottle. Ask if lunch is included; it depends on the guide.

KIDS: Yes, as long as they're old enough to hike. You won't cover as much territory, perhaps, but you'll be aware of much detail you'd otherwise miss.

SKILL LEVEL: All levels. This trip can be tailored to your hiking ability.

ETCETERA: The best wildflower display here occurs during the first two weeks of May; foliage season is the first two weeks of October. Guides' choice for best time is winter, after a snowfall. Early spring (mud season) is the worst time.

"Funny thing about Vermont," said mountain guide Bruce Acciavatti, "about eighty percent of the land, nobody explores. Ninety percent of the people go to twenty percent of the places." They can have their Ben & Jerry's ice cream tours, their factory outlets, their overbuilt resort areas; he'll take the unspoiled territory that's off the beaten path. And for a price, he'll take you with him.

We hooked up with Acciavatti through Adventure Guides of Vermont, an association of professional outdoors guides. If it can be done outdoors in Vermont, Adventure Guides can probably connect you with an expert, whether it's cat-fishing or dogsledding you're after.

Acciavatti is a native New Yorker who took early retirement from IBM to indulge his love of the backcountry. His adopted territory is the northern section of the Green Mountain National Forest. We drove out with him to Bristol Cliffs Wilderness Area, where he takes people bushwhacking (off-trail hiking), snowshoeing, and cross-country skiing.

Acciavatti tailors his bushwhacking trips to his clients' interests, their hiking ability, and the weather. If you want to bushwhack through the heaviest brush, he'll lead the way. If you want to learn compassing, he'll oblige, though he prefers dead reckoning to find his way around. If you suddenly feel the urge to meditate, he'll hang back until you're ready to move on. Left to his own devices, Acciavatti will share with you his astonishing knowledge of this little-known chunk of Vermont: its native plant and animal life, down to the tiniest aphid; the natural history of the area (which, 100 years ago, was a logging settlement); and the myriad ways the forest changes as you reach higher elevations.

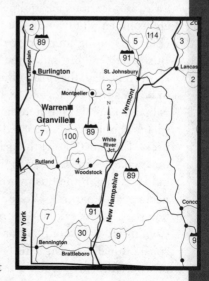

We really put him to the test: we brought along an eight-year-old. "Look at that!" "What's this?" "What does that thing do?" our inquiring child wanted to know. No insect is too lowly, no fungus too insignificant, to escape a child's eye, but Acciavatti was up to the challenge. If you can find it in Green Mountain National Forest, Acciavatti can identify it, and if he's stumped, he'll pull out a field guide and dig until he finds said specimen.

Although trails are blazed through this region of the forest, we steered clear of them, tramping through thick brush, over tree limbs, atop boulders. Bushwhacking is a freer way to explore, because you take the path you're drawn to, not one someone else laid out. We crisscrossed the area, eventually finding a fallen tree near a waterfall (a favorite spot of Acciavatti's) to stop for a snack break. He'd packed homemade gorp, figs, plums, berries, and fruit juice. (On full-day hikes, lunch is part of the deal.) We took a look at his map and realized we were far from Gilmore Pond, where we'd planned to take a swim before heading back. Getting there would mean sprinting through the woods and back, not exactly the mellow meander we'd had in mind. But, hey, we'd been moving at our own pace, stopping to look and touch, and it felt right to sustain the mood. The pond would have to wait.

Clearly, Acciavatti is a man in love with nature. This is a guy who, literally, wouldn't hurt a fly. While we slapped away at voracious mosquitoes and sprayed ourselves with environmentally friendly bug dope, Acciavatti soldiered on. (Finally, getting lumpier by the second, he relented, using "just a dab" on his bandanna.) Mention a medicinal use for an herb or, say, the notion that sarsaparilla root is thought to be an aphrodisiac, and he'll bristle. "Why is something valuable only if it has a human use? That's so humancentric. Plants should be appreciated for what they are, not for their uses." But most likely, the prickly stuff you encounter on a bushwhack with Acciavatti will be stinging nettles, not your guide. A day in the bush with him is an exercise in reconnecting with nature. "We're within a days' drive of 100 million people," he said. "Most people work in the rat race. Coming up to a spot like this has a way of renewing the spirit." Ideally, he said, his fellow adventurers will go back to where they live and discover the natural places there.

"Get to love these surroundings, but find the places in your own area that have a special meaning for you."

Why use a guide at all, when anyone can explore the Green Mountain National Forest without one? It's a great way to get far off the beaten path without worrying about getting lost or shot at. And you'll get a real insider's perspective, perhaps encountering a beaver pond or moose tracks that trail-bound hikers would miss.

We mentioned that we'd like to come back in winter for snowshoeing and animal-tracking. Acciavatti's recommendation: leave the ski resort scene behind, and let him lead us to some incredible backcountry ski trails. If we do, chances are we won't see another soul—they'll be crowded into that other twenty percent of the state, remember?

Charlemont, Massachusetts: Tracking Bears in the Berkshires

*Seeking Oneness with the Bears is
the Point of This Safari*

CONTACT: Paul Rezendes Programs in Tracking, Bearsden Road, Star Route, South Royalston, MA 01331; (508) 249-8810. Other programs include wilderness survival skills, tracking, advanced tracking, wild foods foraging, compass and map, and nature photography.

HOW TO GET THERE: The Bear Country trip meets at the Charlemont Inn in Charlemont, Massachusetts. From Route 91, take the Route 2 west exit; continue on Route 2 (Mohawk Trail) to Charlemont. The Charlemont Inn is on the right, on the west side of town. From there, the group will carpool a short distance to Mohawk Trail State Forest.

RATES: The 5-hour trip costs $35 per person; register in advance.

WHAT TO BRING: In a pack, carry lunch and a beverage, rain gear, and a ground pad or space blanket to sit on. Wear hiking boots. For winter programs, dress in warm, layered clothing, and bring mittens. For warm-weather trips, you'll need a long-sleeved shirt and long pants, a hat with a visor, and bug repellent and/or an insect head net. Plan to get muddy.

KIDS: Decided on a case-by-case basis. Rezendes also runs a tracking/earth skills workshop for kids age eight and up.

SKILL LEVEL: This trip involves strenuous hiking, so participants should be in good physical condition.

Y ou're fast asleep in the wilderness. Suddenly, you're awakened by a lot of noise. Something's in camp, raiding the cooler. This furry prowler isn't a pesky raccoon. It's a bear! Do you: (a) play dead; or (b) yell, scream, and bang pots and pans? Answer: depends on the bear. If it's a grizzly, "curl up, roll over, and protect your vital organs," premier animal tracker Paul Rezendes advised. If you run, you've had it—you're acting like prey. If it's a black bear, do not play dead. The bear will eat you. Black bear attacks are extremely rare, Rezendes said, but if it happens, try to intimidate the bear. "Make noise; scare the bear," Rezendes said. Why not just climb a tree? Don't even think about it. Bears are incredibly fast, and they're great climbers. They can jump eight feet from tree to tree, so you'll never outclimb one, Rezendes said.

"One of the most awesome feelings in the wilderness is to be in Bear Country unarmed," the tracker told us. "You're truly at the mercy of the wilderness, and at the mercy of the bear. If a bear wants you," he added, "it's got you."

We weren't intending to be had, by Yogi or any of his brethren. The goal of this hike was to become intimate with bears in a symbolic sense, not a literal one. "There's no better way to get to know an animal than to track it," Rezendes said. When you learn how an animal lives, where it travels, what it eats, you forge a close bond with the creature, he explained. When you learn an animal's relationship to other animals and to the forest, "You start to see the interconnections along the web of life," Rezendes said. "You start to realize that how you live your life affects these animals, and that you are part of the web of life."

Tracking, as Rezendes defines it, isn't just about tracks. "It's all written in the forest," he said. The forest is constantly giving us information about wildlife by the way plants and trees are growing or not growing; trails, tracks, and signs are everywhere if you know what to look for.

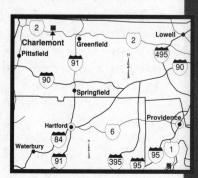

Unfortunately, Rezendes said, we humans have lost the art of seeing. Distracted by our thoughts and inner dialogue, we can walk through the forest and not see a single tree. "People are incredibly disconnected from nature. We're simply not participating in life," he said.

Rezendes embraces the philosophy of being "in the moment" and bringing a quality of attention to our lives. He's so passionate about this subject he's written a book on it, called *Tracking and the Art of Seeing* (Sierra Club Books). "Watch a deer in the forest," he said. "It's incredibly aware, sensitive, alive." That's the essence of tracking, he said, to embrace your surroundings and be one with the territory — like an animal.

Our territory was bear country — Mohawk Trail State Forest, near Charlemont, Massachusetts. We were heading into some of the wildest terrain in the state, bushwhacking through deep forests. We'd find our way back by compass.

We climbed straight up for a while, then gathered in a circle beside a boulder to talk about bears. Most of the group of fourteen had taken part in Rezendes's tracking programs before. He's considered to be one of the most knowledgeable trackers in the Northeast, and his programs are booked far in advance. Bearded and wiry, dressed in a hooded camouflage jacket and well-worn boots, he's an unimposing figure. But he knows the wilderness, and he's generous with his vast knowledge of bears.

Rezendes's real-life bear-encounter stories are hilarious. Picturing this guy naked, chasing a black bear, wielding a canoe paddle, throwing sneakers, and finally surrendering his camp to the bruin is worth the cost of the trip.

The bear facts, according to Rezendes: Bears will gorge themselves until they throw up. Their heartbeat drops from forty to ten beats per minute during hibernation. They lose twenty to thirty percent of their body weight during the big sleep. Female bears have their young during hibernation. Male bears are territorial and solitary. Female black bears typically weigh from 80 to 154 pounds; males tip the scales at 121 to 308 pounds, but can reach 450 or even 650 pounds. (That's a lot of picnic baskets, Yogi!)

We didn't encounter any bears that day, but black bear

sign was everywhere. We saw a beech tree slashed with claw marks. "You'll see hundreds of these around here," Rezendes said. They were arc-shaped, and went surprisingly high. We even saw bear nests in the tops of trees, where limbs were torn out of one side of the canopy and stacked up on the other side. We saw what Rezendes called "whammy" trees, striped maples with bite marks that looked like shots from a .22 rifle. "It's taken me years to learn the things I'm showing you in ten minutes," Rezendes said as we looked closely at trees, inside logs, everywhere, for more bear sign.

We were getting into the search, becoming aware of the details of the forest, asking questions. We fanned out, looking for sign. "Hey, look at this!" someone said. Could that nut-roll-looking thing under the canopy of a tree be . . . bear scat? Finding scat is a big deal in the woods; it can tell you a lot about an animal's habits. Bear scat it was. Rezendes immediately whipped out a tape measure, made an entry in his notebook, and started poking at the specimen with a stick to determine the bear's diet (beech nuts) and how recently it had been here. By now, it had started to rain, but who cared? This was fascinating. We started looking for more. "This is kind of like a treasure hunt, but instead of gold, we're looking for bear scat," one participant said. We found some mystery scat. "Looks like raccoon; doesn't smell like raccoon. Could be fox," Rezendes said, poking and measuring.

The sky was darkening with an approaching storm. Using a compass, we found our way back to the road where our cars were parked. Rezendes gathered us together for some parting words. "I'm glad you all chose to come here, to be more connected with the natural world," he said. "Perhaps this is the beginning of a journey that will draw you into closer intimacy with the wild."

Resources

Wildlife Watching

Champagne Moose Express, Sugarloaf/USA, RR 1, Box 5000, Carrabassett Valley, ME 04947; (207) 237-2000.

Lynn Levine, Forest Care, Partridge Road, RFD #2, Box 764, Putney, VT 05346; (802) 254-4717. Levine also runs tracking programs throughout the winter at Mount Snow Resort, Mount Snow Resort Mountain Road, West Dover, VT 05356; (802) 464-3327.

Moosehead Lake Region Chamber of Commerce, Box 581, Greenville, ME 04441; (207) 695-2702. Ask for a listing of moose-watching opportunities.

Susan Morse, Keeping Track, RFD # 1, Box 263, Jericho, VT 05465; (802) 899-2023.

National Audubon Society, 700 Broadway, New York, NY 10003; (212) 979-3066.

Vermont Institute of Natural Science, Church Hill Road, Woodstock, VT 05091; (802) 457-2779.

Wilderness Survival Courses and Trips

Appalachian Mountain Club, Box 298, Gorham, NH 03581; (603) 466-2725.

Hulbert Outdoor Center, RR #1, Box 91A, Fairlee, VT 05045; (802) 333-3405.

The Maine Conservation School, Box 188, Bryant Pond, ME 04219; (207) 665-2068.

The Mountain Workshop, Inc., Box 625, Ridgefield, CT 06877; (203) 438-1456.

Ray's Guide Service and Wilderness Survival School, RR 2, Box 2700, Canaan, ME 04924; (207) 426-8138.

BOOKS

Commonsense Outdoor Medicine and Emergency Companion. Newell D. Breyfogle, Ragged Mountain Press.

The Essential Wilderness Navigator. David Seidman, Ragged Mountain Press.

Hedgemaids and Fairy Candles. Jack Sanders, Ragged Mountain Press.

Kids Outdoors. Victoria Logue, Frank Logue, and Mark Carroll; Ragged Mountain Press.

Maine Moose Watcher's Guide. Bill Silliker, Jr., Impact Publishing.

Nature Hikes in Southern New Hampshire. Julia Older and Steve Sherman, Appalachian Club Books.

Nature Hikes in the White Mountains. Robert Buchsbaum, Appalachian Club Books.

Outward Bound Map and Compass Handbook. Glenn Randall, Lyons & Burford Publishers.

Outward Bound Wilderness First-Aid Handbook. Jeff Isaac and Peter Goth, Lyons & Burford Publishers.

Tom Brown's Field Guide to Nature and Survival for Children. Tom Brown, Jr., Berkeley Books.

Tom Brown's Field Guide to Nature Observation and Tracking. Tom Brown, Jr., Berkeley Books.

Tom Brown's Field Guide to Wilderness Survival. Tom Brown, Jr., Berkeley Books.

Tracking and the Art of Seeing. Paul Rezendes, Sierra Club Books.

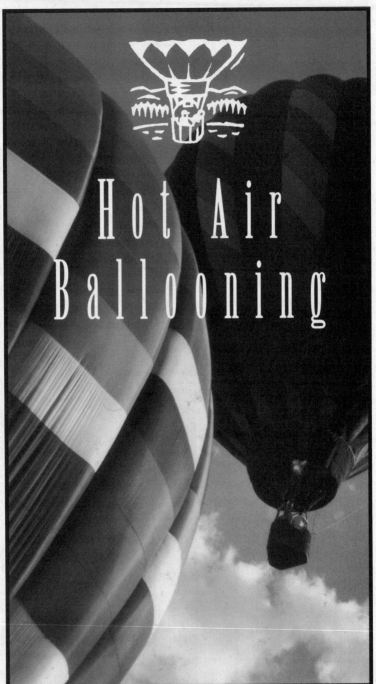

Hot Air
Ballooning

Lewiston, Maine:
Splash and Dash in the Androscoggin

A Balloon Fest in Maine

CONTACT: Sails Aloft, 674 Riverside Drive, Augusta, ME 04330; (207) 623-1136. For dates of the Annual Great Falls Balloon Festival, contact the Maine Publicity Bureau at (207) 623-0363.

HOW TO GET THERE: The Great Falls Balloon Festival is held in Lewiston, Maine. Take Exit 13 off the Maine Turnpike, intersection of Court and Turner Streets. Follow the signs for parking. The festival is free, but plan to pay to park your car.

RATES: Sails Aloft balloon rides cost $125 per person weekdays, $150 weekends. A deposit is required.

WHERE TO STAY: There are several options in Lewiston, including the Ramada Inn, 490 Pleasant Street; (207) 784-2331. Double rooms cost $89. A cozier choice is the Farnham House Bed & Breakfast, 520 Main Street; (207) 782-9495. Double rooms range from $50 to $85 per night.

WHAT TO BRING: Dress for outdoor activity (it isn't colder up in the air). Waterproof footwear is recommended. Bring a camera.

KIDS: Olsen has taken up kids as young as three.

SKILL LEVEL: Anyone can do this.

It's a sensation like no other. You step into the basket, and with a burst of flame, you rise up, up, up, seemingly weightless. This is how it feels when you fly in a dream, but instead of a ringing alarm clock to break the mood, there's the pop of a champagne cork to enhance it. (What's not to like about a sport that involves drinking bubbly before breakfast?)

If you think hot air ballooning is lacking in thrills, consider this: You're 1,000 feet or so above sea level. You're standing in a basket that's tied to a balloon, kept aloft by blasts of fire. And your pilot has absolutely no directional control. It's kind of like being in a small sailboat with a big spinnaker and no tiller; it's just you and the whim of the wind.

Call it serenity spiked with uncertainty. You float bliss-fully along, rising high and dipping low. Believe it or not, low is the greater rush; you dip far enough to pick leaves from treetops, see the faces of waving children, and scare the bejeezus out of dogs; low enough, sometimes, to get wet. Balloon pilots love to catch currents that allow for a dip into water; they call it "splash and dash." As you'd expect, the views are spectacular, especially during a balloon festival, when the sky is a riot of color and townspeople are lined up on the street, faces pointed heavenward, to watch the show.

We caught a ride with pilot Eric Olsen of Sails Aloft dur-ing the third annual Great Falls Balloon Fest in Lewiston, Maine. Could we learn how to fly a balloon in a day or so, we wondered? No way. Learning to be a balloon pilot is like any other aircraft training, Olsen explained. An oral exam, a flight exam, a written exam, and thirty-five inflight hours are required to get a commercial license. Disappointing news for balloonist wanna-bes; great news for nervous nellies.

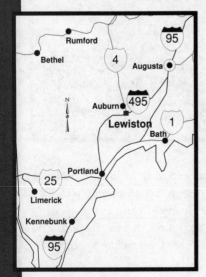

Most balloon festivals last a weekend or so, and include lots of activities that have noth-ing to do with ballooning, like clogging and face-painting. Pick up a schedule of events, then head to a ticket booth to sign up for a ride. Mass bal-loon launches are scheduled for sunrise and sunset. While a sunset ride sounds wonderful, be forewarned: evening launches have a fifty percent cancellation rate due to high

Balloon Festivals

New England hosts several annual balloon festivals, including the Bristol Balloon Fiesta, held over Memorial Day weekend in Bristol, Connecticut (more than 100 balloonists participate, making this the largest festival in New England); the Lake Champlain Balloon Festival, held the first weekend in June in Burlington, Vermont; and the Quechee Balloon Festival, held each June (Father's Day weekend) in Quechee, Vermont. It's a fun atmosphere, and there's nothing quite like the thrill of floating in a balloon-filled sky. Don't miss the nightly "balloon glow," when balloons are lit up, but remain grounded, creating a colorful spectacle in the dark. Other activities might include concerts, square dancing demos, crafts, food booths, fishing derbies, and pancake breakfasts. Souvenirs include balloon-shaped everything. For more information, contact the Balloon Federation of America, P.O. Box 400, Indianola, IA 50125; (515) 961-8809.

winds. The wind tends to be calmer in early morning, so sunrise flights usually take off—eventually. But you may well rouse yourself in the wee hours to catch the 5:30 flight, only to wait two hours to take off because wind conditions aren't right. Under ten knots, pilots say, is ideal. Too much wind turns the balloon, or "envelope," into a spinnaker, dragging and crashing the contraption and its contents.

When the test balloon, or pi ball, has flown successfully, pilot and crew lay out the balloon, hook it to a fan, and blow cold air into it. When it's inflated to eighty or ninety percent of its total volume, the pilot blasts heat into it from the burner. The balloon fills, the basket is upright, the passengers and pilot jump in, and they're flying.

As we ascended, crewmembers Dick and Linda Conant took off in the chase van, trying to keep up with us by land so they could pick us up. (Balloons don't make round trips.) Some might find the chase ride—a merry romp around town with little heed paid to the rules of the road, accompanied by shouts of, "I think they're headed that way! No, over there!"—more exciting than the balloon ride.

Flights generally last from forty-five minutes to an hour-

and-a-half. Ours was long and glorious. The Maine morning was clear and sun-drenched, affording views of Mount Washington, the Atlantic Ocean, and the mist-shrouded valleys of the Androscoggin River. We floated over the river, dazzled by the sight of balloons flying above us, beside us, and, reflected in the water, below us. The loud whoosh! as Olsen periodically cranked the burner made conversation difficult, but we learned a few things: that the pilot can maneuver (but not control) the balloon by picking different altitudes and seeing which way the wind is blowing (a case where spitting into the wind is actually effective). And we learned this sport isn't cheap; a typical unit runs about $25,000, while special shapes, like Malcolm Forbes's Harley-Davidson–shaped balloon, can easily run $100 grand or more. A featured attraction at this festival was a balloon shaped like Noah's ark, filled with animals. Really something to see in the sky.

How safe is a balloon ride? Olsen told us that ballooning fatalities are rare, but accidents do happen. Our research revealed that ballooning is a high-risk sport; a recent survey listed sixty-seven fatalities in 100,000 flights. Most balloon pilots have had a close encounter with a power line, usually during take-off or landing. Not good. "If you touch two lines and you're on the ground, the electricity runs right through you," Olsen said. Another potential problem is high winds during landing, which can lead to a bumpy ride, and bumps and bruises for passengers and crew.

"Danger" isn't the operative word here, but there's a definite unpredictability factor. The day we flew, a fellow balloonist had an unplanned fire, and Olsen himself piloted a later flight that landed bumpily (in about fifteen knots of wind), and deposited him and guests in the middle of nowhere, surrounded by swamp, unreachable by the chase crew. That's part of the thrill of the thing; you just never know.

Some elements are predictable, though. At the end of every flight, there's champagne all around, and a toast from the pilot, "To gentle winds and new friends." Then, more champagne toasts, to the folks whose backyard you happen to land in.

Fairlee, Vermont: Pushing the Envelope with a Champion Balloonist

If You Really Want to See Fall Foliage, Do It in Style

CONTACT: Silver Maple Lodge and Cottages, RR 1, Box 8, Fairlee, VT 05045; (800) 666-1946 or (802) 333-4326. For balloon flights only, call Boland Balloon, (802) 333-9254.

HOW TO GET THERE: Silver Maple Lodge is located off I-91, 21 miles north of White River Junction. From I-91, take Exit 15, and proceed south on Route 5 for 0.5 mile. The inn is on the right, just past Leda's Restaurant.

RATES: The three-day/two-night package, including accommodations, continental breakfast, and balloon ride, costs $225 per person, double occupancy. Inn-only prices range from $49 to $72 per night; balloon rides only are $150 per person. Balloons fly year-round, weather permitting.

WHAT TO BRING: For the flight, rubber-soled shoes are a good idea; also, bring binoculars and a camera. If you plan to eat at the Middlebrook, the area's finest restaurant, bring something nice but not too fancy.

KIDS: Sure.

SKILL LEVEL: None required.

L onging to see Vermont's annual color show, but put off by bumper-to-bumper traffic? Consider rising above the crowds—and the clouds—in a hot air balloon.

From 2,700 feet, Vermont's countryside is a mosaic of fiery hues, and you'll get a bird's-eye view of oaks and sugar maples awash in autumn's palette.

Don't even think about alighting in Vermont from September through October without a room reservation, unless you don't mind spending the night curled up in the back seat of your car. We took care of lodging and balloon ride arrangements in one fell swoop, by reserving with Balloon Inn Vermont.

This package is the brainchild of Scott Wright, who runs the Silver Maple Lodge and Cottages in Fairlee, Vermont. His refurbished eighteenth-century farmhouse is one of the state's oldest continuously operating country inns. It's located right off I-91, which wouldn't seem a great location, but it turns out to be a super base for a balloon-themed getaway; champion balloonist Brian Boland operates out of tiny Post Mills airport, just a pi-ball toss away. Wright offers a three-day, two-night inn stay with a champagne balloon ride (sunrise or sunset) for a flat fee.

The Balloon Inn concept works like a charm for the Silver Maple Lodge—the inn is overwhelmed with business in the fall—and couldn't be easier for guests.

Post Mills airport, situated beside a cemetery (not exactly a confidence booster), is home base for several gliders and some private aircraft. But it's easy to find Boland's digs: his 1971 Volkswagen bus turned hot air balloon grabs the eye immediately. (This contraption actually flies *and* drives, Boland told us.)

In the ballooning world, Boland is a bona fide superstar: besides having 5,000 hours of air-time logged and holding thirty world records in the sport, he designs and builds custom balloons and runs balloon-building camps in Europe. In rural Vermont, though, Boland is just Brian the Balloon Guy.

Aloft under a gorgeous Boland-designed envelope (balloon) of alternating checks in black, green, yellow, blue, red, and orange, we climbed over color-dappled hillsides and saw a couple of deer bounding along. The sudden whooshing of the balloon's burner probably startled them. Boland has seen a bear and several moose from this vantage point. As many times as he's done this route, he said, "It's absolutely different each time you fly."

Part of the fun of ballooning with Boland is hearing tales of this daring not-so-young man and his flying machine. The day before we went up, a couple from Rhode Island got married aboard his balloon. Once, he held a family reunion aloft, but the balloon got hung up in a tree and everybody had to climb down, to be rescued the next day by an all-terrain vehicle. Then there was the dead woman who flew not once but several times, courtesy of her daughters. "She'd always wanted to take a balloon flight, but never got around to it," Boland said. He figured they'd scatter her ashes in the beautiful hillsides, but the daughters treated Mom to annual rides instead. Did Mom ride for free? "Yup. You might say she urned it," Boland said solemnly.

He also has a Century Club; folks age 100 and up ride free. One 105-year-old takes advantage of it every year. Boland also has a wheelchair-accessible gondola, so everyone can enjoy the lighter-than-air sensation of floating above the treetops.

In twenty-five years of ballooning, Boland has had some wild times. He's flown in the Andes, and once flew out of a sinkhole in Brazil for a TV show taping. "We hit a cliffside, and rocks came rolling into the basket," he recalled. "We landed in the jungle like a ton of bricks."

Boland has undertaken the balloonist's version of extreme sport: balloon camping. The idea is to fly from one day to the next, with no chase crew to pick up pilot and balloon, and to follow that the next day with a second flight. This is a risky undertaking, because there's no telling where the balloon will land; you can only play the wind shifts and currents to a certain extent. To do it in the daylight is tricky enough; to do it in the dark, where power lines and other hazards lurk unseen, is life-on-the-edge stuff. "Some pilots think flying in the dark is suicidal," Boland said.

But this guy is always game for a challenge. During our tour de foliage, we couldn't help but notice there were no big clearings that looked suitable for landing, just dense forests and tree-covered hillsides. "Hey, I see a parking space!" said Boland, indicating a postage stamp–size patch of green below us. He had to be joking; between us and the spot were massive trees. "This will be great," he announced, maneuvering us into a tree. "We're perching!" he said, adding, "I did this on purpose."

Sure enough, rocking ever-so-gently on a bough, we tumbled into a VW-sized parking space behind a garage.

Resources

Additional Balloon Companies

Balloon Adventures of New Bedford, South Dartmouth, MA; (508) 636-4846.

Balloon Flights of New England, North Attleboro, MA; (508) 695-3700.

Balloon School of Massachusetts, Brimfield, MA; (413) 245-4846.

Ballooning Adventures of Vermont, Underhill Center, VT; (802) 899-2993.

Ballooning with the Burchs, Dover, NH; (603) 743-0968.

Berkshire Balloons, Southington, CT; (203) 250-8441.

Connecticut Balloon Adventures, Bristol, CT; (203) 583-2518.

Higher for Hire, Berlin, CT; (860) 828-4575.

Kat Balloons, Farmington, CT; (203) 678-7921.

New Hampshire Ballooning, Derry, NH; (603) 434-1910.

Shephard Charter Flights, Mansfield, MA; (508) 339-9546.

Splash & Dash Hot Air Ballooning, Auburn, NH; (603) 483-5503.

Stoweflake Inn & Resort, Stowe, VT; (800) 253-2232.

Stumpf Balloons, Bristol, RI; (401) 253-0111.

Watershed Balloons, Watertown, CT; (203) 274-2010.

BOOKS

Ballooning: The Complete Guide to Riding the Winds. Dick Wirth and Jerry Young, Marshall Editions, Ltd.

Soaring, Gliding, and Skydiving

CHRISTIAN SEWELL

Franconia Notch, New Hampshire: Soaring the Notch

Riding on Silent Wings

CONTACT: Franconia Soaring Association, Franconia Airport, Franconia, NH 03580; (603) 226-2600.

HOW TO GET THERE: Take Exit 3 off the Franconia Notch Parkway; follow Route 18 north. The airport is 3 miles from the exit. You can't miss the airport directional signs.

RATES: A 15-minute flight costs $55.

WHAT TO BRING: A sense of adventure is all you'll need.

KIDS: Yes.

SKILL LEVEL: No experience is necessary, but don't go if you're afraid of heights.

A flock of hawks, hundreds of them, soared on silent wings in a sky the color of morning glories. We watched, mesmerized, as they gracefully, almost motionlessly, rode the invisible winds, performing a majestic, magical aerial dance.

It is this image we took with us as we slid into the sleek fiberglass body of the glider plane for our first flight. It was better than the other images that kept creeping into the black back crevices of our mind: massive winds blowing us into the mountainside; dying winds leaving us plummeting to earth; unexplained equipment failure. . . .

But the seductive promise of riding mountain airwaves, soaring like a bird in an ocean of silence, won out over fear. The tow plane got us started and then quickly dropped the

umbilical cord. Our stomachs dropped, too, as we antici-
pated a freefall to earth, victims of gravity's pull. Instead,
we ascended smoothly on a thermal; it was like a magic
carpet ride.

"The rates of climb for a sailplane can exceed 3,000 feet
a minute," our pilot told us. We were up over 4,000 feet,
above the mountains, banking back and forth as if in a giant
swing over the earth. The pilot flew up and down over spectacular Franconia Notch, a gorgeous jumble of craggy
peaks, fractured granite, gorges, and dense forests. We
floated and soared in incredible silence; we heard only the
occasional whoosh of wind around the wings. "Like being in
the hands of God," our pilot remarked. He had read the
quote somewhere, and didn't remember who'd said it; but
he never forgot the apt description. A half hour later, we
landed softly, back on the tiny Franconia airstrip.

"I've soared all over the world. There's no place better
than right here in Franconia Notch," said Ed Gaffee, a
member of the Franconia Soaring Association. It is the
winds that make this region special, he told us. Most of the
time, sailplanes work with one, maybe two types of winds.
Here in the Notch, Gaffee said, there are often four kinds:
thermal, mountain, ridge, and ocean. This makes for very
good soaring.

A night earlier we heard of other great soaring locations

when we hooked up with the
Franconia Soaring Association.
This brotherhood/sisterhood of
pilots leases a farmhouse for those
who share the passion and sweet
addiction for soaring. Hang
around these folks, and you'll
catch snatches of tales and
dreams.

"I've got a friend who's heading
out to the Sierras next month,"
someone said to the group waiting
at the farmhouse for the right
soaring conditions. A mecca for
engineless flights, the California

City Airport in the Sierra Nevada is where many altitude and distance records are captured. Pilots have been known to solo soar more than 40,000 feet up and ride airwaves cross-country for more than 900 miles.

We also heard deadly tales of gliders getting caught in rotor turbulence, a mass of wind beneath the plane that can toss it out of control; of pilots slipping into unconsciousness when the oxygen system failed; of deep freezes and misjudgments. Our faces must have clouded over with panic, because several in the group hastened to tell us that recreational gliding is "very safe." In fact, it has an accident rate less than one-third that of small airplane flying.

For hours, we talked weather: mountain winds, thermals, ocean breezes, lifts, crosswinds, rotors, lenticular clouds. If you ever want an accurate prediction of the climate, forget the weather station and look up a sailplane pilot.

But why, we asked, are they so hooked on engineless flying? Why do they chase mountain waves?

"It's complete, absolute absorption," said one pilot. "When I'm up there, everything else disappears."

"It's cheaper than therapy," another joked.

"It's the quiet and the beauty."

"It's indescribable; you'll have to try it yourself."

And so we did. "What do you think?" they asked as we climbed out of the plane.

We thought of soaring hawks . . . costly elixirs . . . sweet addictions. "Can we go again?" we asked.

Burlington, Vermont: (Para)Flying Like an Eagle

On a Wing and a Prayer

CONTACT: Parafly Paragliding, P.O. Box 191, Burlington, VT 05402; (800) PARAFLY.

HOW TO GET THERE: To reach Cobble Hill in Milton, Vermont, take I-89 to Exit 17; turn left off the exit, then left again onto Route 7 north. Continue about 5 miles to Bombardier Road. Take a right; go 0.25 mile to the first intersection and take another right. Cobble Hill will be in front of you. Take an immediate right onto Cobble Hill Road, and follow it up the hill through the gate.

RATES: The first lesson is $125; subsequent lessons are $90. A novice package, including six lessons, is $500.

WHAT TO BRING: Comfortable clothing, running shoes, a light lunch, and a water bottle.

KIDS: This adventure is not suitable for children.

SKILL LEVEL: No experience is necessary, but you should be in strong physical condition. Paragliding requires strenuous running and hiking back up the hill.

Avid hang glider Rick Sharp wanted to make his passion pay. In 1984, he bought Cobble Hill in Milton, Vermont, with the dream of turning it into a school for hang gliding pilots. He took off on his first Cobble Hill flight, and immediately got into trouble. Heading for the houses in a nearby subdivision, with a series of power lines in his path, he stalled the glider at forty feet. What went wrong? It turns out that the logistics of Cobble Hill just aren't right for hang gliding. Sharp was devastated. Then, a friend suggested he try paragliding, instead. No way; ridiculous, he thought. But finally, he gave it a whirl. He hasn't looked back since.

"It is the closest way we have to flying like a bird," Sharp explained.

Paragliding, a cross between parachuting and hang gliding, is the newest rage in our ancient quest to fly. Launched in 1985, paragliding was developed by European mountaineers who sought a more direct, easier way down from their summit ascents. Weighing only about twenty pounds, the paraglider is the lightest aircraft in the world, and can easily fit into a backpack. Today, there are more than 90,000 paragliders in Europe and another 50,000 in Japan. But the sport has just begun to catch on in the United States, where only about 2,000 pilots participate in the sport.

That number will rise if Sharp has his way. He and his wife, Ruth Masters, own Parafly Paragliding, and they are teaching hundreds of earthbound souls the intoxicating joy of taking flight.

"It is the most incredible thing I have ever done," said Ailsa Bennel after her first launch. "It's indescribable . . . an exhilarating sense of freedom."

Unlike hang gliders, paragliders have no rigid supports or fixed wings. Instead, pilots sit in a harness and control the glider with lines that run to a wing-shaped canopy. Pilots say it's easier and quicker to learn than hang gliding, and less expensive. And there's that business about hill logistics: Hang gliders need a twelve-one glider ratio, while paragliders can get aloft with only a six-one pitch (in average conditions, paragliders need to travel six feet forward for every foot they descend). This means paragliders can find a lot more places to practice their sport than their hang

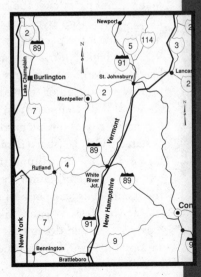

gliding cousins can. While paragliders have not achieved the astounding records of hang gliders, their flights have been known to reach heights of almost 15,000 feet, and to travel more than 175 miles.

We showed up for Parafly's one-day introductory lesson with flights of fancy dancing through our heads. Lesson number one: be ready to cancel all plans. Paragliding is weather-dependent; if conditions are not perfect, class is canceled. You have to have wind, but not too much wind. And it has to be blowing in the right direction; Cobble Hill is currently flyable only in north and northwest winds. Sharp hopes to open the south and west sides of the hill in the future.

It took three tries before our class was held. Ground school included instruction on paragliding technique, safety, and aerodynamic theory. It ended with an inspiring video showing spectacular flights in incredibly beautiful areas. Now, this is more like it, we thought; let's skip aerodynamics and get to the good stuff. We were psyched to soar. We were off to Cobble Hill before we knew it.

In theory, it's easy: Run into the wind, allowing the canopy to inflate, and you're off. In practice, it's much tougher. First, we practiced without the canopy, running down the hill a short distance, carrying out Sharp's commands, and practicing the sequence of tasks that would get us airborne. After five or six tries, when Sharp thought we had the idea, the paraglider was attached.

We wiggled into a seat harness, while Sharp laid out the brightly colored canopy and checked the lines to make sure none were tangled or twisted. "Run, run, run," Sharp shouted. "Lift your arms; now, let go of the lines." We ran as fast as we could down a gradual slope; the canopy filled, then deflated. "Good," Sharp commended. "Let's try it again."

And so it went. Run; lift; deflate. Gradually, we worked our way up the hill, until we were at the midstation, where the incline was sharper and required less running.

"Faster, faster, faster," Sharp shouted. We pumped as hard as we could down the slope. "Arms up! Arms up!" The canopy billowed, feet left the ground . . . we were flying! It was a foot, maybe two, of height, and only a second of air-time. Still, it was a rush.

If the weather remains favorable, and you learn your lessons well, the day will end with a flight off the top of 900-foot Cobble Hill. It took seven years to clear the jumble of scrub brush, wild bushes, and pine that blanketed the nob. From the top, there's a pretty view of Lake Champlain and the Adirondack Mountains. But who can soak up scenery when it's time to soar?

We were prepared for a real launch. From the top of Cobble, the pilot has only about twenty to thirty feet before the hill drops off. No wonder we practiced running fast, we thought. If we don't catch the wind in this distance, we'll land in the middle of the brush and have to crawl up the side of the mountain. Sharp gave detailed last-minute instructions. Run; accelerate; hands up; launch . . . 900 feet in the air. Our sixty seconds of flight felt like hours. Then, plunk! Not a graceful landing, but who cared? We had flown like the birds.

Pepperell, Massachusetts: Ready, Set, Jump!

For Many, Skydiving Is the Ultimate Thrill

CONTACT: Pepperell Skydiving Center, Route 111, Pepperell Airport, Pepperell, MA 01463; (508) 433-9222 or (800) SKY-JUMP. In addition to the tandem skydive class, they teach a seven-level accelerated freefall skydiving course and a static line training course.

HOW TO GET THERE: Take Route 128 or Route 495 (depending on where you're coming from) to Route 3 north, into New Hampshire. Take NH Exit 5 west onto Route 111 (this will take you back into Massachusetts). The airport is 5 miles west on the left.

RATES: A tandem skydive costs $195; a videotape of your jump costs $75. Reservations are a must, and a deposit is required.

WHAT TO BRING: Wear casual, comfortable clothing and a good pair of athletic shoes. You can bring a couple of friends to ride along.

KIDS: In the state of Massachusetts, you must be eighteen to skydive.

SKILL LEVEL: You should be in good physical condition. Recommended weight is 70 to 240 pounds for a tandem training jump.

The next time you're on a plane and the captain says, "We're at 11,000 feet and climbing," take a look out the window. Notice how small everything looks from more than two miles up, how the ground looks like a patchwork quilt and the houses look like toys? Now, imagine jumping out. That's how it feels to prepare for a parachute jump.

For many, this is the ultimate adrenaline rush. Lots of perfectly normal people are afraid to even fly in a plane; to jump out of one takes a real leap of faith: faith in your instructor, faith in your equipment, belief in yourself, and the conviction that a higher power will keep you from being squashed like a bug on a windshield.

Pepperell Skydiving Center's Tom Cahill told us that some people jump as a rite of passage, to celebrate a marriage, a milestone birthday, or beating cancer. Some claim skydiving has curative powers; that they've been cured of blindness or multiple sclerosis during a parachute jump. (Of course, some people are cured of the urge to ever want to do it again.)

Powerful stuff, yet skydiving is amazingly accessible. Sign up for a tandem jump, where you'll be tethered to an instructor under a parachute built for two, and you'll get the thrill of a freefall with a minimum amount of ground training required.

First, we watched two videos. The first—and longest— featured an attorney explaining the release-of-liability form participants are required to sign. The next video covered skydiving basics, and showed an actual tandem jump.

Cahill, our instructor, had completed more than 1,500 jumps in five years. He had all the requisite licenses and certificates (FAA, United States Parachute Association, Massachusetts Aeronautics Commission), as well as a friendly, easygoing manner. He led us through the steps necessary to prepare for the jump, outfitting us with a jumpsuit, a helmet, goggles, gloves, and an altimeter. We reviewed the parachute equipment, and were pleased at how high-tech it looked. If, for any reason, the primary parachute failed to open, a reserve chute would automatically activate.

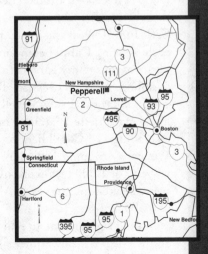

Next, we practiced jumping out of a Cessna airplane door, part of an old grounded plane. (We tried not to think about what might've happened to the rest of it.) Then we practiced "arching," lying belly-down on a table covered with a foam pad, back arched, head, arms, and legs as high as possible. "Arching helps keep you stable during the freefall, and keeps you from tumbling," Cahill explained. We committed the pose to memory, wondering if it would ever come in handy for anything other than skydiving.

Next came ripcord-pulling practice. "When we fall to 5,500 feet, pull it," Cahill said. (He'd be wearing a parachute too, just in case.) We'd be clipped together at four different places; industrial-strength clips, we hoped.

After thirty minutes of instruction, we met the plane, a Cessna 205, on the runway. We were accompanied by Christian Sewell, a skydiver so skilled he can jump and take video and still pictures at the same time. (This option is definitely worth the extra cost; you'll want to have a visual record of your adventure.) A solo skydiver also joined us.

As the plane ascended, we could see the Boston skyline, Cape Cod, and mountains in all directions. The Pepperell Airport was starting to look mighty tiny. At 9,000 feet, the door opened and the solo skydiver jumped. As we watched him drop away from the plane, the intensity of this experience suddenly sunk in.

Eleven thousand feet, the target altitude for our jump. Cahill motioned me to kneel beside the door. "Are you ready?" he asked. I took a deep breath and gave him a thumbs-up. It was now or never. The door opened. "Ready! Set! Jump!" Was this really happening? I remembered to arch, sensing Cahill behind me. The air was rushing loudly past, roaring in my ears. Strangely, there was no real sense of falling, perhaps because of the lack of reference points.

To my right, I saw Sewell shooting the video, suspended like a marionette, matching our altitude. Freefalling . . . freefalling . . . Cahill had said this is what skydivers live for. We were dropping 120 miles per hour, reaching a maximum velocity of 1,000 feet every five seconds. My cheeks were being sucked into my ears. After forty-five seconds, we fell to 5,500 feet.

Cahill signaled me to pull the ripcord. I heard a whoosh, and we began a slow, quiet ride under the parachute. Now I could sightsee a bit; in the arched position, you're looking straight ahead. "Pull to the left," Cahill said. "Let go and pull to the right." Hey, you can actually steer these things. It was fun. After several minutes, Cahill guided us between the target marks on the landing field. By pulling the chute's left and right cords at the same time, we slowed our descent, and our landing was surprisingly gentle.

I felt shaken and spent, the way one does after a close call with a big truck on the highway. Mostly, though, I felt exhilarated.

The reality is, skydiving isn't as dangerous as most of us imagine. The Pepperell Skydiving Center is the site of more than 15,000 jumps a year, with an injury rate of five to fifteen incidents annually (mostly, sprained or broken ankles). Thanks to advancements in skydiving equipment, fatalities are rare. With an injury rate of less than one-tenth of one percent, jumping out of a plane is safer than driving in rush-hour traffic.

All that's academic, though. Skydiving evokes an emotional response. When we jump, we confront our fears, our faith, and, ultimately, the notion that some things are worth the risk.

Winsted, Connecticut: Hang Gliding for Beginners

Here's How It Feels to Be a Human Kite

CONTACT: Tek Flight Products, Colebrook Stage, Winsted, CT 06098; (203) 379-1668. You can take a single lesson, a four-lesson course, or a Spectrum course including fourteen lessons and a credit toward the purchase of a Spectrum hang glider.

HOW TO GET THERE: Take Route 44 west from Hartford to Winsted; from Winsted, follow Route 183 north. A small sign marks the place where you turn off the road to park, at the base of the hill.

RATES: A single lesson of 4 to 8 hours, including ground school, simulator training, ground handling, and flying (as conditions permit) costs $85. A four-lesson course is $200.

WHAT TO BRING: Comfortable clothing, rubber-soled shoes, and a snack or a bag lunch.

KIDS: This adventure is not suitable for children.

SKILL LEVEL: Although Tek Flight stresses that physical strength isn't a priority, you should have enough upper body strength to carry the apparatus on your shoulders while running. With today's fairly light, easy-to-control gliders, 100-pounders can manage it.

Humankind's urge to fly probably predates Icarus. But we've come a long way since the days of wax and feathers. We've even come a long way since the early 1970s, when hang gliding had a poor safety record and was called "sky surfing" by the daredevils who took up the sport with little or no formal training.

Hang gliding has evolved. "The gliders have become

higher-performing, stronger, and more stable, but also more complicated, more expensive, and a lot harder to learn to fly," according to Mike Meier, who writes for *Hang Gliding* magazine. Today's high-tech gliders are safer, and most pilots learn to fly from a professional instructor. But this sport is far from tame.

When accidents do occur, they usually are caused by gross pilot error. "Just about every year at least one pilot kills himself by simply neglecting to attach himself to his glider before flinging himself off a mountainside," Meier wrote. Recent studies show that the fatality rate for hang gliding is about twenty-two deaths per 100,000 attempts; driving a car results in twenty-eight deaths per 100,000 trips. Students under instructor supervision are, statistically, safer than drivers.

With our fear put into perspective, we drove to Tek Flight, in Winsted, Connecticut, for an introductory lesson. Ben and Alegra Davidson, certified as instructors by the U.S. Hang Gliding Association, have been teaching the sport for twenty years. Their property, atop a steep hill, had a neglected look that suggested the owners' attentions were focused elsewhere. Aging vehicles were parked around the house; inside, the living room was heaped with bagged gliders, racks of aluminum tubing, harnesses, helmets, and gear. Nobody answered the door, so we walked right in.

"You're late," Alegra said icily. She introduced us to Ben, and they ushered us into the office/classroom to look at some videotapes. We signed a waiver form, and noticed that the training tape was self-produced. In fact, everything in the place looked to be homemade, antique, or recycled. Ben and Alegra are among the last of the rugged individualists.

Another student showed up, really nervous, having second thoughts about learning to hang glide. Alegra assured

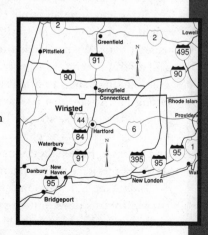

him, "We won't let you try anything if we're not sure you can execute it safely."

Ground school included more videotape and lots of discussion about hang gliding as a sport, and the thrill of flying, "Unlike anything you've ever experienced before," Alegra said. Her passion for the sport melted her frosty reserve, and she and Ben fell into the roles of guides, gurus, and chums.

Next, we moved to simulator training. We were strapped into a harness, which supports the body, sling-like, from shoulder to knee, with several straps leading to a large clip behind the back. The clip connects to the kite. Advanced hang gliders wear harnesses that look like sleeping bags; ours were smaller and easier to run around in.

The simulator was an aluminum frame like a porch swing, with a glider control bar and harness hookup loop mounted on a gimbal. We took turns getting used to it, while the instructor moved the frame from side to side and forward and backward. "Try it with your eyes closed," said Ben. We did, wondering why on earth anyone would jump off a mountain with his eyes shut. We practiced the landing maneuver, learning how to "flare" the kite while lowering the landing gear (our feet).

Time for the bunny hill. The property has three wide, grassy hills: the A hill (bunny slope), which features a cable system that attaches to the top of the glider to break a student pilot's fall in case of mental meltdown; the higher, longer B hill; and C, a launching spot higher up than B.

After watching a couple of demo flights, we decided this might not be so bad. Even the terrified guy had lost his ashen pallor. We proceeded to the bottom of the hill with a glider strapped on. Our instructions were to run as fast as possible, then slightly pitch the glider up until it created enough lift to support its own weight and put upward pressure on the harness straps. Then, we were supposed to push hard, forward, on the control frame to create flare. This is an awkward little ballet; must be how a dancer feels when doing grand jetés with a partner on his shoulders.

Balancing a fifty-pound, twenty-five-foot kite takes some effort, as does building up high speed in just six or eight steps. Combining these is a real trick. And carrying the gliders back up the hill to do it all over again makes this a strenuous workout. Some stretching and warm-up exercises wouldn't have hurt, nor would a bite of lunch. We'd been on the road or in the lesson all day without a morsel of food. Famished, we asked for, and got, a snack. (Tip: Bring your lunch, or eat a huge breakfast before you get here.)

We'd gained some confidence with our runs on the lower part of the hill, so we proceeded to the top, like baby birds ready to leave the nest. We went through all the steps: running launch; pitch the glider up; keep running until you're off the ground; lean into the harness; let gravity take over. Next thing we knew, we were gliding down the hill into the landing area, about forty or fifty feet away.

We weren't exactly soaring like eagles, but we weren't dragging along the ground, either. After several more runs, we were getting the feel for it, losing the sensation of trailing legs and feet and replacing it with something that felt buoyant. Delicious. Imagine what it must feel like to fly off a real mountain. . . .

Resources

Additional Places to Soar

Berkshire Soaring Society, Pittsfield Airport, Pittsfield, MA 01202; (413) 443-5788.

Cape Cod Soaring Adventures, Cape Cod Airport, Marstons Mills, MA 02648; (508) 540-8081.

Captain Eli's Glider Flights, Pepperell Sports Center Airport, Pepperell, MA 01463; (508) 433-9222.

Connecticut Soaring Center, Waterbury-Plymouth Airport, Plymouth, CT 06782.

Island Soaring, Bar Harbor Airport, Bar Harbor, ME 04609; (207) 667-7027.

Stowe Aviation, Morrisville-Stowe Airport, Morrisville, VT 05661; (802) 888-7845.

Sugarbush Soaring Association, Warren, VT 05674; (802) 496-2290.

Additional Places to Paraglide or Hang Glide

Morningside Flight Park, RFD 2, P.O. Box 109, Claremont, NH 03743; (603) 542-4416.

Sky Ambitions, P.O. Box 479, Madison, NH 03849; (603) 367-8791.

Additional Places to Skydive

Airborne Adventures Skydiving School, Northampton Airport, Northampton, MA 01060; (413) 586-1889.

Boston-Providence Skydiving Center, North Central Airport, 380 Jenckes Hill Road, Lincoln, RI 02865; (401) 333-3663.

Central Maine Skydiving, Maine Flight Center, Pittsfield Airport, Harrison Avenue, Pittsfield, ME 04967; (207) 487-5638.

Massachusetts Sport Parachute Club, P.O. Box 122,
   Turners Falls, MA 01376; (413) 863-8362.
Skydive Lebanon Maine, Upper Guinea Road, RFD #1,
   P.O. Box 1255, Lebanon, ME 04027; (207) 339-1520.
Skydive Shelburne, Shelburne Airport, Shelburne, VT
   05482; (802) 985-2100.

INFORMATION AND BOOKS

For more information on paragliding and hang gliding,
contact the United States Hang Gliding Association
(USHGA), P.O. Box 1330, Colorado Springs, CO 80901;
(800) 616-6888 or (719) 632-8300. USHGA also distributes
a number of books, including:

Alpha Flight. Mark Wright.
Hang Gliding Flying Skills. Dennis Pagen.
Hang Gliding for Beginner Pilots. Peter Cheney.
Paragliding: A Pilot's Training Manual. Wills Wing.
Paragliding: Flight-Walking on Air. Dennis Pagen.

Cross-Country Skiing

306

Bethel, Maine:
Skinny Skiing at the Telemark Inn

With Killer Skiing, Sleigh Rides, and Hot Tubs,
Who Cares If It's Too Cold to Sleep?

CONTACT: The Telemark Inn, RFD 2, Box 800, Bethel, ME 04217; (207) 836-2703.

HOW TO GET THERE: Take the Maine Turnpike to Exit 11 (Gray). Take Route 26 north to Bethel (roughly 40 miles). Approaching town, look for a sign for Route 2; go north on Route 2 for about 4 miles, then turn left on Flat Road. Go 2.6 miles and turn right. At 0.6 miles, turn right, then watch for the Telemark Inn sign.

RATES: A two-day weekend package, including trail passes and meals from Saturday breakfast through Sunday lunch, costs $198 per person, double occupancy. A trail pass alone (for nonguests) costs $15 per person.

WHAT TO BRING: Cross-country skis, ice skates (or you can rent them from Telemark Inn), warm clothing for layering, a swimsuit, a towel, and casual warm clothes for après ski.

KIDS: Yes, at reduced rates. Children especially enjoy skating on the pond, the marshmallow roast, and feeding the inn's animals.

SKILL LEVEL: All levels. Ski lessons are available for novices; all skiers will find challenging runs on the groomed lower trails or the backcountry terrain.

Remember playing King of the Mountain as a child? We met the kid who won. His name is Steve Crone, and he's got a nice patch of Maine mountain all to himself.

He doesn't actually own the hill, but his lodge, the Telemark Inn, is tucked inside White Mountains National Forest at the base of Caribou Mountain. Want to play? Bring skinny skis and polar fleece, and prepare to be wowed by this unique property.

The Telemark Inn & Ski Touring Center is ten miles from Bethel, Maine, but this tells you nothing. Somewhere in the village, you take a left and keep going and going and going, until someone in the car exclaims, "This can't be right!" At that point, you're almost there. Look closely for the small, hand-lettered Telemark sign, then point your vehicle straight up the hill.

As you drive up, you'll pass a skating rink and a menagerie of resident llamas, horses, and goats. The lodge itself, a turn-of-the-century Adirondack-style retreat, was built by Prudential Insurance Company founder Leon Blanchard. Its most intriguing feature is a huge stone fireplace that's usually bedecked with wool socks and boots that need thawing. The overstuffed chairs, hand-built cabinetry, and abundance of books create a cozy escape from the harsh Maine winter. The weekend we visited, the mercury never budged above the ten-degree mark. But that didn't stop us from running around outdoors in our swimsuits (more about that later).

As Nordic skiers, we were naturally more concerned about snow than cold. New Englanders have suffered through enough snow-drought years to be mighty wary of planning a cross-country ski trip in advance. "We've got piles of snow," Crone had assured us on the phone. He wasn't exaggerating. We couldn't wait to carve trails in the fresh carpet of white.

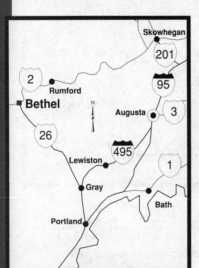

Crone's property has won rave reviews for its twenty kilometers of wide, scenic hillside trails, which are tracked for traditional and skate-style skiing. There's also direct access to ungroomed terrain in the backcountry of White Mountain National Forest.

The Telemark Inn caters to the skier looking for a peaceful getaway. To preserve the alone-in-the-wilderness feel of the area, Crone limits the number of trail passes he sells. If a long day of skiing followed by an energetic game of Scrabble is your idea of the high life, this is your kind of place.

The inn has six bedrooms and sleeps sixteen. The weekend we were there, there were only four guests, plus Crone and innkeeper Jo Faubert. We found ourselves wishing for a full house, simply to generate body heat. The inn is heated by woodstoves, but our rustic room didn't sport one, so we spent much of the night piling on layers of clothing, shuffling back and forth to the dining room for a hit of heat, and trying to lure the resident puppies into bed with us. Getting up in the morning was the hardest part; we could actually see our breath. Fortunately, Crone and Faubert had arisen early to stoke the fire and make pancakes for breakfast.

Outside, snow was falling; several inches had accumulated since our arrival. Crone was long gone. He had set out on his grooming machine to track the trails. "He's a maniac," Faubert said sweetly. So far, Crone had been a phantom host, plowing the road by night and grooming the trails by day. The most we did was exchange a few wisecracks about our classic wooden skis versus his flashy short jobs, and the length of his ponytail compared to ours (he won by several inches).

The skiing was sublime. Dry, fluffy snow created a cushiony surface and a dreamlike landscape. Snowy skies and humpy trails melded into one. Snow continued to fall as we sampled long, steep runs; wide, tree-lined, twisty trails; and just enough climbs to keep us warm and limber. Another couple from the inn was out skiing, too, but we quickly lost sight of each other. Visibility was low, so the uncertainty of what lay ahead added a spooky dimension to the trails. Now and then, Crone passed by on his snow machine; he looked like a wild-eyed cowboy in a ski cap. We skied until we were spent, then stopped to visit the llamas before we went in. One particularly adorable creature stuck out its tongue, catching snowflakes.

Cross-Country Skiing

After doffing ice-crusted duds and warming up in front of the giant fireplace, we gathered for dinner. We made short work of the meal, then began to ponder what to do next. Skating, perhaps? The rink, illuminated by kerosene lanterns and offering a pondside fire, was an inviting option. Too ambitious, we decided. Should we bundle up for a horse-drawn sleigh ride, maybe? No, we'd save that for tomorrow. The other couple retreated to a Scrabble game, leaving us and the hot tub. No contest.

"You know, this is crazy," one of us said as we pulled off Icelandic woolens and pulled on swimsuits. The temperature had dipped into the single digits and we were going outside to get wet? We put ski jackets on over our Spandex and ran, barefoot, through knee-deep snow to the wood-fired hot tub. The air was numbingly cold. The tub was awesomely hot. "Some say the world will end in fire, others say in ice," New England poet Robert Frost wrote. At that moment, we wouldn't have budged if the devil himself had appeared on a Sno-Cat.

"Wonder what it would feel like to roll in the snowbank, then jump into the hot tub?" someone said. There was only one way to find out. Flesh tingling, eyelashes frosted with ice, we giggled in the moonlight. You can have April in Paris. We'll take the rough-hewn romance of a hot tub in Maine any day.

Gorham, New Hampshire: Backcountry Skiing in the Whites

Go Off-Trail for Solitude and Scenery

CONTACT: White Mountain National Forest, Androscoggin Ranger District, 80 Glen Road, Gorham, NH 03581; (603) 466-2713. The Appalachian Mountain Club (AMC) can also supply information on trails and weather conditions; write them at P.O. Box 298, Gorham, NH 03581, or call (603) 466-2725. The state of New Hampshire offers a recorded cross-country skiing report; call (603) 224-6363.

HOW TO GET THERE: Directions to trailheads are available at the Androscoggin Ranger Station in Gorham, on Route 16, about 0.5 mile south of Route 2; or at AMC headquarters in Pinkham Notch, on Route 16, about 18 miles north of North Conway.

RATES: Access to trails and parking at the trailheads are free. Overnight accommodations at the AMC Zealand and Carter Notch huts are $18.

WHAT TO BRING: Carry a compass and map (and be sure you know how to use them), winter survival gear (do some research into specifics), an emergency ski repair kit, food, drink, winter gear, and snowshoes. Leave your dog home.

KIDS: Consider their abilities, and use your judgment when selecting trails.

SKILL LEVEL: Varies, depending on trail selection.

It's Saturday morning and you're heading to the mountains for adventure, skinny skis clamped to the car rack. If you want to get your heart pounding, bypass the well-traveled, impeccably groomed trails that are as wide and smooth as a golf fairway. Instead, head into the woods and mountains, where the snow is deep and the crowds are thin, and untracked trails aren't exhausted by noon.

The White Mountains of New Hampshire offer back-country skiers hundreds of forested hideaways in which to slide, skin, and skate for miles on snow that's never seen the claws of a Cat.

"There are lots of backcountry trails, from flat carriage roads to steep, expert terrain," said Andrea Muller, the winter course instructor for the Appalachian Mountain Club. "The thing to remember is that it's high elevation, and trail conditions can change radically on any given day."

All backcountry skiers should check in with the Androscoggin Ranger Station in Gorham or the folks at the Appalachian Mountain Club headquarters in Pinkham Notch. They can suggest routes and provide up-to-the-minute trail conditions.

Beginners will like skiing to pretty Zealand Notch. It's a thirteen-mile round-trip on moderate to easy terrain. Follow the unplowed Zealand Road, off Route 302, just east of Twin Mountain, for about four miles, until it intersects with Zealand Trail. You'll twist your way through a hardwood and balsam fir forest, paralleling the Zealand River. The trail skirts the banks of a frozen beaver pond (a favorite hangout

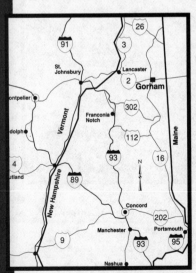

for moose), then heads to the top of the notch. The steep ascent up to Zealand Falls is worth the climb. The falls are a wintery menage of ice and trickling water, surrounded by shimmering sheets of black-gray granite. Think ahead and reserve a spot at the hut, one of only two in the Appalachian Mountain Club system that remain open for the winter. You'll enjoy the warmth, provided by propane heaters, and the use of kitchen facilities.

This is not a trip for silence

and solitude. The trail is popular with skiers; the hut is often full during winter weekends; and Zealand Road is open to snowmobilers. Still, it's a nice excursion for beginners, and for families looking for their first taste of backcountry terrain.

If you're an intermediate skier, eschew the road and ski Spruce Goose Trail to Zealand Trail. This wide up-and-down track parallels the road, so you'll avoid other skiers and machines. Take Zealand Road over the bridge; as you start uphill, look for Spruce Goose Trail on your right.

The hushed beauty of the Great White Hills will be all yours if you venture farther into the Pemigewasset Wilderness, where you can go for miles without seeing another two-legged traveler. From Zealand Falls, follow Ethan Pond Trail; then, take your pick. There are lots of trail choices; most are easy to moderate grades. We liked Shoal Pond Trail, which winds around the pond, passing through marshlands, and then follows old tote roads and railroad beds. As you skirt Shoal Pond, be on the lookout for moose, especially in the open, swampy areas along the edge of the water, where they feed on twigs, bark, and stems. Observe from a distance so you don't disturb them; you don't want to make a moose angry. These magnificent beasts are five to six-and-one-half feet tall at the shoulders; males, on average, weigh more than 1,000 pounds; and the record antler spread is more than six feet.

Follow Shoal Pond Trail for four and a half miles, until it intersects with the Wilderness Trail, one of the easiest and prettiest routes in the Whites. The Wilderness Trail meanders along the East Branch of the Pemigewasset River and provides access to other trails. This is a great place for winter camping. (The closer you get to the Kancamagus Highway, the more day-trip skiers you're likely to encounter. If it's solitude you want, stay away from the Kanc.)

Ready for a challenge? Intermediate and advanced skiers can hike up Tuckerman's Ravine Trail or skin up the John Sherburn Trail. This is beautiful country, especially in winter. Lion Head is to the north; Boott Spur is to the south. Point your skis toward the Pinkham Notch Visitors Center and follow the wide, twisty trail back to where you began. You never know what conditions you'll encounter on this trail. If the snow gods have smiled, there will be fresh dumps of white powder. If an emergency vehicle has tucked and rolled the trail, it will be a choppy ski.

After a good night's sleep and a bowl of Wheaties, you might be ready to tackle the tough, tortuous terrain of the Gulf of Slides. This steep, wind-slapped, exposed run is not for the faint of heart. Attempt it only on friendly days, preferably when the sun is shining and the wind is dead. The very best skiers can skin up Gulf of Slides Trail (the trailhead is located at the south end of the Pinkham Notch Visitors Center), ascending into a series of slides south of Tuckerman's Ravine. A giant bowl invites expert skiers to take the plunge. Before you head out, be sure to ask the folks at AMC headquarters or the Androscoggin Ranger Station in Gorham about snow conditions and avalanche danger.

For a classic White Mountain winter wilderness experience, reserve a space at the AMC Carter Notch Hut, pack your gear (including snowshoes), and head for the Wildcat River Trail in Jackson, New Hampshire. Intermediate skiers will like this meandering, up-and-down route to Carter Notch. The trail leaves Carter Notch Road and weaves back and forth through the woods, crossing several brooks, before entering more open terrain. The trail becomes too steep to ski about a mile before reaching the hut. Don those snowshoes and persevere up the radical incline into Carter Notch. This is a great base for exploring and appreciating the gorgeous mountain scenery, all the more spectacular dressed in its winter finery.

Stowe, Vermont:
Snow Cave Camping and
Telemarking on Mt. Mansfield

A Thousand Stars in the Sky, and
No One on the Slopes

CONTACT: Outdoor Adventure of Vermont, RR 5-2147, Bear Swamp Road, Montpelier, VT 05602; (800) 639-9208 or (802) 223-4172.
HOW TO GET THERE: Outdoor Adventure of Vermont offers a variety of year-round trips, including cross-country and downhill skiing, hiking, and rock-climbing adventures. Meeting spots vary. We met in Stowe, Vermont. Take I-89 to Exit 10; follow Route 100 north into Stowe.
RATES: The trip, including one night's snow cave lodging, one dinner, two breakfasts, and trail lunches, costs $125 per person.
WHAT TO BRING: Winter clothing, a backpack, sleeping bag and pad, a water bottle, and ski equipment. (Equipment rentals are available.)
KIDS: Older kids with experience and gumption are welcome.
SKILL LEVEL: Intermediate backcountry skiing skills are required for this trip. Participants should be active and in good health.

It was late February, and the temperatures were hovering near zero. We were on top of mother Mansfield, the highest peak in Vermont. Who would have thought we'd have a choice of accommodations? There was an older (circa November), one-room abode with hard-packed walls. There was a domed multiroom suite with connecting tunnels and low ceilings. And there was an elaborate high-walled, two-room dwelling with built-in shelves, sculptured cupboards, and an outdoor kitchen. It was a tiny village of snow caves, built by Vermont locals in search of backcountry solitude and untracked powder.

That night we were alone on the mountain; the locals had gone home. It was surprisingly roomy inside our snow home; there was enough space for four sleeping bags and gear in the first cave, and for four more in the connecting dome. A lone candle illuminated the cave, its light reflecting off the white walls, filling the air with flickering ice crystals. The candle was also our source of heat; in just a short while, we were sitting around in nothing but long underwear and heavy socks.

Before falling asleep, we threw on our parkas, crawled out into the cold, clear night, and stood in a giant black amphitheater. A thousand stars exploded across the inky background, lighting up a virgin white moonscape that rolled, soared, and dropped for miles and miles. There's nothing quite like spending a winter's night in the wilderness.

We were on an overnight backcountry ski excursion with Outdoor Adventure of Vermont. We had met our guides, Hal Leyshon and Smith Edwards, and the rest of the group at a Ben & Jerry's ice cream shop in Stowe, Vermont. It was an appropriate send-off, we thought, for a trip that would burn 5,000 calories per person, per day. "You're the heat source; you need a lot of calories," Leyshon reminded us several times during the next two days.

We headed over to the Stowe Mountain Resort, bought a one-way ticket, and hopped on the summit chairlift. At the top, we took the Auto Toll Road, followed Bruce Trail, and headed out of bounds. Not too many people do this; tourists rarely cross the trail lines, and even dare-devils had better know where they're going before heading off piste. But we had Leyshon and Edwards with us to guide the way.

When backcountry skiing, it's safest to hire a guide or go with an experienced, knowledgeable friend. Assess your abilities honestly, too. "You don't have to be an expert back-country skier, but you should have some experience with ungroomed terrain," Leyshon advised.

Just as important is your mental attitude. "This trip isn't for everyone," Leyshon said. "There are those who wonder what it would be like to sleep in a snow cave, and who crave the challenge and solitude of the backcountry. Others just think we're loony." (We confess that our thoughts fell some-where in between.)

Outdoor Adventure of Vermont conducts a friendly pre-trip screening to find out about each participant's back-ground, experience, and expectations. This helps to avoid mishaps and disappointments once a trip gets under way.

There's a practical side to snow cave camping: because of the warm shelter of the cave, you don't need to ski with a lot of alpine equipment. We carried personal items, a ground pad, and a sleeping bag. The guides had packed in food earlier—lots of food. Lunch begins right after break-fast and ends just before dinner, the guides quipped. It was hardly a joke.

We spent the next two days skiing the wild terrain near the top of Mt. Mansfield. No groomed corduroy; lots of fresh powder, hard scrabble, and a little bit of breakable crust. We had to pick and choose our way around.

We dropped off the backside of the mountain and headed down Teardrop. "The top is tough," Leyshon warned. Indeed. Narrow and steep, the trail is squeezed by snow-laden trees on both sides. We discussed kicking off the skis and donning the snowshoes Leyshon had brought along. Instead, we all decided to take it cautiously. Eventually, the snow alley widened and the scrabble turned to velvet.

Mount Mansfield, a popular recreation area in the sum-mer, becomes a quiet, snow-covered wilderness when the mercury drops. We stood in the silent woods and looked out at the shimmering waters of Lake Champlain and the peaks of the Adirondacks. In the other direction, we could see the craggy, white-capped summits of the White Mountains of New Hampshire.

We cruised backcountry trails, crudely cut and barely maintained. Then we headed down to Ranch Valley, a groomed cross-country ski center, and reluctantly returned to civilization.

Later, as we sat at the counter of Ben & Jerry's watching the tourists order up scoops of Cherry Garcia, we smugly entertained ourselves with the knowledge of our secret hiding place. "Nyah nyah, nyah nyah, we know something you don't know," we thought. Shame on us.

Brandon, Vermont: Country Inns Along the Trail

Ski Inn-to-Inn in Green Mountain National Forest

CONTACT: Country Inns Along the Trail, RR 3, Box 3115, Brandon, VT 05733; (802) 247-3300.

HOW TO GET THERE: Take Route 7 north to Brandon, then follow Route 73 east through Forest Dale; the Churchill House Inn is on the left.

RATES: Country Inns Along the Trail will custom-design a trip for you, including lodging, dinner, breakfast, trail lunch, car shuttle, and gratuities. Prices vary according to inn selection. In prime season, a double room at the Blueberry Hill Inn is $112 per night; at Churchill House, $115. Country Inns Along the Trail also offers guided cross-country and hiking trips. Five-day guided trips cost about $750 per person, double occupancy.

WHAT TO BRING: Ski gear (rentals are available at the Blueberry Hill Inn); a small pack to carry inn-packed lunches and personal gear; a swimsuit; and a water bottle.

KIDS: Yes; inquire about special rates for children under thirteen.

SKILL LEVEL: All levels; no experience is necessary.

We sat at a large, antique oak table, still flushed from our challenging trek through thick forest and the soothing warmth of the sauna. Birch logs crackled and popped in the fireplace, sending out a sweet, woodsy aroma. The scents that came from the kitchen were even more wonderful.

We were at the Churchill House Inn in Brandon, Vermont. Outside the door lay miles of trails—loops, circles, and climbs that would take us through the forest and on to the roaring fire and fine cuisine of the Blueberry Hill Inn, our second-night destination.

In the Moosalamoo region, 20,000 acres nestled in the Green Mountain National Forest of Vermont, cross-country skiers do not have to compromise. They can ski a spider web of trails that climb snowy peaks, drop into valleys, skirt lakes and streams, and wander deep into solitude and silence. They can skip carrying their homes on their backs and avoid the challenges of winter camping. If they plan it right, at day's end they'll glide to the doors of one of New England's finest country inns.

We had Country Inns Along the Trail design a trip for us. This organization of ten fine country inns has twenty years' experience in providing hikers, bikers, and cross-country skiers with detailed information on trails, guides, accommodations, and shuttles from point to point.

Our trip began at the Churchill House Inn, a farmhouse that has been a haven for weary travelers since 1871. Innkeepers Lois and Roy Jackson carry on the tradition of country hospitality.

After an exquisitely prepared four-course dinner, we sat in the den, poring over trail maps and talking about the next day's routes with Lois. We could spend the day skiing twenty-five kilometers of groomed trails maintained by the inn, or we could shuttle to a nearby touring center or to more rugged backcountry terrain. We decided, instead, to take the Leicester Hollow ski trail, an eight-mile route to Silver Lake. From there, we mapped a route—a series of groomed and rough trails—that led to the front yard of the Blueberry Hill Inn in Goshen, Vermont. We liked the idea of skiing door-to-door. We left our car keys and suitcases with the Jacksons; these items would be waiting at the Blueberry Hill Inn when we got there.

The Jacksons packed our lunch, supplied a map, and took care of our gear. We traveled light, floating across the hard-packed, groomed snow surrounding the inn, and onto the Leicester Hollow trail. It ascended gradually, an easy kick-and-glide through the woods. Alas, a group of snow-mobilers shattered our peace, whizzing by in a fury. We followed in their tracks until the noise subsided and the smell of exhaust was replaced by the fresh scent of pine. The trail broke out of the trees on the south bank of Silver Lake, then meandered the steep, rocky ridge around its eastern edge. Silver Lake, 1,250 feet above sea level, was once a Native American hunting and fishing ground. It proved to be a fine place to stop for lunch.

More choices: Continue up wide, unplowed Silver Lake Road to the frozen Falls of Lana? Tackle the trails up Rattlesnake Point and Mt. Moosalamoo (for experienced backcountry skiers only)? We decided to make tracks on the up-and-down intermediate Churchill House trail into the vast array of the Blueberry Hill cross-country network. We entered a world of towering white pines, frozen bogs, snowy fields, and narrow, forested passageways. We traveled for hours without seeing another soul, only the occasional tracks of a squirrel and, once, the footprints of a snowshoe hare. By the time we reached the Blueberry Hill Inn, an alpenglow sunset was reflecting off the snow, painting the landscape a warm pink.

The Blueberry Hill Inn is a treasure. The restored 1813 farmhouse nestled at the foot of Romance Mountain is a wonderful combination of colonial charm and modern elegance, with cozy rooms, a glorious candle-lit dining room, and a sunlit greenhouse. Just outside are more than seventy-five kilometers of groomed and ungroomed trails for skiers of all abilities. There's also a fully equipped ski center, with a rental and repair shop, a waxing area, and friendly staff.

Despite our busy day in the woods, we couldn't resist a moonlight stroll and a before-bed session in the sauna. "What should we do tomorrow?" we wondered. The legendary Catamount Trail? Spectacular Hogback Mountain? Maybe we should head north to the Water Tower trails, click off our skis, and take a peek at the Robert Frost Interpretive Trail. We'd decide tomorrow. We grabbed a giant homemade cookie out of the never-empty jar and slipped under the thick antique quilts covering our beds.

Ahh . . . life is good, we thought.

Resources

Information

For a complete listing of cross-country ski areas, contact individual states:

Connecticut Tourism Office, 865 Brook Street, Rocky Hill, CT 06067; (800) CT-BOUND.

Maine Publicity Bureau, Inc., P.O. Box 2300, Hallowell, ME 04347; (207) 623-0363.

Massachusetts Office of Travel and Tourism, 100 Cambridge Street, 13th Floor, Boston, MA 02202; (617) 727-3201.

New Hampshire Office of Travel and Tourism, P.O. Box 1856, Concord, NH 03302-1856; (603) 271-2665. For cross-country ski conditions, call (800) 262-6660.

Rhode Island Tourism Division, 7 Jackson Walkway, Providence, RI 02903; (800) 556-2484.

Vermont Chamber of Commerce, Department of Travel and Tourism, P.O. Box 37, Montpelier, VT 05601; (802) 828-2651.

BOOKS

Classic Backcountry Skiing. David Goodman, Appalachian Mountain Club.

The Cross-Country Primer. Laurie Gullion, Lyons & Burford.

Cross-Country Skiing, A Complete Guide. W. W. Norton and Company. (A Trailside Series guide.)

Cross-Country Skiing in New England. Lyn and Tony Chamberlain, Globe Pequot Press.

Short Hikes and Ski Trips Around Pinkham Notch. Linda
Buchanan Allen, Appalachian Mountain Club.
Wilderness Skiing and Winter Camping. Chris Townsend,
Ragged Mountain Press.

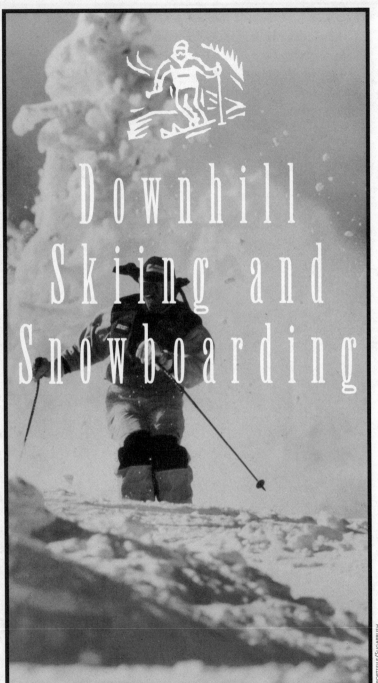

Downhill Skiing and Snowboarding

Tuckerman's Ravine, New Hampshire: Doing Tuckerman's Is a New England Rite of Spring

Thrills in Thin Air

CONTACT: Androscoggin Ranger Station, 80 Glen Road, Gorham, NH 03581; (603) 466-2713. The snow rangers who work out of the headquarters can supply up-to-the-minute snow conditions and avalanche warnings.

HOW TO GET THERE: The ranger station is on Route 16 in Gorham, approximately 0.5 mile south of Route 2. Tuckerman's Ravine Trail begins at the Pinkham Notch Visitors Center on Route 16, about 18 miles from North Conway.

RATES: Camping at the Hermit Ranger Station costs $8 per person. You can get camping permits at the Appalachian Mountain Club headquarters in Pinkham Notch.

WHAT TO BRING: Nerves of steel; and be prepared for severe weather. You'll also need food and water for the day. If you camp at the Hermit shelter, you'll need winter camping gear.

KIDS: Those who are athletic and like to hike might enjoy the trek up to Picnic Rocks, where they'll be treated to a great ski show. Older teens with lots of skiing experience and skill might attempt Tuckerman's Ravine; use your judgment.

SKILL LEVEL: Experienced, expert skiers only.

The crocuses were up. The robins were back. The sidewalk vendors were hawking bouquets of tulips and daffodils. And we were shouldering pounds of ski gear, ascending slippery ridges of granite with slopes as steep as fifty-five degrees. Below us lay the vast and open bowl of Tuckerman's Ravine.

Every spring, when avalanche danger subsides and the sun crests the edge of the bowl and softens the ice, this wild and challenging region in northern New Hampshire opens to daredevil skiers. This backcountry powderhound paradise sometimes draws more than 2,000 skiers on a spring Saturday—and that's not counting the spectators. In April and May, and some years into June, crowds gather at Picnic Rocks, a jumble of giant boulders at the base of the ravine. They come to enjoy the surrounding winter splendor and to ooh and ahh as a skier successfully maneuvers the mountain—or to gasp and groan as another slips, slides, tumbles, and turns into a fast-moving human snowball.

"Doing Tucks," as it's affectionately dubbed, is not for the faint of heart. The craggy, untamed wilderness of Mount Washington's granite ridges and summits is known for its severe, fickle weather, record-breaking winds, and snow depths of seventy-five feet or more. The infamous ravine, an enormous glacial cirque on the southeast side of the mountain, has sudden fall-line shifts and precipitous

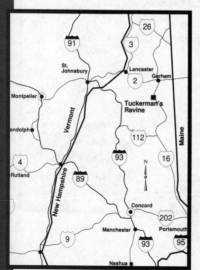

drops. Each year, Tuckerman's claims its victims; unfortunately, not a season goes by without word of a serious injury or a fatality percolating through the mountains, to be verified later in news accounts.

But the lure of Tuckerman's Ravine tugs at the spirit, and backcountry skiers from all over the country come East to feast on what Mother Nature dishes out: pure, savage, over-the-head powder skiing.

If you're into winter camping, you can stay at the Hermit Ranger Station, two-thirds of the way up. This is not condo-living, boys and girls; it's first-come, first-served accommodations at a lean-to turned snow hut. A giant snow wall often closes in the front of the lean-to, in which case you'll have to crouch your way in the small opening at one end of the wall, and grab a spot for your sleeping bag. Cozy.

The shelter might just have the best occupancy rate in northern New England during spring mud season. Powder addicts and thrill-seekers, hungry for virgin snow, often fill it to capacity. Campers not only get first tracks, but they awake to the crystalline splendor of the mountains, an incredible expanse of white powder and shimmering ice. (If you elect to camp out, you'll need to purchase a ticket at the Pinkham Notch Visitor's Center.)

If winter camp-outs are not your thing, don't worry. As long as you're willing to cram the perilous hike up the mountain and the steep plunge down into short daylight hours, you can go for the day. Start out early and hike from Pinkham Notch, up the well-packed Tuckerman's Ravine Trail. It's about a three-mile trek to Picnic Rocks. Then, it's decision time: stay with the nonskiing hordes, eat, and be merry; or strap your skis to your back and go for it.

We decided to hike to the summit. It turned out to be a tortuous, one-step-at-a-time climb. Though it is a short distance, it seemed to take forever; halfway up, our knees were wobbling and our sense of adventure waning. "Just pick a spot and go down anywhere you want," our friends had told us. Yeah, right. Our boots were jammed in icy crud, our faces in the snow; it was way too steep to put skis on. We trudged, single file, to the top of the ravine. It took a little over an hour.

At the summit, above the ravine, it flattens out. The view, of course, was incredible. We looked out at an endless expanse of white-capped mountains, jagged spires, rugged gardens of craggy granite, and, beyond, rolling valleys, icy ponds, and pine forests. Despite the summit-struck hikers who clustered on the ridge, we felt alone in the wilderness. For a moment, we let the quiet and solitude of the mountains envelop us. Then the whoops and hollers of skiers going over the edge, and the buzz of anticipation, shook us out of our reverie.

Mother Nature offers a warm-up run before the drops—the Alpine Gardens are vast snowfields that fall down from the summit of Mt. Washington. It's a nice place to test your ski legs and regain your nerve. As we neared the ravine, the group of skiers began to spread out; everyone was searching for his or her own way down the giant bowl.

That's it: pick a line; point your skis; take a deep breath; and plunge into the ultrasteep, sometimes icy, deep dumps of powder. If you're lucky, you'll make the first turns tight and precise. Then, rhythm will take over. All you'll hear is the schuss of skis over snow and the sound of your heart beating. You'll emerge with a grin on your snow-covered face, to the whoops and hollers of the Picnic Rock crowd.

That's if you're lucky. More often than not, the mountain wins. Still, it's worth every tumble.

"Incredible," exclaimed one skier. He was covered head to toe with snow; it took him fifteen minutes to find his ski, after somersaulting a quarter of the way down the ravine. "I'm going up again," he said.

Waterville Valley, New Hampshire: Riding the Storm Out

*Keep Putting on Airs and You'll
End Up in the Boneyard*

CONTACT: Waterville Valley, 1 Ski Area Road, Waterville Valley, NH 03215; (603) 236-8311. The season typically runs from mid-November through late April. Special features for snowboarders are the Boneyard park on Lower Periphery trail on Mt. Tecumseh, and Snow's Mountain Snowboard Park.

HOW TO GET THERE: Waterville Valley is about 2 hours from Boston and 6 hours from New York. Take I-93 north to Exit 28, then take Route 49 east 11 miles to the resort village.

RATES: Snowboard lessons cost $24. Snow's Mountain snowboarding lift passes are $29 for adults, $25 for teens (ages thirteen to eighteen), and $20 for juniors (ages six to twelve). Snowboard rental is $30. A one-day lift ticket is $37 per adult midweek, $43 weekends and holidays; teens pay $32 midweek, $38 weekends and holidays; juniors, $24 midweek, $28 weekends and holidays. Kids' programs range from $40 to $65 for one day. Packages are available.

WHAT TO BRING: Snowboarding gear (rentals are available) and warm, layered clothing that will not restrict your movements.

KIDS: Many kids begin to try out this sport at age nine or so.

SKILL LEVEL: All levels. A good sense of balance and some physical coordination will help.

Quick: What's giving the downhill ski business a much-needed lift? Hint: It's not snowmaking, off-piste skiing, or newly opened snowbowls (though those things help). Answer: It's those baggy-pants-wearing kids who say things like "Let's grab fat air, dude!"

Snowboarders (call 'em riders, never shredders), once banned from the slopes for their wide, splashy boards and in-your-face antics, are bringing a whole new edge to the mountain. Ski resorts are wooing these (mostly) teenaged renegades with state-of-the-art snowboard parks, camps and events, and even snowboard-only mountains. Resorts are now tailoring their advertising to riders as well as skiers, a sure sign that snowboarding has carved a niche in the $1.5-billion ski equipment market. Not bad for a sport that was started in the barn of a surfer from Vermont, a man named Jake Burton.

Snowboarding is finally getting some respect. It's become an Olympic event; before long, people will be talking fakies, shifties, and stiffies around the breakfast table. Some industry insiders believe that, at its current rate of growth, snowboarding could overtake skiing as the favorite alpine activity. Ski purists, however, dismiss it as a fad that fickle teens will toss aside once it loses its counterculture cool.

In New England, never a bastion of coolness, snowboarding is enjoying an avalanche of interest. This was readily apparent on a recent Saturday at New Hampshire's Waterville Valley. A free "learn to ride" season opener pulled in more than fifty people, young and old, eager to taste the freedom of riding the air and willing to eat some snow in the process.

"Prepare to fall, then fall again, then fall some more," said Charlie King, our instructor. "Sadly, there is no graceful way to do this." We were split up by age into three groups: twelve and under; teens; and grizzled types (thirty and over). Quickly, age ceased to matter; we were bonded by our determination to conquer the bunny slope on these strange-looking snow surfboards.

In soft, black boots, on boards of bright yellow (the better to see under mounds of snow), we baby-stepped on the flattest terrain on Mt. Tecumseh. We practiced going across the hill, one foot on the board, digging our uphill edge into the mountain. "If you dig in your downhill edge, you'll do a face-plant; it's automatic," King said. Back the other way. Then, our first turn and . . . spectacular wipeouts all around.

"Man, this is humbling," said one of the grown-up students. "I've been skiing for thirty years, and I've eaten more snow today than I did in a lifetime."

"You gotta get in the power position!" King said, meaning, stand over the board, knees bent, arms up, like you're ready to hug a bear. "Reach where you wanna go!" One at a time, we careened down the mountain, growing humbler by the minute. "Fall before you hit a tree or a person," King advised. "You'll be sore tomorrow, but the first three days of this sport are by far the toughest."

Waterville Valley is clearly convinced this flamboyant sport is no flash in the pan. Named "best place in the East" for snowboarding by *Outside* magazine, this resort has won many awards for snowboarding terrain and park design. On Mt. Tecumseh, the Boneyard snowboard park has gaps, table tops, kickers, and railsides. (If you have to ask, don't go there.) "Most intense" is how the park's designer, Waterville Valley snowboard coordinator Matt Gormley, described the Boneyard, calling it a Shangri-La for East Coast rippers.

Across the street is Snow's Mountain, a 2,050-foot peak for snowboarders only. Here, "the jumps are good, huge, pro-level," Gormley said. Features include steep pitches and a half-pipe, a snow-capped chute laid in the ground where riders dip and dive off mounds of snow. Snowboarders have their own base lodge at Snow's Mountain, with beanbag chairs and music that would make the old guard cringe. And riders are welcome to ski the trails on Mt. Tecumseh, the main mountain, too. With all this going on, little wonder that snowboarding currently accounts for nearly a quarter of skier visits here.

Downhill Skiing and Snowboarding

Ever mindful of the potential for discord between skiers and snowboarders, King, like the other snowboard instructors at Waterville Valley, is a goodwill ambassador for his sport. "Don't cut across the entire mountain or you'll cut off other skiers," he warned. "Be helpful; if you see a skier lose a pole, pick it up for them." King, a skier for twenty years and a rider for two, splits his slope time between the sports. "My body feels better after a day of boarding," he said. "When you ski, you twist a lot. There are a lot of knee injuries. With riding, the body is moving in harmony."

Once we progress along the learning curve from baby steps to freeriding, launching airs, and ripping, perhaps we'll experience the true euphoria of the sport—what King blissfully described as "an incredible sensation, so free." Someday we'll see for our ourselves—unless King is making a mountain out of a mogul.

Various Sites: Out-of-Bounds Skiing

Been There, Done That? It's Time to Head Off-Trail

CONTACT: You won't find any trail maps or circles, squares, and diamonds on this terrain—that's why they call it off-trail. Your best bet is to connect with a friendly member of a ski patrol or ski school. For information about the options mentioned here, including ski conditions, lift rates, and directions, contact the following organizations.

Androscoggin Ranger Station, 80 Glen Road, Gorham, NH 03581; (603) 466-2713 (for information on the Gulf of Slides and Tuckerman's Ravine).

Appalachian Mountain Club, P.O. Box 298, Gorham, NH 03581; (603) 466-2725 (for information on the Gulf of Slides and Tuckerman's Ravine).

Cannon, Franconia Notch, Franconia, NH 03580; (603) 823-5563.

The Department of Environmental Management at Mount Greylock Visitor Center, Rockwell Road, Lanesboro, MA 02137; (413) 458-3123 (for the Old Thunderbolt Ski Trail).

Stowe Mountain Resort, 5781 Mountain Road, Stowe, VT 05672; (802) 253-3000.

Sugarloaf/USA, Carrabassett Valley, ME 04947; (800) THE-LOAF.

WHAT TO BRING: It's best to bring an experienced, knowledgeable friend or guide into the backcountry, as well as heavy-duty ski equipment; warm, waterproof, layered clothing; an extra hat, gloves, and goggles; food; and water. If you plan to head into avalanche terrain, carry a radio transceiver and shovel.

KIDS: Probably not, unless they're older teens, very experienced, and accompanied by an adult.

SKILL LEVEL: Advanced intermediate to expert. There's some backcountry terrain for intermediate skiers, but you have to know where to find it. Again, go with someone who knows the territory.

Off-piste, OB, backcountry, off trail, out of bounds—whatever you call it, it means the same: deep dumps of untrammeled snow where the meek perish, tourists never go, and the way down is not a ski run, but an adventure.

Think you have to go West to go off trail? Think again. You just have to know where to head those 205 boards.

The locals in Stowe, Vermont, have been skiing off-piste terrain on the backside of Mt. Mansfield for years. This mountainous region is favored by the snow gods, who dump an average of 250 inches of the white stuff here each year. Backcountry skiers can find miles of uncut powder runs through unspoiled wilderness—if they work at it.

Mt. Mansfield resembles the profile of a man's face. To reach the best and most challenging backcountry skiing, you have to hike up The Chin to 4,393 feet, the highest point in Vermont. It's a one-hour traverse from the top of the Stowe ski resort gondola, but worth every grunt and groan—and the price of the lift ticket. On top, catch your breath and take a look at the million-dollar, 360-degree view. On a clear day, you can see across three states and into Canada; jumbles of white-capped peaks and miles of snow-blanketed valleys spread out in every direction. But gravity's tug and the lure of wild terrain won't let you linger for long. Experts can take the plunge down Profanity, a pulse-quickening chute with sudden drops and unpredictable conditions; or ski the steep, narrow Hellbrook Trail, a tight, twisty, skinny route through the woods, guaranteed to leave your legs shaking and thighs burning.

Ready for more? Hop back on the gondola and strike up a conversation with someone who doesn't look like a tourist. In the summer and fall, Stowe-area locals (illegally) snip and trim for rough-cut runs in the surrounding state forest. Hook up with a local and perhaps you'll be led to the outback, an ungroomed paradise of five-foot-wide swatches of four-mile-long, winding glade runs. Pick a line and point 'em down.

Across the border in New Hampshire, powderhounds drop off the backside of Cannon into the unmarked, untrammeled territory of the Kinsman Range. Take the Cannon aerial tram to the 4,180-foot summit of Cannon Mountain. The resort trails head off to the left; you keep going straight.

"They're not on our trail map," Dick Andros, Cannon's mountain manager, said of the backcountry runs. "But we don't tell skiers they can't do them either."

The rugged off-piste runs are part of the old Mittersill Ski Area, cut by the Civilian Conservation Corps in the 1930s. We like them best when the sun is in the western sky, painting the granite-slabbed mountains pink and lighting the way down the old-fashioned, one-at-a-time narrow runs through the woods. Watch out for quick, sharp switchbacks and launchable rocks. If you have trouble finding your way (or just feel more comfortable with a guide), look for someone with a Cannon season pass and long skis.

Purists who scoff at lift-accessed, just-out-of-bounds skiing can challenge the tough, high alpine drifts in the New Hampshire Presidentials. The steep, icy headwall of Tuckerman's Ravine draws gaggles of powder addicts and peak skiers in early spring, when the danger of avalanches subsides. (See "Doing Tuckerman's Is a New England Rite of Spring" on page 325.) Or avoid the crowds and head up the Gulf of Slides trail from the Pinkham Notch Visitors Center. Avalanche activity occurs often here (hence the trail name), and skiing is for experts only. It's a workout up the trail; you'll gain 2,000 feet in elevation on the two-and-a-half-mile climb. The trail ends just beneath the headwall, where a giant, open bowl of powder pleasure awaits. Best when splashed with morning sun, and after a good night's rest.

For years, regulars at the Sugarloaf Ski Resort in Carrabassett Valley, Maine, have ducked under the out-of-bounds tapes (and risked getting their tickets pulled). Recently, the resort has opened up the boundaries; you can ski anywhere on the mountain, off-trail or on. "It's a way to add some thrill, fun and excitement for adventure seekers," says Nancy Marshall, spokesperson for the resort.

For gnarly, ungroomed tree skiing, experts can head out of the double-diamond snowfields of Bubblecuff into the pine-speckled chutes. Intermediates can try the glades off Bucksaw. Even kids can get a taste of backcountry skiing in the Everglades, a gladed kids' park in the Whiffle Tree and Moose Alley areas.

There's only one catch to out-of-bounds skiing at the

Loaf: If you get in trouble, you pay for your rescue.

Southern New Englanders in search of wild, virgin snow don't have to travel far north to get it. Just head to Adams, Massachusetts, and hike up the Old Thunderbolt Ski Trail. Cut by the Civilian Conservation Corps, it was once a famous racing course. Today, it takes you from the top of Mt. Greylock, the highest point in Massachusetts, straight down an unpredictable snowy maze rough-cut through the forests. Don't even think about attempting this in a light snow season; in the best of winters, you're liable to get slapped by saplings on the plummet down.

Of course, that's what makes it an adventure.

Resources

There are more than 100 ski resorts in New England. For state-by-state listings, contact:

Maine Publicity Bureau, Inc., P.O. Box 2300, Hallowell, ME 04347; (207) 623-0363 (ask for the state's winter guide). Or call the Ski Maine Association snow phone at (800) 533-9595.

New Hampshire Office of Travel and Tourism, P.O. Box 1856, Concord, NH 03302-1856; (603) 271-2665. For current promotions, contact SKI NH, Box 10, North Woodstock, NH 03262; (800) 88-SKI-NH or (603) 745-9396. For up-to-the-minute snow conditions, call (800) 258-3608.

Vermont's complete winter guide is available from the Department of Travel and Tourism of the Vermont Chamber of Commerce, P.O. Box 37, Montpelier, VT 05601; (802) 828-2651. For snow conditions, call (802) 229-0531.

The Massachusetts Office of Travel and Tourism offers a complete listing of ski areas; write them at 100 Cambridge Street, 13th Floor, Boston, MA 02202, or call (617) 727-3201. The statewide snow phone is (800) 632-8038. Berkshire Ski's 24-hour phone is (413) 499-SNOW.

In Connecticut, contact Connecticut Tourism Office, 865 Brook Street, Rocky Hill, CT 06067; (800) CT-BOUND.

Rhode Island has one ski mountain, Yawgoo Valley, at 160 Yawgoo Valley Road, Exeter, RI 02822. For information, call (401) 294-3802.

BOOKS

The Centered Skier. Denise McCluggage, Tempest Books.

Classic Backcountry Skiing. David Goodman, Appalachian
Mountain Club.

Eastern U.S. Ski Country Access. HarperPerennial.

The Good Skiing Guide, edited by Peter Hardy and Felice
Eyston. The Overlook Press.

Learn Downhill Skiing in a Weekend. Konrad Bartelski and
Robin Neillands, Knopf.

The New Guide to Skiing. Martin Heckelman, W. W. Norton
and Company.

Winter Adventure

339

Newry, Maine:
Mushing in Maine

Out Here, Going to the Dogs Is a Good Thing

CONTACT: Mahoosuc Guide Service, Bear River Road, Newry,
ME 04261; (207) 824-2073.

HOW TO GET THERE: Take the Maine Turnpike to Exit 11 (Gray),
then Route 26 north to Bethel (roughly 40 miles). Mahoosuc Guide
Service is 7 miles west of Bethel on Route 26.

RATES: The five-day trip in Rapid River Country is $750. Four-day
trips are $375; three-day trips, $295.

WHAT TO BRING: Just your own personal items. They'll supply
everything else, including parkas, gaiters, sleeping bags, sleeping
pads, Nordic skis, and snowshoes.

KIDS: Not on overnight trips. Ask about day trips for families, or
private group trips for four or more people.

SKILL LEVEL: None required, just the ability to learn and a good
attitude about being outdoors in the winter. Expect to work hard,
though; this is a fairly strenuous trip.

G ee! Gee!" we shouted to our team of Alaskan Huskies.
(That's "turn right" in musher-talk.) The dogs veered
to the right, led by capable Lonnie, lead dog extraordinaire.
We leaned into the turn, guiding the sled with body English. "Har!" We zigged to the left, two novice mushers and a
team of energetic dogs who, amazingly, seemed to trust us.

We were winding our way along a riverside trail from
Richardson Lake to Lake Umbagog, amid Maine's
Mahoosuc Mountains. Fortunately, we were running on
hard-packed snowmobile trails. If we had been chugging

along for several miles in deep, heavy snow, we would have collapsed in the sled and let the dogs drive us to the Yukon, or to the dog food section of the nearest supermarket.

"You don't have to raise your voice," said Polly Mahoney of Mahoosuc Guide Service, who, with partner Kevin Slater, ran our five-day dogsledding journey. "Talk in a quiet, gentle voice, and the dogs will respond. If you scream 'Whoa!,' they'll get all excited," she said.

Mahoney knows her stuff. She and her dogs were featured in the movie *Never Cry Wolf*, which was released a few years ago. A native Mainer, she lived a subsistence lifestyle in the Yukon bush, where her Huskies were essential to survival. They hauled wood and water and provided transportation. Equally important, she told us, "The dogs were great company. They're like my children."

Mahoney isn't too keen on competitive mushers, some of whom, she said, "treat their dogs too roughly." Nor does she believe in pushing dogs hard, as happens in competitive dogsledding. But someone on our trip asked, "Do dogs really like this?" Mahoney replied, "They definitely like it. It's in their breeding to pull."

That was obvious to us from the start. The beautiful animals were raring to go. Before we could say "Hokey hay!" ("Let's go!"), we were off and running. Mushers caught unawares ended up head over heels in a snowdrift.

On five-day trips like ours, there are two people on each dogsled, one on one runner, one on the other, holding tight to the wooden handlebar and ready to brake at any moment. Slater hand-crafts the Quamatik sleds of ash. Each takes about a week to construct.

A good driver knows when to get on and off the runners, and when to stand on the brake to slow the sled down. Mushers also spend a lot of

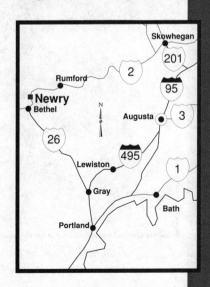

time "pumping," stepping on one leg to get the sled going. "Kind of like riding a scooter," Mahoney said. This keeps the dogs moving at a steady pace.

All Mahoosuc Guide Service trips incorporate traditional practices and materials, and some are run by local Native American guides. Current offerings include trips with the Cree of James Bay and the Inuit of Hudson Bay and Baffin Island, in Canada's Northwest Territories.

Our overnight shelter, a traditional Cree winter camp called a *mithogan,* was heated by a woodstove to cozy com-

*Tranquility base: bright sun, open space, clean snow,
and a spirited dog team.*

fort. At night, the fire went out, so the temperature was the same indoors as out—around twenty degrees below zero, typical for northern Maine in early February. Cocooned in arctic-weight sleeping bags, we stayed toasty. The dogs—Ootek, Kipmik, Lonnie, and chums—sprawled happily in the snow on the spruce bough beds we'd made for them.

At the beginning of the journey, we each drew a slip of paper with the name of a dog who'd be our buddy for the trip. We lavished that particular furry beast with love and attention. We didn't need to be coaxed; they were affectionate, nose-rubbing, playful dogs, and their good nature added a lot to the spirit of the trip.

Indeed, some people come on these trips "just because they love dogs," Mahoney said. Once they're out there, they realize they can experience the north woods of Maine in winter and be comfortable. "It builds self-confidence. I see this a lot on all-women trips," she said. You don't need to be a triathlete, or even an experienced winter camper, to enjoy this. "This isn't about survival, it's about fun," Mahoney said.

If five days, or even a weekend, seems too long to subsist on freeze-dried, instant food, never fear; there's no elk jerky for dinner on these trips. Simple fare like baked beans, brown bread, and chicken stir-fry are prepared by the guides on a campfire or Coleman stove.

Typically, first-time mushers, and families, start out on a day trip, where everybody travels on a dog team. This is a nice introduction to dogsledding, offering beautiful mountain vistas and a campfire lunch. The next step might be a three-day, two-night adventure, combining lots of mushing and some Nordic skiing on lakes and mostly flat terrain. Then, there's the five-day trip we took. At the next level is a ten-day journey with the Inuit or Cree, for those who want to improve their driving and dog-handling skills. And for mushers hankering for a dog team of their own, Slater teaches a workshop on dogsled construction.

Our trip took us from the north end of Richardson Lake to Smooth Ledge Falls, along the Rapid River to Umbagog Lake and Black Island Cove. We skirted the water's edge for most of the journey, in the shadow of the Mahoosucs, amid forests of spruce, birch, and evergreen. Our second day was a layover, affording us the chance to explore on cross-country skis and snowshoes and look for signs of deer and moose.

At Smooth Ledge Falls, where the water doesn't freeze, we saw otters at play. Endless blankets of virgin snow muffled the sounds of the forest. All we heard was the soft swish of sled-runners as they slid through sugar-white snow. We lost ourselves in the tranquility and overwhelming beauty of this scene.

"Whoa!" We had startled a deer, not uncommon on the crossing from Lake Richardson to Umbagog. The dogs went on a merry chase, oblivious to the two people hanging onto the sled, braking mightily and shouting "Whoa!" Oops — Mahoney had said "no shouting," but it was too late. Like their car-chasing city cousins, the dogs went into a frenzy, playing the ancient game that runs deep in their veins.

Such is the way of the wild. On this dogsledding trip, these rambunctious canines, related to the wolf and half-wild themselves, surely tuned us into the winter woods.

Pinkham Notch, New Hampshire: Building the Perfect Snow Shelter

High Price of Snow-Country Real Estate Got You Down? Take Matters into Your Own Hands

CONTACT: Pinkham Notch Visitor Center, Appalachian Mountain Club, P.O. Box 298, Gorham, NH 03581; (603) 466-2727. Currently, this course is offered only once per season, but the AMC runs dozens of workshops on similar topics.

HOW TO GET THERE: This workshop meets at the Joe Dodge Lodge check-in desk, Pinkham Notch Visitor Center, on Route 16. It's 18 miles north of North Conway, New Hampshire, and 10 miles south of Gorham, New Hampshire.

RATES: A $130 fee includes lodging Friday night and breakfast Saturday. Reserve early; this one fills up far in advance.

WHAT TO BRING: Complete winter backpacking gear, including a large-frame pack, boots appropriate for wet snow, snowshoes or skis with climbing skins, and a sleeping bag rated to minus 100 degrees Fahrenheit. AMC will send you a complete equipment list upon registration.

KIDS: Generally, no; discuss with AMC personnel.

SKILL LEVEL: You must be in excellent physical condition, have winter camping and backpacking experience, and be able to carry overnight gear for several miles on snowshoes or skis with skins.

Call it *This Old Igloo*. On the last morning of the Appalachian Mountain Club's snow-shelter building workshop, the twelve participants, along with guides Aaron Glazer and Hans Bengtsson, took a house tour of each other's architectural marvels. Featured homes included Green Acres, a snow cave studded with green M & Ms; the more upscale Ice Palace, a well-wrought igloo painstakingly created by three up-and-coming snowmasons; and, alas, the least-desirable property, a snow trench dubbed "The Tomb" by its owners.

At least the neighborhood is nice, and very secluded. To get there, you have to snowshoe or ski along an old ski trail for three or four miles, from Pinkham Notch to a campsite on the slopes of Mt. Washington. Elevation gain is roughly 2,000 feet. Then go up to the Gulf of Slides, an east-facing ravine just above the tree line. The Gulf gets tons of snow, making it a perfect place to undertake the ancient craft of snow-shelter building.

The best preparation for this trek is winter backpacking and tent camping experience. "Mt. Washington can be brutal in winter," Glazer said, "with temperatures hovering around twenty-five or thirty degrees below zero." And this was March, nearly spring. "The most important thing we want people to know is, we can't instruct them in how to deal with the cold."

Surprisingly, though, cold wasn't the biggest problem; wetness was. We were literally in the snow all the time, up to our waists and our elbows. Underneath, we sweated. This was hard work, about a hundred times more strenuous

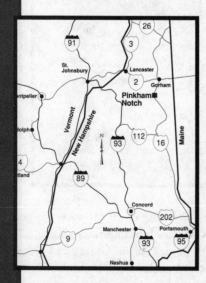

than shoveling the driveway after a blizzard. It was also a lot more fun.

"We try to show people how snow can be fun and creative," Glazer said. The idea was to convince us that snow is something we could sleep in. We had to visualize empty snow as a protective house.

Our adventure began at the AMC's Pinkham Notch Visitor Center, where Glazer and Bengtsson gave us a two-hour overview of shelter building and safety gear. We spent the night at the lodge and rose before 8 o'clock Saturday morning to begin the arduous hike to the Gulf of Slides. We were laden with fifty-pound packs containing stoves, food, fresh clothes, and other gear. The group ranged in age from twenties to sixties, and included ice climbers, avid cross-country skiers, and backcountry snowshoers. Some were dressed in the latest high-tech fabrics, with $400 packs on their backs and special shoes on their feet; others, including the guides, were decked out in well-worn heavy woolens.

Glazer and Bengtsson have been running this workshop for more than fifteen years. Early on, it attracted lots of hard-core mountain-man types, Glazer said. Now it draws men and women who love winter and want to expand their repertoire of outdoor skills.

"This isn't about winter survival," Glazer cautioned. "If you have to 'survive' in the snow, you've done something wrong."

Glazer, who has worked for Outward Bound as well as AMC, described the biggest mistakes people make when winter camping: not bringing enough food, so caloric intake dips too low to provide warmth; not wearing warm enough clothing; and not bringing sleeping bags made for extreme temperatures. "You get cold, tired, wet, and, if it's too dark to start building a shelter, you're in trouble. I've learned a lot out here by being dumb and making mistakes." With this workshop, he said, "We're trying to shorten the learning curve."

When we got to the Gulf of Slides, we looked for deep, strong, slablike snowdrifts. Like giant white Legos, these offered the best construction possibilities. We drew slips of paper to see who got to build what: snow trench, quinzee, snow cave, or igloo. Everybody wanted to build the igloo. "It's such an elegant dwelling," Glazer said. The guides suggested we build our shelters in a circle, about 100 yards apart. "For a nice esthetic sense, and also if anyone wants any privacy," Glazer said with a wink. As if.

After lunch, a high-calorie binge of salami, cheese, and M & Ms, we set to work, in teams of two or three, building our homes for the night. We realized why this workshop was given in March; the days are longer, and we needed every minute of light to finish our colony.

To describe the features of each type of dwelling doesn't do the process justice. In a general sense, a snow trench is like a tomb. To make it, you mine big slabs of snow, layer them, then hollow the whole thing out. The quinzee is a simple but time-consuming shelter that can be built on flat ground. Essentially, it's a big, igloo-shaped snow pile; you shovel snow up and out to make an entrance. A snow cave is a quick and dirty number that can be made in a drift of snow. With an ice-ax or ski pole, you measure the depth of the drift; you need six to eight feet of snow to mine so you can go in and hollow it out.

Then there's the igloo, the showplace of snow shelters. You need at least 100 blocks of the right size and shape; these are angled and shaped with a snow saw. The higher you build, the steeper than angle is, to achieve the characteristic rounded look. Typically, it takes three people from three to four hours to do this. Done right, an igloo this size will sleep three people, with an entrance that goes down, then up to the sleeping chamber, which is blocked off for the night.

"This is no place for someone who gets claustrophobic," Glazer noted. However, he said, when it's very cold, there's little danger of a snow shelter collapsing on its inhabitants. "The worst thing for us is to have the temperature go above freezing, because the snow gets soft and won't breathe," Glazer said. Severe storms can also be problematic. In 1993, a major blizzard collapsed two shelters when the weight of heavy, wet snow proved too much for them. The occupants burrowed into neighbors' dwellings that night.

Satisfied that our little homes were snug, we made dinner, sharing stoves among us. There was no campfire sing-along. "Never a fire in the winter!" Glazer declared. Fire doesn't keep people warm outdoors in the winter, he said, and it isn't prudent to light one in a house made of snow. Snowball fights were another no-no. After all, people living in ice houses. . . .

Before we retired gratefully into our sleeping bags at 6 P.M., we surveyed the frozen landscape. The lights of North Conway twinkled below us. "Let's go to the Red Parka Pub for the night!" someone whispered.

We were awakened in the morning by a guest who came bearing a treat: ice cream.

North Conway, New Hampshire: Alpine Mountaineering and Ice Climbing

Enter the World of Frozen Waterfalls and Giant Snowfields

Contact: Alain Gomeau, Mountain Guides Alliance, P.O. Box 266, North Conway, NH 03860; (603) 356-5310 or (207) 935-2008.

How to Get There: Climbers meet at Ragged Mountain Equipment, 3 miles north of North Conway, on Route 16.

Rates: One-day rates are $165 for a one-person, private lesson; $125 for a group of two; and $110 for a group of three.

What to Bring: Wear comfortable, warm clothing; bring lunch and water. Technical equipment, including footwear, a harness, a helmet, and ropes, is supplied.

Kids: Twelve and up.

Skill Level: No experience is necessary, but you should be in good physical condition.

They stepped and rested, stepped and rested; took deep breaths and exhaled. The moisture that escaped their mouths quickly crystallized. They climbed with ice axes and crampons, up the steep, snowy path, through a nasty brew of stinging ice and blinding snow. A biting wind chased them up the mountain, howling in their ears and blowing them off balance, sending them scrambling for footholds. Several hours later, they reached the summit and gazed down into the clouds, out across great white sweeps of ice and snow. "It was like walking on the moon," the student climber said. "A one-of-a-kind joy."

Enter the wintery world of alpine mountaineering and ice climbing. Whether to claw up frozen waterfalls or climb snowy peaks, more and more outdoor enthusiasts are heading into the mountains when the mercury drops.

"People are amazed at how enjoyable it is," said Alain Gomeau, an American Mountain Guide Association–certified alpine and rock guide, and a founder of the Mountain Guides Alliance, a referral agency representing professional guides in New England. "There really is something for everyone in this sport."

Winter climbing has a lot to offer: access to solitude and the quiet beauty of the mountains in winter; the chance to learn and improve skills and endurance; and the opportunity to turn outdoor pursuits into year-round endeavors.

Sound too—brrr—tough to tackle? Cast aside images of ax-wielding men with ice-caked beards. The sport is more about grace than power. It takes patience, not force; mental rather than physical strength.

"Most people are intimidated by winter conditions," Gomeau said. "We live in comfort zones. Start to leave the zone and we become anxious.

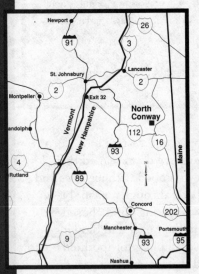

"The key is to expand your comfort zone little by little," he explained. "People are surprised at what they can do. It's very exciting."

Whether you have visions of ascending vertical sheets of ice, or simply taking a winter hike in the mountains, first sign up for a winter mountaineering/ice climbing course, where you'll learn about proper clothing; use of equipment; and basic techniques of traveling in snow and ice.

"Underestimating the severity of the mountains in winter" is the biggest mistake beginners make, Gomeau said. "The uninitiated can quickly find themselves in a world they're not ready to handle."

Gomeau has climbed extensively around the world, and is responsible for many first ascents. He has also served on the board of directors of the Mountain Rescue Service. He's the kind of guy you want to have next to you when you venture into the world of snow and ice. His beginner's course stresses minimal use of equipment, emphasizing technique rather than technology. ("Today's technology allows people to do things they shouldn't; it gives them a false sense of security," he said.) His students practice walking on ice and climbing snow slopes. They also learn to use an ice ax, including the technique of self-arrest—using the ax to stop a freefall slide down the side of the mountain.

Gomeau conducts the one-on-one course on Willey's Slide, in the Crawford Notch region of New Hampshire's White Mountains. Willey's is popular with climbing schools for its wide, low-angled ice and snowfields. The best thing about Willey's might very well be the reward you get for your efforts: beautiful views of white-capped, craggy peaks and snow-blanketed valleys.

Those who've completed the basic course and want to expand their comfort zone just a little more can accompany Gomeau on a day-long trek into Crawford Notch. The long climb will take you up Shoestring or Hitchcock Gully, narrow channels that fill up with snow and ice. You'll work your way up the vee to the upper ridges and summit of the mountain.

For some, working up steep walls of ice is the ultimate thrill. "It takes a different mentality to ice climb on vertical, forty-degree ice," said Gomeau. "The joy comes from the climbing itself, the sense of body movement, balance, and effort."

If you're ready to take the plunge up, Gomeau conducts instructional guides on Frankenstein Cliffs, near North Conway. Named for the nineteenth-century painter of White Mountain scenery, not the monster-creating doctor, these cliffs can nevertheless prove beastly. They offer a wealth of short, steep routes up walls of vertical ice, around hanging icicles, and through caves, allowing climbers to practice balance, footwork, efficiency of movement, and, Gomeau says, "the pure, simple enjoyment of the sport."

Imagining a harrowing, spectacular climb up a towering, tenuously frozen waterfall, we asked Gomeau about his best day on the snow and ice. He told us that a woman had come to him one winter, wanting to climb Mt. Washington. A short way into the trek, she gave up. The following year she trained; come winter, she booked another guided ascent of the meanest and mightiest peak in New England. "We began the climb at 5 A.M.," Gomeau said. "It was tough, a steep trudge through deep snow. Finally, we broke through the clouds and onto the peak."

It was like Mother Earth held her breath for a moment, he said. The wind died and the sun appeared in the deep-blue sky. They were the only ones up there.

"It was a turning point for her," Gomeau said, "and one of the most exciting days I've had. It's these kinds of experiences that keep me going back to the mountains; it's why I teach."

Various Sites:
Frostbiting—the Name Says It All

The Snow Is Flying, the Wind Is Whipping —
A Perfect Day for a Sail

It was a wintry Sunday morning in New England, a Currier & Ives print come to life. Indoors, folks were putting logs on the fireplace, clutching steaming mugs of java, divvying up the Sunday paper. Outside, others were rigging their boats and going sailing.

Say what?

Details like frigid temperatures and howling winds don't cool diehards' ardor for the sport. "For some people, it's their favorite season to sail," said Tom Robinson, race chairperson of the Winthrop/Boston Harbor frostbiting club. "I like it better than summer sailing; there's more wind," he added.

How hard is it to leave a warm house for the cold North Atlantic? For Robinson, it's a no-brainer. "It's what I do. I don't do brunch," he chuckled. "I turn on the Weather Channel to get psyched up, listening for those magic words, 'cold and windy.'"

Frostbiting, as the sport is known, draws mostly experienced racing sailors looking to maintain their competitive edge. "You have to be a little sharper or you'll get wet," Robinson cautions. Even if you sail sharp as an ice-skate blade, there's no guarantee you won't take a dunk anyway. With the fierce and fluky winter winds, capsizes are common. The possibility hovers in the air—so to speak—and gives frostbiting an adventurous edge.

There's a lot of action, since as many as five races are run a day instead of the typical one or two in summer. And there's the incongruity of the thing. As Robinson says, "It's kind of a rush to sail while it snows."

CONTACT: Frostbiting fleets sail from several harbors in the region. For information and directions, contact one of the following organizations:

Barrington Frostbite Sunfish Fleet #155 sails Sunfish out of Barrington, RI; (401) 245-9237.

Boston Sailing Center sails J/24s from Lewis Wharf, Boston MA; (617) 227-4198 (Dave Franzel).

Bristol's International Penguin Fleet sails Penguins out of Bristol, RI; (401) 245-5865.

Coasters Harbor Navy Yacht Club sails Rhodes 19s out of Newport, RI; (401) 841-3134.

Cottage Park Yacht Club (includes Marblehead fleet) sails Interclubs and Lasers out of Winthrop, MA; (617) 646-6418 (Tom Robinson).

Courageous Sailing Center sails Rhodes 19s and J/22s from Charlestown, MA; (617) 242-3821.

Edgewood Yacht Club sails Sunfish out of Cranston, RI; (401) 781-9626.

Essex Corinthian Yacht Club sails Interclubs out of Essex, CT; (860) 767-7757 (Ed Birch).

Narragansett Terrace Yacht Club sails White Horses out of East Providence, RI; (401) 433-0528.

Frostbiters are not a tiny bunch of zealots who've swallowed too much seawater. Some fleets get fifteen or more boats out each week, some as many as thirty.

Traditionally, frostbiting was done in Interclubs, and at many clubs, they're still the winter boat of choice. An Interclub is a twelve-foot, two-person tub rigged with mainsail, a tiller, and a centerboard. They have rounded bottoms and no keels, so they're notoriously tippy. An Interclub can be had cheap, around $400 for a used charter boat for the season. Some frostbiting clubs sail other boats, such as Sunfish, Rhodes 19s, J/22s, J/24s, and Lasers. Most clubs are organized locally, usually with a yacht club

Newport Yacht Club sails Turnabouts out of Newport, RI; (401) 846-9410.

Newport's Laser Fleet #413 sails Lasers out of Newport, RI; (401) 847-1613.

Scituate Harbor Yacht Club sails Interclubs from Scituate, MA; (617) 740-1766 (Dave Lewis).

Vanguard 15 Class Association sails Vanguard 15s out of Bristol, RI; (401) 254-0960.

Wickford Yacht Club sails Sea Dogs out of Wickford, RI; (401) 294-9010.

RATES: Dues vary, depending on the fleet. If you'd like to give frost-biting a try before you buy or rent a boat, some clubs, such as Newport Yacht Club and the Penguins, offer a club boat to borrow and a complimentary day of racing. Make arrangements in advance.

WHAT TO BRING: Some sailors layer lots of wool or pile under foul-weather gear; some wear drysuits. Dress warmly with a waterproof layer on top. Also, wear boots and sailing gloves.

KIDS: Parent-child crews are typical. Children should know how to swim and sail.

SKILL LEVEL: Some sailing ability is preferred. Some fleets are extremely competitive, and made up of very experienced sailors. With others, the focus is on fun.

or sailing club as a base for launching boats and warming up after racing.

Just when the rest of the sailing community is bidding a fond farewell to summer and having their boats shrink-wrapped for the winter, the frostbite crowd is getting set to sail. The season runs from late October to April, with races held on Saturdays or Sundays, starting at 1 P.M.

Call it a Yankee thing; we're suckers for the opportunity to pit ourselves against the harsh elements. But frostbiters are not crazy. For safety's sake, there's the twenty-twenty rule: if it's blowing twenty knots or more, or it's colder than twenty degrees, racing is canceled. The race course is set on an inner harbor, just a few yards from the sponsoring yacht club. And rescue boats (Boston Whalers with motors) are out there to save sailors as needed.

On a recent Saturday in February, suffering from a bad case of winter doldrums, we let ourselves get talked into frostbiting. Some friends had an Interclub and couldn't sail that day; could we fill in? What we really needed was a cruise to St. Bart's, but Massachusetts would have to do.

It had snowed overnight; we had to clean the snow and ice out of the boat before we sailed it. A group of hard-core racers had shown up, ready for a 1 P.M. start. The wind was picking up, about an eighteen-knot northwesterly by now. To invoke the twenty-twenty rule, or to race? "Let's race one race and see what happens," a race committee member suggested. The committee holds forth from a little barge topped with a heated hut. Our starting line was set up between the barge and a buoy. Three minutes to go, signaled by three horn toots . . . two minutes to go . . . finally, ten short toots, counting down to the start.

The first mark was set into the wind, so the boats had to tack, and strategize against wind shifts and competitors. We got a good start at the weather end, hiking out hard to flatten out the boat. We tacked to port and, a minute later, back to starboard, with two other boats in close pursuit. The three of us pulled away from the fleet.

Close to the windward mark, the wind became very shifty. After three more tacks, we rounded the windward mark in first place, another boat close behind.

On beam reach now, all the boats moved to the second mark. Rounding it, we increased our lead, the excitement of the race keeping our adrenaline pumping and keeping us warm. Could we actually win this thing?

We headed downwind to the third and final buoy. The wind was really howling now, so we had to keep our weight in the back of the boat to keep it stable. Huddled together, we managed to make the right moves. We caught a huge puff, the boat trimmed right, and we moved ten boatlengths ahead of the pack. To think we hadn't been keen on coming out here! This was great.

We looked behind us at the rest of the boats, and saw

big gusts of wind traveling down the harbor toward the fleet. As the gusts hit, the boats went down like dominoes into the frigid sea.

We sailed down to the final mark, hoping that, before the puff hit us, we'd round the mark and sail into the wind, out of harm's way. Steady . . . steady . . . splash! The skipper got up on the high side of the dinghy and stayed dry. The hapless crew was submerged completely in the icy water before scrambling on top of the overturned hull.

Eventually, we were picked up by a Whaler and whisked to the warming hut. The rescue boats had their hands full, rescuing seven other soggy crews. So we bided our time, gazing around the harbor. It was quite a picture: dignified Marblehead mansions in the background; and in the foreground, a comical scene of overturned boats bobbing in the water, with wetsuited sailors clinging to them in a most undignified fashion.

Now this is a scene Currier & Ives never captured. Mathew Brady, maybe.

Resources

Other guides, companies, and organizations offering ice climbing, mountaineering trips, and winter adventures include:

Craftsbury Center, P.O. Box 31, Craftsbury Common, VT 05827; (800) 729-7751.

The Green Mountain Club; RR 1, P.O. Box 650, Route 100, Waterbury Center, VT 05677; (802) 244-7037

Hulbert Outdoor Center, RR 1, Box 91A, Fairlee, VT 05045; (802) 333-9840.

Ian Turnbull, Mountain Guides Alliance, Box 266, North Conway, NH 03860; (603) 356-5310 or (603) 466-3949.

Kurt Winkler, Mountain Guides Alliance, Box 266, North Conway, NH 03860; (603) 356-5310 or (207) 935-3853.

L.L. Bean Outdoor Discovery Program, Freeport, ME 04033; (800) 341-4341, ext. 6666.

Maine Outdoors, RR 1, Box 3770, Union, ME 04862; (207) 785-4496.

Michael Jewell, Mountain Guides Alliance, Box 266, North Conway, NH 03860; (603) 356-5310 or (603) 356-7738.

Mountain Hawk, P.O. Box 81, Jericho Center, VT 05464; (802) 899-3617.

Northern Pack and Paddle, P.O. Box 624, Woodstock, VT 05091; (802) 457-1409.

Outdoor Adventure of Vermont, RR 5-2147, Bear Swamp Road, Montpelier, VT 05602; (800) 639-9208.

Peak Concepts, P.O. Box 338, Jeffersonville, VT 05464; (802) 644-5385.

T.A.D. Dog Sled Services, P.O. Box 147, Stratton, ME 04982; (207) 246-4461.

The White Memorial Foundation and Conservation Center, P.O. Box 368, 71 Whitehall Road, Litchfield, CT 06759; (203) 567-0857.

BOOKS

AMC Guide to Winter Camping. Stephen Gorman, Appalachian Club Books.

Climbing Rock and Ice. Jerry Cinnamon, Ragged Mountain Press.

Mountaineering: The Freedom of the Hills. Don Graydon, ed., The Mountaineers.

NOLS Wilderness Mountaineering. Phil Powers, National Outdoor Leadership School Publication and Stackpole Books.

A Snow Walker's Companion. Garrett and Alexandra Conover, Ragged Mountain Press.

Wilderness Skiing and Winter Camping. Chris Townsend, Ragged Mountain Press.

Winter Adventure. Peter Stark and Steven M. Krauzer, W. W. Norton and Company. (A Trailside Series guide.)

Index